Intelligent
Multimedia
Databases

Intelligent Multimedia Databases

From Object Orientation and Fuzzy Engineering
to Intentional Database Structures

Dimitris N. Chorafas

PTR Prentice Hall, Englewood Cliffs, New Jersey 07632

Library of Congress Cataloging in Publication Data

Chorafas, Dimitris N.
 Intelligent multimedia databases : from object orientation and
fuzzy engineering to intentional database structures / Dimitris N.
Chorafas.
  p. cm.
  Includes index.
  ISBN 0-13-031188-X : $24.75
  1. Multimedia systems. 2. Database management. 3. Object
-oriented programming (Computer science) 4. Fuzzy systems.
I. Title.
QA76.575.C47 1994
658.4'038'02856—dc20   94-1017
                                                        CIP

Acquisitions editor: *Paul Becker*
Cover design: *Wanda Lubelska*
Cover design director: *Eloise Starkweather-Muller*
Copyeditor: *Betsy Winship*
Art production manager: *Gail Cocker-Bogusz*
Production coordinator (Buyer): *Alexis R. Heydt*

© 1994 by PTR Prentice Hall
Prentice-Hall, Inc.
A Paramount Communications Company
Englewood Cliffs, New Jersey 07632

The publisher offers discounts on this book when ordered in bulk quantities.
For more information, contact Corporate Sales Department, PTR Prentice
Hall, 113 Sylvan Avenue, Englewood Cliffs, NJ 07632.
Phone: 201-592-2863; FAX: 201-592-2249.

Printed in the United States of America

10 9 8 7 6 5 4 3 2 1

ISBN 0-13-031188-x

Prentice-Hall International (UK) Limited, *London*
Prentice-Hall of Australia Pty. Limited, *Sydney*
Prentice-Hall Canada Inc., *Toronto*
Prentice-Hall Hispanoamericana, S.A., *Mexico*
Prentice-Hall of India Private Limited, *New Delhi*
Prentice-Hall of Japan, Inc., *Tokyo*
Simon & Schuster Asia Pte. Ltd., *Singapore*
Editora Prentice-Hall do Brasil, Ltda., *Rio de Janeiro*

Contents

CHAPTER 2

CHAPTER 3

CHAPTER 4

CHAPTER *5*

PROMOTING INNOVATION
IN DATABASE OPERATIONS   80

CHAPTER *6*

GETTING A BETTER UNDERSTANDING
OF AVAILABLE DATABASE RESOURCES   99

CHAPTER 7

PART TWO
TECHNOLOGICAL SOLUTIONS

CHAPTER 8

CHAPTER 9

CHAPTER   10

SETTING THE STAGE
FOR CROSS-DATABASE FUNCTIONALITY   170

CHAPTER   11

KNOWLEDGEBANKS AND DATABASES   188

CHAPTER *15*

PHYSICAL, LOGICAL, AND GRAPHIC USER
INTERFACES   266

CHAPTER *16*

OBJECT ORIENTATION, HYPERMEDIA, AND SEMANTIC
MODELING   286

CHAPTER 17

CHAPTER 18

Foreword

Production and consumption play a significant role in economic and social activites. But as the importance of information becomes ever greater, it is being recognized that its management also has a strong influence on the development of corporations, and that the effective use of information is a key to success in private life.

This paradigm shift, for which the omens have long been visible, is now clearly established as a result of the emergence of *multimedia technology*, such as two-way cable television. Such technology seems to be leading us toward another level of communications capabilities. Fulfillment of its potential requires:

- The provision of sophisticated databases in an easy-to-use environment, and
- The establishment of high-speed any-to-any networks.

Of course, there are as well many issues involving the protection of intellectual property and the establishment of security.

Starting from the above premises, this book provides a systematic understanding of databases in today's new circumstances. The author, D. N. Chorafas, is a distinguished scholar and businessman with significant achievements in the fields of computers and communication technology, knowledge engineering, free-market financial products, and environemtnal protection. His book discusses present conditions and is full of creative and instructive ideas.

The author deals mainly with the following topics: Why should we care for multimedia databases? What is the role of database intelligence? What is meant by distributed deductive databases? Why do knowledgebanks and databases integrate? He also examines the concept of intentional and extensional databases, explains how to design the global databases in heterogeneous environments, and outlines the service provided by intelligent networks. In short, he provides the reader with the notions he or she needs for applying new technology in business.

This book will be very useful for leading-edge technologists and executives responsible for data processing, office automation, communications, and database management—specifically, for people who are interested in multimedia and distributed deductive databases. I would also like to recommend it to academic institutions, particularly as a text or a reference book for courses in information science, engineering, and mathematics at the graduate level.

Shigehisa Hattori
Executive Director
The Center for Financial Industry Information Systems
(FISC), Japan

Preface

"To make money the dealer has to have an edge," suggested Stanley Ross in his Edmond Israel Foundation lecture. The same is true of the company as a whole. The edge is being provided by the able use of human capital, but also through low cost, innovation, and high technology.

This book focuses on one of high technology's most promising aspects: Intelligent Multimedia Databases. It is addressed to practicing professionals in all fields, not only computer, communication, and software specialists.

Written in a comprehensive manner, the book's 18 chapters require no previous knowledge of the subjects they treat. Any computer-literate person can benefit from their contents.

The book starts with business fundamentals. Manufacturing companies, merchandizing concerns, insurance firms, and financial institutions that deliver better than expected profits do so largely by cutting costs to bring more revenue to the bottom line. But with humans substituting for technology—rather than the other way around—companies are falling behind in the race. Therefore,

- They cannot effectively cut their costs;
- Neither can they gain an edge in a market place more competitive than ever.

The other pillar of survival is innovation. For innovation to have an impact, the implementation of information technology must be moving forward at a fast pace. This means facing new challenges and solving new problems, rather than making the status quo supreme and losing control of the business.

Promoting innovation and swamping of costs have prerequisites. One of the most fundamental is the subject of corporate databases. Databases are so valuable today because management has a lot of critical information as well as competitive knowledge locked in them. Without online, interactive access to multimedia information, managers, professionals, and even clerks cannot function properly.

Few people appreciate that the nature and content of databases have radically changed over the last 10 years. Not only has user visibility tremendously increased, but the database structures themselves have become too voluminous to be exploited without the use of intelligence.

As this book demonstrates, object orientation and knowledge engineering—as well as the tools connected with them—have been providing a valuable assistance to those who wish to exploit database contents in an able manner. But are companies taking advantage of the capabilities that technology now offers?

The 18 chapters of this book are divided into three parts. Part One addresses the applications challenges, starting with the identification of the nature of complexity and proceeding with an explanation of why this calls for new concepts in software engineering. This is done in Chapter 1.

Chapter 2 presents to the reader two practical implementations of object-oriented approaches in business planning. Both are generic research projects which aim to revamp the whole aspect of information technology, placing it on a rational and integrative basis. The first case study is in banking; the second is in manufacturing.

The focal point of Chapter 3 is on how to use intelligence to exploit database resources, most particularly, how to capitalize on the contributions fuzzy engineering can make to this issue. It also introduces the concepts of intentional and extensional databases, which will be elaborated on in Part Two.

The theme of Chapter 4 is the new generation of long transactions in business. Even if there was no other reason for innovative database technologies, the handling of complex transactions would have been enough to justify the change. Chapter 5 presents practical examples of how companies promote innovation in database operations, for instance, Project IMKA, which includes participation by Ford, USWest, Digital Equipment, and Texas Instruments.

Chapter 6, too, is a case study. This chapter focuses on the excellent work on the organization of heterogeneous databases, as well as the definition of homonyms and synonyms, done at the Agro Division of Switzerland's Ciba-Geigy. Based on lessons derived from practical implementations, Chapter 7 examines global and local issues in database management, and how they impact on the enterprise.

The technological solutions that Part Two proposes have been developed to answer the problems brought to the reader's attention in Part One. The concept of distributed deductive databases is introduced in Chapter 8, which demonstrates why the synergy provided by object orientation and knowledge engineering offers significant opportunities in database management.

Are companies following the path that Chapter 8 suggests? To answer this query in a positive manner, Chapter 9 takes examples from the air transportation industry—first, with American Airlines as a leader in artificial intelligence implementation, which is now active with object-oriented languages, and second, with COVIA of United Airlines—and the need it has found to handle long transactions through supercomputers.

Chapter 10 introduces the reader to the mechanics of how to set the stage for exploiting deductive resources, obtaining a cross-database functionality. This is further expanded in Chapter 11 which introduces the issue of knowledgebank management and the benefits to be derived from it.

The goals to be attained through knowledgebank management systems (KBMS) are presented in Chapter 12, leading toward a consideration of the relative merits and demerits of object and relational database management systems (DBMS). Also explained is a pioneering fuzzy associative memory project elaborated in Japan. From Japan come, as well, the practical implementation concepts of intentional and extensional databases presented in Chapter 13.

The first 13 chapters of this book introduce the reader to the new wave of database technology and the value-added benefits it makes possible. By doing so, they set the stage for the study of how to handle polyvalent media in our disposition. This is the issue of Part Three.

Chapter 14 introduces a subject of growing importance to every person working with computers: Graphic User Interfaces (GUI). The text explains why they are a friendly tool, and also brings into perspective integrative graphics solutions and frameworks.

The theme of Chapter 15 is that of multimedia approaches. One of the novelties that it includes is that of knowledge robots (knowbots). This concept of steady innovation is further extended in Chapter 16 which blends object orientation and hypermedia.

By answering the query, "Why should we care for multimedia databases?" Chapter 17 opens a window to the exploitation of this domain of growing importance to any business. Chapter 18 addresses the issue of text and image warehouses. The underlying reference is that of managing compound electronic documents. The Appendix compares Graphic User Interfaces to Character User Interfaces (CUI).

The approach and purpose of this book are different from those of the many other publications on databases. The book is not intended primarily to describe theoretical aspects, although the basic concepts are discussed. Rather,

- It explains the most up-to-date developments in technology that directly affect database management, and

• It tends to separate profitable from unprofitable computer applications which will characterize the 1990s.

The writer feels indebted to a great number of systems experts and corporate executives who participated in the research that led to this book. American, Japanese, English, and Continental European leaders in business and industry, as well as technologists, have contributed ideas; they have also reviewed selected chapters.

The list of professionals who gave insight and advice is too long to include in the Preface and therefore it is presented in the Acknowledgments. The writer expresses his thanks to Paul Becker for his initiative to publish this innovative book. To Eva Maria Binder goes the credit for typing, artwork, and assistance in preparing the index.

February 1994   Dimitris N. Chorafas

1

Identifying the Nature
of Complexity

1–1 INTRODUCTION

Throughout the First World, business and industry feel the need for collecting, storing, and accessing multimedia information spread over widely distributed heterogeneous databases. Many of these databases have grown like wild cacti, though they belong to the same organization and may be used every day by lots of its people.

But the database landscape is changing. While endusers do not wish to be bothered with technical details and are demanding seamless access, technologists must be able to assure a growing number of ad hoc analytical queries. Increasingly such queries are polyvalent and unstructured, requiring both database intelligence and multimedia response.

No miracle solutions to this problem exist, but one of the better approaches is to use semantically rich models that are applicable to a variety of existing computer implementations as well as to those under development. These are recently available through *object-oriented* databases and programming languages.[*]

Another major factor in the new strategies adopted in regard to distributed databases is that, in a growing number of cases, user organizations are better qualified than vendors to provide solutions for the 1990s. For example, the development of *Dectrade* was done by Bankers Trust, whose aim was to assure a fully distributed database whose database management systems (DBMS) are relational but programming is object-oriented.

This is not an isolated reference. The foremost Japanese banks (Mitsubishi, Dai-Ichi, Fuji, Sumitomo) and securities houses (Nomura, Nikko,

---

[*]The object approach is explained in Section 1–7. See also D.N. Chorafas and H. Steinmann, *Object-Oriented Databases,* Prentice-Hall, Englewood Cliffs, NJ, 1993.

Yamaichi) each have under development a *total dealing system* which combines forex, treasury, and securities. It addresses in a seamless manner heterogeneous databases and uses an impressive number of object-oriented tools.

Endusers increasingly require from the information system at their disposal uncommon capabilities—whether it is to restructure database contents along specific customer lines, evaluate widely distributed statistics on market share, or look into the Profit and Loss of major products and customer accounts under pressure. Solutions must be:

- Suitable to a range of sophisticated applications,
- Observant of maximum data independence,
- Able to serve multimedia requirements, and
- Integrative of different database models: object, relational, networking, and hierarchical.

Supported functions should be capable of representing entities, attributes, and relationships, as well as performing computation of widely distributed objects. They should serve an environment that is steadily characterized by polymorphism, being able to handle both local and foreign functions, in formerly disperse applications.

As these introductory state-of-the-art references suggest, the information technology environment we are seeking is a far cry from the one we have known in the past. New concepts and the proverbial long hard look combine to provide significant innovations which in turn translate into competitive advantages in the marketplace.

1–2 NEW CONCEPTS IN SOFTWARE ENGINEERING

Software engineering and database management have traditionally been seperate disciplines. The original file-handling approaches concentrated on static issues of information storage. In contrast, software engineering modeled the dynamic programming aspects.

However, since the development of relational database models and the evolution of fourth-generation languages, these two disciplines have been combining, converging towards systems that model both processes and data. This has been further underlined with object-oriented solutions which assure a finer mesh of integration capabilities.

In addition to introducing dynamic information management concepts, object-oriented databases represent a significant increase in our ability to capture the semantics of information elements. As a result, they are leading towards semantic modeling.

- The interest in object databases has arisen from application areas where traditional database systems fail to meet the growing user requirements.
- Since these requirements continue to expand, the evolving new application areas require an enhancement of object-type implementation concepts.

But transition to the new information management environment is not a matter of simple changeover in preferred database models. Today,

1. Many applications exist that are not properly supported by databases.
2. Others are even unfeasible because the needed database contents are not or cannot be effectively linked together.
3. Often, data transfer is done in a rather primitive manner, with no dynamic exchange between local databases.
4. In many cases, applications interfaces are substandard, or even nonexistent.

Yet, both database connectivity and process flexibility are very important. As implementations in computers and communications tend to establish their own specific data types, it is not easy, or even wanted, to have one central clearance authority. Increasingly we appreciate that we are better off if we:

- Improve the usefulness of old applications through knowledge engineering and
- Promote the ability to integrate old and new applications in a seamless manner.

This means that we have to work with common formats as well as to observe the standards which are finally under development. There are, as well, other basic requirements.

To process increasingly complex applications that employ *soft-data**
and respond to queries that are *not crisp*† in any meaningful sense, we have to use more powerful tools than those to which we have been accustomed

---

*Forecasts, projections, extrapolations, inferences, and hypotheses that have not yet been verified.

†A query is crisp if it is asking for a yes or no, 0 or 1 response. This is not the type of query that management usually asks.

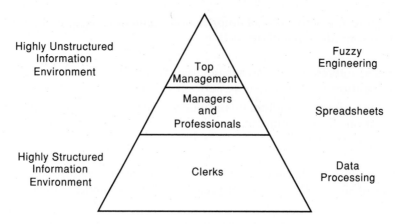

Figure 1.1   Knowledge and information requirements are deterministic at the bottom, but stochastic and possibilistic at the top.

during the last 40 years. This means models of a fuzzy or at least nondeterministic nature with:

- Stochastic concepts,
- Conditional probabilities, and
- Qualitative reasoning.

In short, these models are able to account for vagueness and uncertainty, hence fuzziness. Such developments are going to characterize high technology applications in the mid- to late-1990s.

As we will see in Chapter 3, *fuzzy engineering* has emerged as a new theory with an increasingly practical usage, suited to represent uncertainty contained in the meaning of words and deeds. This concept can be related to the structure of an information environment as shown in Figure 1.1. At the bottom of the pyramid it is highly structured, which means we can deal with the issues it involves in a procedural way.

This is typical of clerical work, as we will see through examples in Chapter 3. It is an area where deterministic approaches are not only acceptable but also mandatory. Midrange the information environment is semistructured; some issues are crisp, others fuzzy. At the top of the organizational pyramid, the information environment is highly unstructured, involving a good deal of vagueness and uncertainty. This is typically the top management level which has been so far badly served through data processing, precisely because procedural and deterministic approaches are not able to answer information requirements at top level.

With the emphasis now placed on senior management support through computers and communications, during this decade the application of fuzzy engineering is expected to play an important role in the establishment of an intimate relationship between executives and artifacts. It will provide solutions to problems we could not tackle at an earlier date because of lack of appropriate tools.

Cognizant people foresee a growing use of fuzzy engineering in configuring more flexible and more friendly computers, but also in speech-recognizing artifacts, for instance, in factories, branch offices, and as home helper robots. Fuzzy engineering can also be used in developing intelligent tools which support human experts in a number of activities such as:

- Financial analysis
- Treasury management
- Securities dealing
- Sales forecasting
- Scheduling
- Production control
- Quality assurance
- Medical diagnosis

Similar statements have been made in connection to neural networks, another tool of second generation expert systems. These new media are no matter of curiosity or modernity. They are there to help solve problems which could not be tackled efficiently with older tools, be it classical data processing or rule-based expert systems.

But as it has been emphasized in the introduction, the design and implementation of more efficient processes are only part of the story. The other pillar on which rest innovative solutions for the 1990s is cross-database management. A data management extension architecture should provide for cooperation between multimedia storage distributed in a network-wide sense, and applications which preserve their functional autonomy but must cooperate.

Object orientation and fuzzy engineering work in tandem. The notion of object identification and its underlying concepts are basic components of a solution to the problems posed by distributed databases, the handling of fuzzy queries, and the production and usage of soft-data.

1–3 GRAND DESIGN AND MACROSCOPIC KNOWLEDGE

One of the key reasons for past failures with computers and communications projects is the avoidance of taking the proverbial long, hard look by those who had the responsibility of doing so. Able planning requires a *grand design* under which all specialized or parochial solutions will be fitting—being subservient and inheriting some or all of the embedded characteristics of the master plan.

The grand design should dominate the project, setting objectives, constraints, and guidelines. It should also account for the fact that many life processes are complex and ill-defined. Therefore, it is hard to analyze them *quantitatively*, and sometimes even *qualitative* evaluations have to be rather vague.

Today we have available the necessary means to map vague and uncertain situations into the computer by *fuzzifying** them. However fuzzification and defuzzification require a *different culture* than that classically possessed by information scientists.

To approach complex, only slightly comprehensive situations in the first place, we have to learn how to live with *uncertainty* and accept *vagueness* as part of the real world—and of our job. We also have to master the tools which are now becoming available for this type of study.

Much of the challenge lies in complexity. Some of the processes with which we deal or intend to deal cannot be correctly recognized even if they are divided into components, each being studied in detail but in a manner reminiscent of old deterministic procedures, to which most people are accustomed.

Some systems experts proceed through subdivision, but the more we divide large projects into smaller and smaller pieces, the harder it becomes to understand the *mutual relationships* of the component parts. Knowledge acquisition is also getting more difficult, and we have to deal with uncertain knowledge, obtaining an effective representation through *fuzzy cognitive maps*. This is the conclusion reached by current research conducted by the Laboratory for International Fuzzy Engineering (LIFE) (Yokohama, Japan), which is sponsored by the Ministry of International Trade and Industry (MITI) as well as a number of blue-rubbon Japanese industrial firms and financial institutions. Other projects recently done by leading-edge corporations confirm the aforementioned concept.

Studies done in America, England, and Japan converge toward the conclusion that perception of the complex problem or system under study as well as its cognition needs to be based on two different levels of reference:

1. *Macroscopic* knowledge
2. *Microscopic* knowledge

Macroscopic knowledge should take precedence, and this is the reason why *strategic planning*—which focuses on macroscopic views—is so important a

---

*The process of fuzzification is explained in Chapter 3.

prerequisite to other more specific plans, for instance, plans for financing, product development, marketing, human resources, technology, and other logistics facilities.

Strategic plans are typically long range and reflect the grand design. In contrast, specific plans made in each critical sector tend to be shorter range. For instance, the budget is a one-year financial plan and, since it closely connects to accounting, it follows a microscopic view—with precision rather than accuracy being the overriding characteristic.

In general, microscopic plans are more limited in terms of interdependencies that they reflect and the crucial factors that they involve—one of them being the time frame that they cover. Macroscopic and microscopic plans differ in a number of important dimensions:

> *Macroscopic* plans involve a great deal of intuition, the definition of concepts, and the recognition of patterns. They are elaborated in the right hemisphere of the brain.
>
> *Microscopic* plans address the commonsense part of logic, but also calculation, language, and speech. They are analytical and originate in the left hemisphere.

Research done at the Laboratory for International Fuzzy Engineering not only confirms this division of our concepts into macroscopic and microscopic, but also brings under perspective a number of other interesting issues. "When we deal with large scale complex systems, we cannot see anything without a *macroscope* which is the conceptual approach," said Toshiro Terano.[*] An old Hindu proverb talks about the blind men who felt the elephant. They all described it differently, for each of them touched only a small part of the animal. None of them was correct in his description.

1—4 AVOIDING THE TRAPS POSED BY TUNNEL VISION

Typically, a specialist will address himself or herself in a detailed manner to a small issue concerning only part of the problem, as Figure 1.2 suggests. The problem is that this often leads to tunnel vision. Looking at the details of building blocks is, indeed, a very important function and somebody has to do it, but at the same time, too much specialization and narrowing of the field of investigation blurs the big picture, which is no more kept in view.

---

[*]The term *macroscope* is excellent. Dr. Terano, who coined it, is general manager of LIFE and a professor at Hosei University.

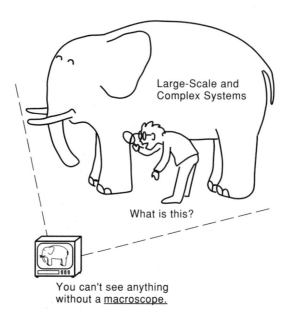

Figure 1.2   This illustration exemplifies the difference between macroscopic and miscroscopic views. (Adapted from LIFE.)

Here exactly lies the strength of a first–class implementation project carried out by the Agro Division of Ciba-Geigy, in Basel, Switzerland.* Through an Entity-Relationship analysis and design tool, it has been possible to *build a macroscope* which permits management to look at the grand design, therefore avoiding tunnel vision traps.

There are a host of other differences between macroscopic and microscopic cultures and mentalities, as well as tools, which should be kept in mind. For instance,

   1. *Microscopic* knowledge is focused on one domain in which there is little or *no contradiction.*

The variables entering into a microscopic landscape are exact, logical, and systematic. They are more or less objective, such as cases with analytical and largely quantitative expressions. Hence they can be easily processed by computers. Furthermore,

   2. *Microscopic* knowledge is often considered to be "obvious" to persons with experience in a given limited domain.

---

*Presented in Chapter 6.

Yet, although microscopic knowledge addresses a narrow field, there is difficulty in knowledge acquisition. Also while there is only one or at maximum very few established patterns, there exists, at times, less than realistic reasoning. Finally,

3. *Microscopic* knowledge is fixed in several ways. By consequence, it is *crisp.*

As stated in Section 1–2, crisp means of a yes/no, 0 or 1 type of answer. The information such reasoning uses is also crisp and by majority *hard-data.** There is little room for vagueness and ambiguity—or at least so it seems.

All this peddles the cause of certainty and greatly contrasts to the perspectives opened by *macroscopic knowledge.* In the macroscopic domain, conceptual approaches dominate and with them the broader view as well as the recognition of patterns. Precision takes the backseat, accuracy comes to the foreground—but not only accuracy.

1. *Macroscopic* knowledge is, by and large, fuzzy and so are the models which it uses.

Macroscopic knowledge concerns not only the grand design, but also projections, extrapolations, inferences, deductions, abductions, and inductions. By consequence, it deals with *soft-data*, which sometimes is vague and uncertain. This explains how much the macroscopic view helps us avoid the tunnel vision trap. It is difficult to be opinionated if we are not certain of a given situation and its evolution. The best way to guard against uncertainty is to hedge, keep flexible, and have an open mind.

2. *Fuzziness* characterizes the macroscopic knowledge itself, its goals and constraints.

One of the two basic differences between conceptual people and analytical people is that the conceptual person can live and even thrive with uncertainty and vagueness. The second major difference is in the macroscopic view that conceptual people take—and the two issues are related.

Macroscopic knowledge is not a collection of microscopic knowledge, like the summing up of a supermarket bill. It is *a long experience* crystallized into a *qualitative rule* or rules. Furthermore,

3. *Macroscopic* knowledge is essentially philosophical and interdisciplinary.

---

*Statistics, vouchers, accounting records, and so on.

It is qualitative and logical, often suggestive, allowing for contradiction in concepts and references, even vagueness. But it is also *flexible* and *adaptive* to the changing environment and its evoluting rules.

Right after the Korean War, two U.S. Air Force colonels, John Boyd and Chuck Yaeger,* demonstrated on the basis of combat-kill results in Korea that what a fighter airplane could do—climb, roll, dive—was less important in combat than how quickly it could change from doing one thing to doing something else.

- This quick change requires a spirit that is *agile, fluid*, and *alert*—and is characteristic of *macroscopic knowledge.*†

By contrast, climb, roll, and dive are specific acts which call for specialist skill mapped into *microscopic knowledge.*

A slower and theoretically less capable plane could often beat a "better" plane, if the pilot's skill and the craft's own design permitted it to switch quickly from one maneuver to another. The goal is that of catching the enemy by surprise, executing a master plan.

Yaeger and Boyd provided convincing evidence that a similar principle applied to combat on a larger scale. It did not really matter whether an army attacked by land, by sea, on the flanks, or from the air. What mattered was whether it could change its behavior more quickly than its adversary could do.

That is the role of a grand design: Put together aims, conditions, and boundaries which, macroscopically viewed, may be rather fuzzy, but together they make a flexible and responsible system. Such solutions can give real supremacy in combat, as well as in business.

$1-5$ FLEXIBILITY, METACONCEPTS, AND BEHAVIORAL VIEWS

What is true of aerial combat finds a counterpart in finance as well as in the manufacturing industry. The big contrast is between the *monolith* (that may even be perfect) and the *flexible structure* that can change readily as demanded by competition and market evolution.

Interestingly enough, the foregoing statement remains valid even if the flexible structure has in itself certain imperfections and some of its concepts have embedded into them an amount of uncertainty. "Profits,"

---

*The American test pilot who broke the sound barrier.
†"Our success depends on our ability to *turn on a dime*," Sam Walton, the man who in 20 years built Wal-Mart, the largest retail chain in the world, advised his associates.

I was taught 40 years ago by my professors at the University of California, "are the reward for taking risks." And risks are characterized by uncertainty.

- Risk taking can only succeed if we are fast and flexible, otherwise it leads to catastrophies.
- But to be fast and flexible in our decisions, we have to have deep knowledge and timely information—even if that information is uncertain.

Similar arguments contrasting monoliths to flexible solutions can be made on a number of other issues, for instance the implementation of technology. Flexibility and adaptation should characterize our own thinking and our acts, as well as the language and the tools that we use.

- Flexibility is the key to competition.
- The business advantage lies with the side that is more adaptable.

Because it is flexible and adaptive and includes concepts that might be vague, macroscopic knowledge is not so easily understood by the average person. "Use your common sense"* is the preferred argument, but common sense is more microscopic than macroscopic.

Many people are adverse to uncertainty because it destabilizes them. But as we will see in Chapter 3, fuzziness can be *equilibrated*. Equilibration is truth maintenance.

- If there exist contradictory rules and/or contraditory facts and values, we must adjust our knowledgebase to weed out inconsistency.
- Alternatively, we may develop *metarules*, that is, rules about rules, which assure that at a higher level of reference our base of knowledge is indeed consistent.

In down-to-earth terms, the effects of vagueness as well as of uncertainty are compensated through *metaconcepts*, that is, concepts about concepts which set the framework. Macroscopic knowledge has layers of conceptual definitions on which we can capitalize.

Precisely because of being conceptual, macroscopic knowledge is by far more important than microscopic in making decisions about complex problems and in investigating their solutions:

---

*Common sense is that which a proverb says is the most widespread commodity on Earth, and that is why each one of us has so little of it.

- Macroscopic knowledge focuses on *behavioral views* by taking the aforementioned *grand design* perspective.
- *Attention to analytical detail* is the domain of microscopic knowledge under the condition of appropriate skill availability.

At the macroscopic (or hyper) level, the query is not "how" but "what." By contrast, at the microscopic (or lower) level, the basic query is "how." To be used effectively, detail must be provided not in a one-layer flat sense, but with a technology permitting one to zoom through successive levels.

To a "how" query responses have to be given step by step, as it is done in accounting. The procedure defines the reference. This is totally different from what is really demanded by a "what" query, which by its nature is conceptual.

An effective response to the question, "what?" will be given by guidelines, by means of examples (analogical reasoning) and through icons, hence multimedia. It will be characterized by heuristics rather than algorithms. Figure 1.3 exemplifies this reference: *Behavioral views* are translated

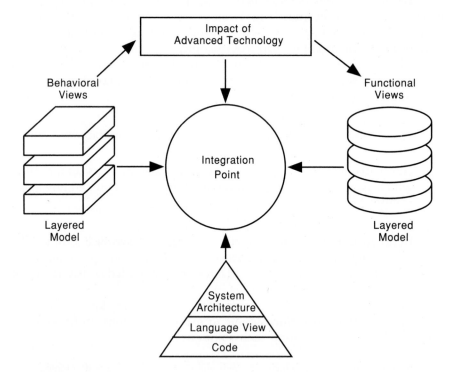

Figure 1.3   A macroscopic approach to behavioral and functional views.

into *functional views* through the right technology, and they are supported by a system architecture.

- The more advanced the technology is that we have available, the finer is the grain of the transformation.
- The more backward the technology is, more coarse is the grain, longer is the lead time, greater is the cost, and lower is the quality of the product.

Unfortunately, these issues are not being taught in school; people have to learn by experience. But many individuals are deprived of the opportunity to gain such insight because, as Dr. Harold D. Koontz, one of my professors at UCLA, used to say: "For lots of people 20 years of experience is just 1 year of experience repeated 20 times."

1-6 METAKNOWLEDGE AND OBJECT KNOWLEDGE

Object knowledge is the usual description, hence a basic level knowledge. For instance, typical logic programming is an expression of object knowledge. By contrast, *metaknowledge* is of a higher level, which includes generalizations and constraints.

Metaknowledge, that is knowledge about knowledge (which essentially is contained knowledge), is very important because it controls the inference processing mechanism in humans as well as in machines. As such it can be instrumental in the transformation of behavioral views, whose need has been underlined in Section 1-5.

In a similar manner, *metadata* is data about data. Metadata is critical for the effective management of data resources, and also for defining the best structures to be adopted for logical and physical databases.

The focal point with databases is their organization, utility, and service in a marketplace that is steadily becoming more competitive and more demanding. Emphasis must be placed on applications to which the evolving high-power database systems can be put, particularly focusing on the effective use of distributed resources for:

- Improving service quality,
- Reducing costs, and
- Increasing productivity.

New object-oriented and knowledge-enriched database solutions can relieve the constraints inherent in current information technology applications. This is particularly important in handling the evolving class of *long transactions* and *complex queries* as well as their implications in database management.

Attention has to be paid to the contributions offered by new database technology, examining how it can be exploited to provide tangible benefits, assessing the opportunities the new technology creates. Such opportunities have to do a great deal with the definition and exploitation of patterns as well as of behavioral views.

The transformation of behavioral views by means of metaknowledge is of significant importance both in technology and in business. But with low level tools at our disposition and without the needed online controls, it is very difficult if not outright impossible to assure that such transformation does indeed take place.

The problem of course is that the low technology, Classical Data Processing, provides tools which can help in the satisfaction of past premises—not the challenges of the present and the future. Part of the problem is that past premises are no more important in terms of sustained business competitiveness since:

- Scientific breakthroughs continue,
- Products and processes evolve, and
- The organization itself changes.

As a result, people and companies who concentrate on looking at the past are stumbling backwards into the future. The organization for which such people work is missing the opportunity switch—paying the costs of technology but not reaping the benefits.

People and companies able to face the challenges of this decade and capture its opportunities appreciate the wisdom of interactive solutions that permit *quick visualization* and a flexible, focused response, instead of following a cookbook course of action.

- Macroscopic views are typically taken at the *metadata* level.

As we have seen in the preceding paragraphs, the concept of metadata is fundamental to the effective use of information technology and also to human thinking at large.

- Effective microscopic level decisions are made under the light of macroscopic ones that act as the metalayer.

When the macroscopic views are misguided, the microscopic ones too will be misdirected. Although they might be quite precise, they will be off-center, hence quite *inaccurate.*

Macroscopic representation gives an integrative view, but to do so it needs concepts and tools. These are provided by fuzzy logic, fuzzy reasoning, heuristics, the process of intelligent control of unstable systems, and future course understanding through *feedforward*.

Feedforward helps in projecting on concepts and events, and as such contrasts to *feedback*—no matter if the latter is done real time.

- The better known feedback permits the exploitation of an analytical and largely quantitative input based on hard-data.
- A feedforward capability helps in the preevaluation of complex systems, from development of a scenario to establishing fuzzy associations.

Feedforward produces soft-data and is needed in domains such as the prediction of possible events; the modeling of their most likely action, reaction, or evolution; and in connection to social and managerial issues.

Model identification; knowledge representation; the understanding of meaning, evaluation, and diagnosis; and prediction as well as learning are examples of domains where fuzzy engineering can provide solutions. The same is true of language and image understanding, all sorts of modern communications, and the inference of intentions.

Based on the research projects it has undertaken, LIFE suggests that macroscopic knowledge and metaconcepts are necessary to model systems which are growing quite fast. Their often uncontrolled explosion challenges our ability to take hold of resources at our disposition, an example being databases. The basic reason of *complexity* lies in this short sentence.

1–7 AN OBJECT-ORIENTED APPROACH FOR MICROSCOPIC DETAIL

Quite recently, object-oriented design and programming are being adopted by user organizations and software developers due to the benefits they present in terms of the integration of applications. They also contribute to development productivity and the maintainability of programming products, enabling software companies to:

- Develop more powerful commodity offerings, and
- Deliver them faster to the market.

Object design and programming make it feasible for user organizations to take hold of their data resources, analyzing them under the grand design and its associated macroscopic view, integrating them in a more efficient manner than could otherwise be possible.

The open, extensible architecture of object solutions helps as well in microscopic evaluations, permitting developers to merge object-oriented techniques into existing development environments. This offers more potent solutions for the assurance of software quality as well as productivity.

Object databases and associated programming languages permit a feature-oriented design. This enhances the ability to effectively implement pattern recognition and to automatically generate network-wide instances of selected objects.

The approach that has been briefly described allows an easier handling of complex databases with relations between objects as important as the objects themselves. But this approach also necessitates tools that are both powerful in their functions and easy in terms of implementation. Such duality should prevail in terms of facilities and tools, whether they are oriented towards the more general case or are domain-specific, whether they are transferable or more restricted.

Transferable tools, that is, those capable of integrating with other similar database designs and programming media, are the preferable solution. One of the fundamental requirements of a modern design is the ability to proceed with incremental modifications without a break to the functionality of the system.

Written within the perspective of a software environment, this strategy closely emulates the Boyd–Yaeger *flexibility* principle:

> Quickly changing from doing one thing to doing something else, rather than being locked into climbing, rolling, or diving—and losing the business opportunities which develop.

Object orientation is key to the ability of effectively employing different instances as well as of assembling common protocols which facilitate interoperability in a distributed environment. It also permits process reversal.

As Figure 1.4 suggests, at the level of greater   abstraction program specification can start with a paradigm, then proceed towards general process definition, specializing on types and classes. This leads to rather flexible operational characteristics during execution time.

At the microscopic level, at least theoretically, the inverse procedure is followed in going from operational characteristics to idealization of the successive steps that will essentially be:

1. Software objects
2. Specification at instantiation time
3. Software application code
4. A class library
5. Overall software architecture

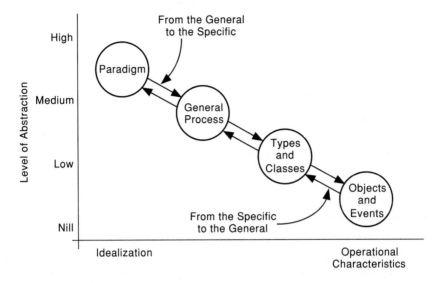

Figure 1.4   Idealization is characterized by a high level of abstraction, while the operational characteristics must be pragmatic.

6. Implementation paradigm(s)

This 1 to 6 course of events is essentially what we call *reverse engineering*. However, the reverse engineering of old code is a process that has been often discussed, but practical cases are not around to document that it is able to be done in a meaningful sense. The whole issue seems to involve much more hope than reality.

Old computer programs, which have typically been written in the procedural languages of the 1950s and 1960s,[*] cannot be reverse engineered in any practical way. This does not necessarily imply that code written in object-oriented paradigms will be successfully reverse engineered, but it does stand a better chance for being able to do so.

Eventually object decompilers will be developed which apply the path, from the specific to the general, that has been shown in Figure 1.4. It is too early to say how successful they may be. But the process of decompilation might stand a better chance if compilation has observed basic requirements embedded in an object specification method, including:

- Necessary formal foundations which are fully observed
- Expressive language to represent a degree of abstraction

---

[*]COBOL, FORTRAN, PL/1, and the like.

- A formal path from design specification to code implementation
- Use of knowledge engineering approaches driven by operational concepts and supported through reversible software tools

This goes beyond the now classical advice of expressing complex concepts based on simpler concepts. It requires a formal but flexible methodology with associated rules specifically studied for being reversible.

In conclusion, *software flexibility* is most crucial as we enter a period of fast growing, but also rapidly changing, enduser application requirements. These increasingly involve:

- Multimedia systems dealing with text, data, graphics, image, animation, and voice
- Information elements grouped into small nonsequential units stored in a network of database nodes interconnected by links
- Response to ad hoc queries displayed through windows, which can be navigated by following microscopic links (Hypermedia)
- Fuzzy queries to which may be many answers, essentially alternatives due to the fuzziness of data

According to available evidence, there is no better approach than using object databases as the medium. This has to be enriched with an intelligent kernel modeling system which provides full support to user interactivity and visualization—therefore to the path towards the macroscopic view.

Prior to seeing what these concepts can do for business, we have to complete the paradigms and definitions which enter into the more powerful tools and solutions available today. Key among these issues is a clear understanding of the role played by object-oriented solutions, which are presented in Chapter 2, and by fuzzy engineering, which is discussed in Chapter 3.

2

Rearchitecturing Business Operations Through Object Orientation

2–1 INTRODUCTION

Since the mid-1980s, object-oriented approaches have been used by leading-edge organizations in system analysis and programming. Also in structuring and managing distributed databases. The background reasons for this trend are in the fact that objects provide competitive advantages over relational solutions:

1. They help create a *flexible* infrastructure which can answer ad hoc requirements.
2. They make feasible the implementation of *meta* concepts which act both as higher level references and as constraints.
3. They put in action an *inheritance* mechanism for repetitive descriptions.
4. They enhance and promote the usage of *knowledge engineering* artifacts, and thus the development of more powerful systems.

These four basic reasons, which make advisable the use of object solutions in databasing and in programming, can be instrumental in developing dynamic architectural solutions for business systems.

Object-oriented approaches to business planning effectively deal with the concept of entities and relationships, their types and categories. They assist in handling problems related to naming, identification, and description as they turn up in daily practice.

Business planning developed with the dual objectives of meeting market requirements and making them easily handled by computer is one of the hardest software engineering problems companies are facing today. This is particularly true as certain types of problems require software solutions that are time consuming to implement, awkward to maintain, and difficult to extend. These situations are characterized by two needs:

1. To represent a class of problems which due to their complexity do not fit into a traditional information technology (IT) structure
2. To develop a flexible representation that evolves as the problem scenario or solution changes

Working along these premises, Citibank used object orientation in rearchitecturing its retail banking system. This chapter describes the path followed by this project and the results that have been reached. To help generalize the application, it also adds a recent experience from Ciba-Geigy along the same lines.

The outcome has been positive. Based on the initial results, Citibank decided to initiate a second project in architecturing through object models. It addresses global finance for wholesale banking. This second project is in process, benefiting from the results of object orientation in retail banking.

2–2 WHY AN OBJECT APPROACH IS ARCHITECTURALLY SOUND

Few people are ready to admit that the ways financial business systems have been implemented on computers have grown like wild cacti: left and right with unrelated and often heterogeneous components. This largely reflects accounting practices but rarely answers endusers' requirements in a practical manner.

We have today both the experience and the technology to remedy this situation. But semimeasures will not help. After a thorough study of the issues that the needed thorough restructuring of core financial business applications would involve, Citibank decided to focus on the following key issues:

1. *Rapid development of a banking model.* Top management asked for an open model with knowledge-enriched capabilities. It should not only involve processing chores but also, if not primarily, communications and *electronic money monitoring* activities.
2. *Integration of fundamental business factors.* Based on an analysis which was made in the retail banking operations bottom-up, a new business

design was implemented. This implementation took place through a top-down business object model, starting with the *fundamentals of banking business.*

3. *Embedded flexibility, able to assure that the business architecture is adjustable over time.* Object orientation was instrumental in reaching this goal. Taligent—the IBM and Apple subsidiary which designed the new, fully object-oriented framework—did a survey of object projects in the United States. This study found that Citibank had adopted a more fundamental approach than any other organization. Interestingly enough, among 500 American companies engaged in object-oriented work, Taligent also found that the results of their experience underlined the need that the *object Enterprise Model should come first*, that is, before programming approaches are undertaken.

This emphasis on object-oriented analysis and design in connection to business objectives permits greater rationalization and sets the basis for a flexible system. My own research among leading-edge organizations confirms such results.

The contribution of object-oriented approaches starts from the fact that business domains require appropriate definitions. Each financial product represents the bank's offering with respect to a single or a multiple channel[*]:

Each financial asset is associated with a set of business terms.

These terms are organized into procedures and the procedures into documents.

Compound electronic documents must be able to execute the activity of the product and of the channel to which this product belongs.

This is true in terms of communications, storage, and processing. There should be an uninterrupted continuity in online activity from client to bank and from bank to client, without manual intervention.

Banking facilities bring documents and terms together with services provided not only by the institution; they also impact on the financial assets which the bank manages. Such services, which should be executed online, have objects as their component parts.

A basic issue underpinning this whole procedure is the ability to state explicitly, but in a programmable sense, the business requirements. The problem is that no single person can define all of the requirements at a given point in time, and teams of people are not necessarily coordinated.

---

[*]Financial product line.

From this basic fact of business life results the system strategy Citibank has recently followed. It is applying object-oriented technology to *handle the objects identified by different specialists each in his or her own domain*. And it is using object orientation to bring together these business definitions and their component parts toward integration.

The procedure which has been established to serve as a platform for object-oriented business planning in retail banking, can be described in the following basic steps:

1. Identify what exists in terms of business requirements.
2. Catalog these information elements but also establish synonyms and homonyms.
3. Provide a platform for cross-integrating which can be used bank-wide.
4. Document the fundamentals of the business—by business domain and as a whole.
5. Within each domain and cross-domain describe the fundamental business concepts.
6. Map into the computer the financial and business policies, interconnecting their constituent parts.

Made in an object-oriented manner, this mapping addresses the vital issue of how the financial business is to be managed and how the retail banking practice relates to its parts, for instance, how senior management operates and controls the business as whole. This description of basic elements and procedures helps in answering queries such as:

- What is a financial business architecture?
- Which are the goals to be reached through a thorough restructuring?
- How can the different retail banking components integrate together in a flexible and dynamic manner?

The way of reaching the goals stated in the preceding paradigms starts with a description of the business which is sufficiently detailed to specify *client and bank requirements* but also general enough to illustrate the salient business goals and associated subgoals.

An integral part of this approach is the ability to map designs such as business organization, operations, process flow, and resources. In the background of this work has been the aim to produce very flexible and adaptive software. Correctly, Citibank looks at this subject as today's critically important enabling mechanism.

2-3 DEVELOPING A FLEXIBLE AND ADAPTABLE SOFTWARE BASIS

The object-oriented approach discussed in Section 2–2 makes business sense. It is needed to build processes and systems that are expressed in an adaptable form, fit together, and can be shared. By being flexible, this approach is able to survive leapfrogs in technology, organizational changes, and product and market evolution.

Not only does a flexible software approach facilitate business evolution, but also it permits the mapping into on-line computer resource processes which are driven by business principles. Central to the issue is the ability to represent an adaptable long-term management strategy.

As Citibank has aptly underlined, a long-term management strategy can never be monolithic. It has to be able to adjust to changing business circumstances, without losing its precision. Therefore, it requires tools and procedures that permit the *reverse engineering of solutions to requirements*—a challenge which can be effectively answered through object-oriented approaches.

Domain by domain, the business planning specialists, to whom reference has been made in Section 2–2, have been involved with each local and with each interdepartment concept, for instance, interdepartmental concepts necessary in making business agreements which refer to seemingly simple issues such as demand deposit accounts (DDA).

A demand deposit account is a business object.

It is also a *financial asset.*

Each DDA has *terms*, for example, fees on checks.

A diagram of interacting objects can be created on the basis of these premises as in Figure 2.1. If we have an agreement on DDA this may address the position holder, hence the client, but also the general ledger. This is true both in terms of transactions and of balance.

An agreement made on DDA may as well have an impact on the Future Business File, because this client may not have been served so far by all channels. By contrast, *database mining* and/or a current ongoing transaction may suggest that the client's dealings may be much more extensive than those currently handled by our bank.

A different way of making this statement is that there may exist a wider implementation of the object business model. This can involve:

- Cross-financial instruments,
- Cross-client handling, and
- Cross-market requirements.

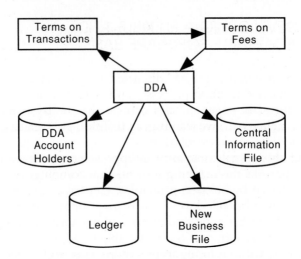

Figure 2.1   Each demand deposit account has terms that can be treated as objects.

Apart from the object orientation of the business model, the able handling of these functions calls for the development and use of a common business language. As Citibank was to suggest, such language should permit system-to-business communication adding a considerable degree of accuracy to financial business interactions.

One of the aims of the object business model under development is that such interactions should be *source-to-source* in opportunity representation, that is,

- Source of the transaction originating at client site, and
- Source of the business functions to serve that transaction, at the bank.

This eliminates lots of inputs, hence manual labor, errors, delays, and costs. Such an approach can be effective if the model takes care that variables and their attributes are effectively expressed in the form of objects. The same strategy applies all the way to the presentation of results for management reporting purposes, for example,

- *Operating Cost* and *Revenue Earned* versus *Client*
- *Market Cost* and *Market Share* versus *Prospect*
- *Banking Service* and *Party Engaged to Buy* versus *Buyer*

The goal of the Citibank financial business project in terms of such representations is to animate the objects and put behavior in them. Once more, the same principle applies both in handling basic operations and in management reporting.

In basic banking operations, for instance, the object *Check* is conditioned by the objects *Payor, Payee, $ Amount, and Date.* Figure 2.2 shows in a block diagram form how an object-oriented business analysis effectively maps the client agreement and helps define the applicable information flows.

Thinking in terms of metalevels in the execution of this work, the higher layer is that of the *Business Architecture* which sets the principles for the enterprise model. The next layer is the *Business Domain Analysis* which attacks the requirements for today's work.

Restructuring the results of the Business Domain Analysis leads to the elaboration of the Application Architecture which should include a legacy transition plan, development priorities, plan for the deployment of the new software, effective resource sharing capabilities, and so on. This should be an integrative approach which assures that *Competitive Systems,* tomorrow's business support, and *Legacy Systems,* computer programs for yesterday's and today's business, work in unison.

Only when this integrative perspective has been achieved can we talk of a valid technical domain analysis regarding the necessary technologies and products. Therefore, we can target a Technical Architecture which

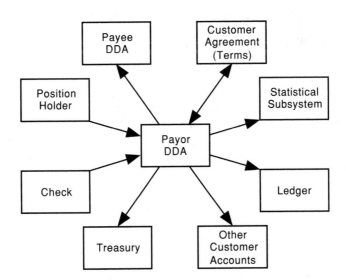

Figure 2.2   An object-oriented business analysis maps the client agreement which defines the data flows.

upholds both the established business strategy and the principles and policies for cost-effective computing and communications solutions.

2–4 ORGANIZING THE BUSINESS ARCHITECTURE

The emphasis on business planning helps focus attention on how the financial business architecture should be organized. In the way Citibank approached this issue, the answer to the organizational challenge started with the proper identification of *business objects*, along the lines of reference discussed in the foregoing sections.

Next, attention has been paid to the elaboration of *business domains*, that is, product lines or channels and their finer grain subdivisions. Closely associated to this process is the mapping of *business policies*—for reasons of management planning and control. In this sense,

- business objects,
- business domains, and
- business processes

constitute three independent but interrelated views of the global business finance environment which the institution must analyze in an integrative manner. This principle has essentially underlined the presentation in Section 2–3.

An object-oriented approach effectively looks at attribute analysis, subtypes, and entity roles exemplifying the problems and concepts that frequently appear in practice. It also emphasizes the role of *metamodels* in information systems design leading to practical applications.

At Citibank, all this work has been done in the understanding that *business and information modeling requires lots of creativity,* a process of discovering the world, as well as a practical epistemology. As the project in reference demonstrares, implemented at the level of planning banking services, object approaches can be profitably applied in:

- Discovering the real-world relationships between the financial institution and its clients, and
- Exploring information models and data structures which strengthen the client-handling perspectives.

At the business planning level an object orientation helps in determining the membership in entity functions. It also assists in identifying problems and therefore can be instrumental in information modeling techniques.

Entity state transitions and data distribution provide a solid background for closely relating project management issues. In the implementation case we have examined, these included:

- Presentation to users
- Quality assurance
- Test case generation

Business objects may be products, resources, and other elements. Characteristics of these products can be bread-and-butter financial services as well as those we steadily create, which add value to our channels. Typically, such products are being offered to a wide range of customers, hence the object-oriented business model should differentiate between the sophistication of *customers* and *services*.

As we have seen in Figure 2.2, a *demand deposit account* product is composed of payor and payee DDA, position holder, customer agreement (terms), checks, ledger, and bank procedures such as a statistical subsystem. Some of these elements can be broken into smaller units—for instance, the terms may include authorized signer.

A *letter of credit* product includes a letter of credit document, a contingent liability reference, and possibly a bill of lading and an insurance certificate. Over and above this are the ledger reference and other atomic elements of the DDA account. In a similar manner, a *forward rate agreement* product encompasses a trade, a counterparty, an offer letter, a deal ticket, a blotter, a ledger, and an asset position—as seen in Figure 2.3.

Resources are general-purpose facilities that enable the bank to do its work. These may be human resources but also buildings, utilities, communications networks, computers, and software.

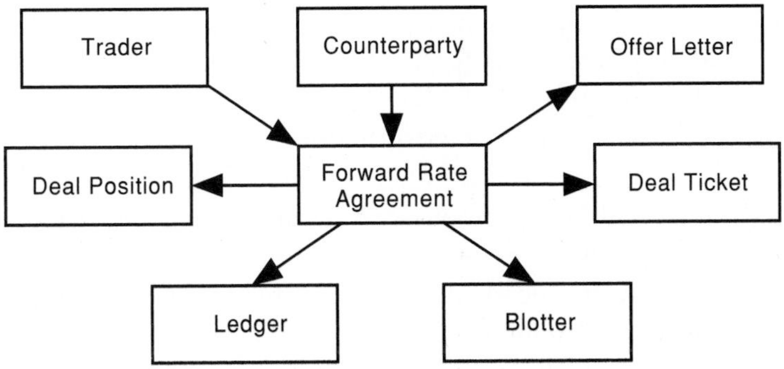

Figure 2.3   Atomic elements entering a forward rate agreement.

Business elements are policies, procedures, and by-laws regarding the banking business. They may affect customer handling and the way we establish documents: checks, accounts, ledgers, letters of credit, securities. They may as well address commodities, prospects, tellers, brokers, marketing people, managers, and so on.

These business elements can best be handled if we look at them as *atomic objects* of which everything else is composed. Typically, a financial product will consist of atomic elements working together, elements that are:

- Stable and persistent
- Established by banking and tradition
- Easy recognizable and defined
- Used on a day-to-day basis

Given the existing banking experience it is relatively easy to organize such atomic elements into a simple *classification* scheme, which permits the business information to work effectively. More complex financial products are composed of a number of atomic elements, and an object approach helps provide the necessary dynamic restructuring capability.

If this is the sense of the atomic elements entering into a financial transaction, how are such elements related to resources? Typically resources hold information reflecting on the qualitative and quantitative *attributes* of each element. They perform work which defines and exhibits the elements' *behavior*. For instance,

- The program running on a computer posts a debit to a check's payor and a credit to a check's payee.
- The DDA file holds the customer's name, address, telephone number, and so on—all atomic business elements.

Accounting for the fact that the top layer (metalevel) in an object-oriented analysis is that of the business architecture, which provides information for the enterprise model by reflecting on products and processes, Figure 2.4 presents a three-layered structure.

- Each of three different products (A, B, and C, is composed of atomic business elements.
- Some of these atomic elements are common to A, B, and C. Others are specific per product.
- The execution of these elements calls for resources that are provided by the lower plane.

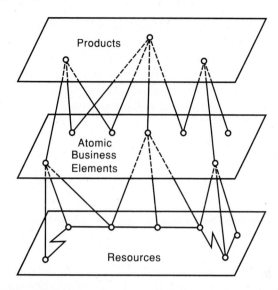

Figure 2.4   A three-layered structure characterizing a financial business, its products, constituent elements, and resources.

The products shown at the upper layer of Figure 2.4 may be unit products in whose case a higher up metalayer can be drawn to represent complex financial services. Unit products are based on a *single financial asset*, but several unit products may come together for marketing and operations purposes.

This integration of products within the bank's same product line or across service lines becomes increasingly important as customers start demanding tightly coupled *product value chains*. Such chains provide the opportunity for value differentiation and permit the bank to make good profits—if the software needed to handle them is flexible and available in a timely manner.

2–5 SUPPORTING CUSTOMERS AND FINANCIAL ASSETS

One of the most difficult queries posed to a bank is to provide in a factual and documented way an answer to the query: *Who is a customer?* It may sound ludicrous that a bank does not know who is a customer—and who are its customers—and yet this is generally true.

In the 1970s, as a consultant to the board of Osram, the lamp company, I was confronted with a similar problem: Defining *what makes a factory* as an autonomous unit. Is a factory defined by the products it makes? The management that it has? The wall that delimits its awe? Or by other criteria, arbitrary as they may be?

In general but fairly ambiguous terms a customer is a *business partner* with one or more roles played with respect to the bank's products. This is not, however, a satisfactory response when we come to specifics. A bank may have 4 million accounts. Do these represent:

- 4 million customers?
- 1 million customers?
- Or something in-between?

A customer company, for instance, has 10 subsidiaries who operate as independent business units. Are these 10 customers, 11 customers, or one customer?

In the retail banking side, husband and wife have an account. Are these two customers or one customer? There are many examples like these whose answer is neither simple nor standard—and above all *it is subjective.*

The business partner may be the final customer, an agent, a service provider, another financial institution, or the regulators. The agents may be pay or settlement participants, broker or trader, custodian, registrar or transfer agent. The service provider may be a communications service, depository, or information service.

The other financial institution, the instrument provider, may be an issuer or assurer. The regulator may be the reserve bank, securities and exchanges commission, or a standards body like the Financial Accounting Standards Board (FASB).

With these elements in mind we can build a tree structure of relationships, like the one shown in Figure 2.5. A dynamic representation is very important and objects permit dynamic construction of perishable

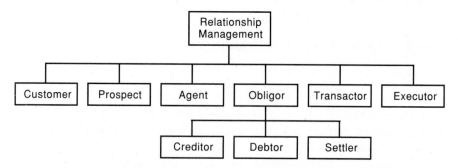

Figure 2.5   A tree structure regarding customer relationships and associated instances.

hierarchical models which serve one query or one transaction and then dissolve into their atomic elements.

For the next transaction, which is different than the one just executed, a new tree structure is constructed which is best adapted to the needs of that operation. This vastly improves upon the traditional hierarchical approach, while exploiting dynamic inheritance characteristics. Such object approaches can be instrumental in terms of handling:

- Financial assets
- Liability ledgers
- Lines of credit
- Legal prerequisites

A similar statement can be made in regard to assigning and following up *revenues and costs* associated with a given *client relationship*; controlling risks and exposure desk by desk[*]; comparing results this year with similar results last year; evaluating product marketing by branch office and/or by salesman assigned, and so on.

There exist as well other important queries that an object orientation can help address. For example, what exactly is the bank's relationship with its customers? Once the customer profile has been properly defined, we are interested in a detailed examination of the positions customers own in financial assets. The next questions then become:

Do we effectively offer products that manage these positions?

Are these products defined in a truly business-oriented sense?

Do we appropriately map the terms comprising the customer agreement?

Positive answers to these queries are necessary to define the customer relationship beyond doubt, and to automate the handling of all aspects characterizing a profitable customer relationship.

A profitable customer relationship will involve the exploration and handling of financial assets which can themselves be treated as objects. Are these really *performing assets* appreciating and paying interest, or does *this* account have *nonperforming assets* such as bad loans?

Relationship management requires *corporate action* which will be expressed in a particular *form* to be mapped into and followed by computers.

---

[*]Many banks have an average risk control system, but this is absolutely inadequate. Risk management must be in *real time*, client-by-client, market-by-market, instrument-by-instrument, desk-by-desk—and in accord with a lot more criteria.

This presupposes thorough preparation through an *information modeling* approach which involves data analysis.

The methodology should be disciplined enough to discover the navigation and access paths through the entities of banking, this being true of any other line of business as well.

The ideas and the solutions underlying these statements are generic. The process best works through situations amenable to analogical reasoning, making effective use of classification and taxonomy of real-life problems in business and industry.

Several topics can be handled in this way, such as representing in data structures time, space, services, history, quantity, and so on. In all these cases a conceptual and high-level view is necessary in order to meet the developing business requirement.

A simple financial asset, such as a demand deposit account, pays interest, involves fees, is subject to transactions, requires the handling of checks, includes the issuance of statements, and must be performing under rules. The associated action must be mapped into systems and procedures:

- Terms are organized by document, and
- Each document reflects applicable rules.

For example, as a financial asset a demand deposit account may include the rule that fees can be waived or alternatively there is a monthly account fee leveled with each statement, or, there is a check fee applied for each debit to the account.

"Fees," too, are objects and the variation in the rules governing them can be embedded in a metalayer. The latter sees to it that all transactions are governed by terms: A check is posted to the ledger but also reflected in the statement. The general ledger and the statement must agree both in terms of transactions and in regard to the balance.

In conclusion, as the Citibank project demonstrates, the support of customers and financial assets can be effectively made through the mapping of essential business element relationships. Object orientation is a valid way of effecting the needed description and business transactions associated to the client relationship.

Financial assets, that is, the *products*, consist of *terms*. These terms govern the actions of parties, such actions and their rules being mapped into *documents*. Products, terms, and actions are objects obeying established rules which must be organized by document to control the actions of contracting parties—that is, of the *bank* and its *customers*.

2–6 OBJECTS AND BUSINESS AGREEMENTS

A business agreement is a set of terms related to a financial asset position. This is essentially the service the bank offers to manage for a customer, using the facilities which it provides for the headquarters and branch offices.

Business agreements typically exist for every position in a financial asset which is owned by a customer. By and large, the terms of position agreement are general, applicable throughout a certain class of assets. But there may exist as well a subset of actual or potential terms that are specific to a given customer or group of customers.

> The *inheritance* mechanism embedded in object-oriented solutions simplifies the implementation of conditions.
>
> The *metalayer* structure permits the establishment of the proper framework as well as outlines applicable constraints.

For instance, through its inheritance mechanism a *portfolio* agreement covers every set of positions. But one or more of these positions and the financial assets they represent may also abide by special rules as negotiated with the customer. These, too, are objects.

The metalayer of this portfolio agreement governs the portfolio, not the individual positions—although it provides the constraints to which each individual position must abide. Entities in the different layers and in the metalayer are, as well, objects.

Such agreements and their mapping in an object sense exist at every business level. The DDA, money market, foreign exchange, and portfolio agreements, for example, can be governed by one or more master agreements.

> A *master* agreement exists when there are terms that deal with many divisional issues.
>
> Every bank has a hierarchy of master agreements at each level addressing the objectives of the institution.

Typically, master agreements govern the set of channels and positions, not the individual products or the detailed transactions these involve. Such master agreements present a hierarchy of atomic elements or parts, with business elements at the top and *fillials* at the branches:

- Parties
- Financial assets
- Banking facilities.

The leafs, fillials, or *parties* may be business partners, enterprises, sovereign nations, or persons. The leafs of *banking facilities* may be channels, products, services, and management.

All items in this hierarchy can be expressed as objects. The structure of a basic business agreement acts as a template for the terms of other, more specific agreements. These agreements may exist in ephemeral hierarchies reflecting the nature of the business arrangement. Some may be *permanent objects*.

> Agreements define customer and bank rights and change slowly.
>
> The rules establish responsibilities mapped in documents and help define conduct.
>
> A document's execution is controlled by the terms of the agreement— that is, by objects.

A business domain is built around objects and rules. *Securities custody* is an account product; it is also a financial asset and an object. The equities and debt that this account contains are also objects in a procedure of investment management.

As defined by the Citibank project, a Structured Financing Advisory Service is a master agreement. The portfolio agreement is part of it, and the position agreement is further detail. A special condition is that the portfolio agreement leads to credit facility expressed in dollars ($), deutsche mark (DM), yen (Y), pounds (£), or other currencies.

All agreements into which the bank has entered are subordinate to its *business policy* which must be at all times under management control. This includes risk management, credit administration, financial accounting, cost accounting, profitability reporting, and so on. Each one of these issues requires a well-defined set of procedures that consist of a set of rules and objects obeying such rules. Hence the generic nature of the project.

2–7 GLOBAL FINANCING AND REGULATORY COMPLIANCE

Regulatory compliance is not just the observance of rules, but also includes government control reporting. This particularly applies to transaction services, specifying the practices which have been followed in the expired period, business and commitments which were made, and possibly business requirements for the next generation funds transfer.

Regulatory compliance is a basic business requirement which too can be expressed through rules and objects. For instance, the Securities and Exchange Commission (SEC) report 13d calls for reporting by business unit the total number of shares of voting or nonvoting equities or nonequities that the bank controls. These are objects. The rules specify that such reporting must take place when:

- The security can be converted into voting equity
- The security is contained on the SEC's 13f list
- The security is to be converted into voting equity

The latter clause is applicable when the total voting equity for any bank unit is 5 percent or more of the outstanding number of shares, or the total controlled by the corporation is 5 percent or more of the outstanding number of shares. Such rules can be easily mapped into the computer through knowledge engineering.

Regulatory compliance for business reporting purposes is the rule, except when the issuer of the securities is exempt under section 12.G.2.g of the U.S. 1934 Securities Exchange Act, or the issuer is a closed end investment company registered as such under the U.S. 1940 Investment Companies Act (ICA).

These rules are easily mapped into the computer as exception to the more generic SEC rule, but their reference to our company is so much more enhanced if we can relay them in a valid manner to *our* business problem. Thus it is necessary to define and treat:

- Equity and nonequity
- Voting and nonvoting stock
- Convertible bonds and associated controls
- Issuers and associated securities

Subsequently, the object-oriented paradigm will find it easier to demonstrate that legal exceptions to rules are effectively used to satisfy business requirements.

Figure 2.6 presents a simplified version of the Entity-Relationship model developed by Citibank in connection to its object-oriented financial business planning system. The entries in this model are business elements subject to the 1934 Securities Act and its amendments.

The U.S. Government represents the sovereign authority requiring name of issuer exempted under 1.2.G.2.g or registered under 1940 ICA. The issuer must specify for instrument issued:

- Title and name
- Kind of instrument
- Number of units issued

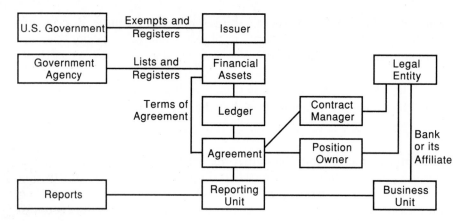

Figure 2.6   Entity-relationship model with entities being the business element.

- Unit of ownership
- Registration number
- Convertibility
- Unit-to-unit conversion factor
- Government agency calling for 13f reporting
- Ledger maintaining position

The financial assets have a name, contract manager, and position owner, and are registered as a legal entity. The agreement has a ledger position which must be recorded. All such items are objects and can be handled as such. The goal of the Entity-Relationship map is to animate the business elements.

The legal entity requires a legal form to be registered by the contract manager. This involves a position owner, reporting unit, ledger that maintains such position, and financial asset including defining terms and conditions. The reporting unit as well has a name and specific duties which, too, are objects.

A similar Entity-Relationship logic can be applied to funds transfers and other issues which define the financial business requirement. Funds transfers are executed through Fedwire, CHIPS, Swift, and telex/cable messages, but as well funds transfers are associated with DDA, especially cash management, and are sold to customers with a number of defined terms and conditions.

The funds transfer line of business, for example, includes two distinct customer types requiring proper identification: Banks using our institution as an intermediary for their own business; and other companies as an extension of their primary business.

This object-oriented approach to the handling of financial instruments fully considers the customer's viewpoint. It helps reorient products to his or her perspective, and is capable of assuring value-added capability for each channel of our bank—and its product(s).

2-8 AN OBJECT-ORIENTED BUSINESS ANALYSIS IN MANUFACTURING

Object solutions provide a flexible approach which transcends geographic differences and is reasonably independent of company size or line of business. They also permit internal services to be measured against the yardstick of external customer service.

The strategy Citibank has followed in redefining through object orientation its business perspectives and their evolution can be just as effectively applied in other industrial environments. As we will see in this case study, the chemical industry gives a good example.

The goal of a recent object-oriented project at Ciba-Geigy has been to create a corporate model of *business objectives* and *functions* as outlined in Figure 2.7. After the objectives and functions in references had been defined, they were related to the company's:

- Organizational units,
- Projects running in these units, and
- Information technology supports.

Figure 2.7 should be considered from a dual perspective: The one examined in the following paragraphs is more generic in regard to management's aims and functions. It is applicable at the corporate level as well as in each unit and subunit. The other, which we will see in the second half of this section, addresses issues at the atomic level and also permits their recombination.

Aims and functions entering into the business definition can be detailed all the way to the level of atomic elements, as the preceding seven sections have shown. Also, as far as *reporting* is concerned, the spontaneous and instantaneous reconstruction of these atomic elements into an ephemeral hierarchy is able to further enhance aims and functions.

Interactively the user of this system can obtain all of the detail that is required in daily work. One can view this detail as one sees best fit, from the perspective of the organizational unit to which one belongs, for instance,

- Research
- Production
- Inventories
- Marketing

The system will use as objects the atomic elements in storage, recombining them in a way which is meaningful to the enduser, and also highlighting those objects which may be crucial to the function making the query, for instance, animal health, insect control, fuel supply, and packing material.

Inventory management executives may wish to obtain characteristics connected to the job they are doing at that moment—all parts and products being handled as objects by the system. Or the query may be procedural, for instance, corporate or local purchasing policy (for a given material and site), bulk or order control production for semimanufacturing, safety instructions, multidivisional financial control, and so on.

Marketing may be interested in customer name, address, relationship, past orders, orders currently in execution, credit limits—or simply in order status. All programs available to handle a given customer requirement are objects that will be interactively presented on the monitor.

Delivery requirements are handled through the networking of objects, permitting transportation executives to interactively interogate the company's databases on who delivers to whom, as well as when and what is

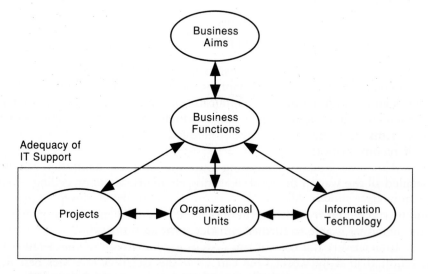

Figure 2.7   A corporate model of business objectives, functions, and support.

being delivered. For their part, the IT people may examine adequacy of support by studying:

- Language in which a given program is written (there are five alternatives)
- DBMS managing the databases accessed by the application in reference (there are four possibilities)
- Type of transaction processing monitor and operating systems under which the application runs

Charting is used to create a concept diagram capable of integrating production sources, transport links, and consumption points. This is expressed in the form that the enduser chooses, not the way the analyst might have decided some years back. The kernel of the answer will be shown as a basic production program with identification of other applications routines which contribute to the handling of a given product and/or function.

Interactively, the object-oriented system provides information elements per application, as well as languages, inputs, updating procedures, reporting conventions, and so on. It also indicates organization units using this application and degree of satisfaction that might have been expressed. The user can also ask:

1. Give me all applications under Unix.
2. List all applications written in C.
3. Identify all applications with low level of user satisfaction.

Furthermore, given its object structure the system can respond to ad hoc queries such as: For each application *list all organization units* employing it (one or more); or, list and define the corporate atomic units with the authority necessary for an application's modification or renewal.

The way the system has been constructed, each query can be expressed as a network of subqueries and their instances. This way, the query, "What do I need to establish the price of product X?," will result in an interactive report which visualizes programs and databases pertinent to the question being made. All queries are constructed graphically by the user through colors and symbols. The response is also given in a visualization sense.

In terms of systems management the facilities are provided for visual inspection of a basic application and its connectivity to subsidiary routines and other basic applications. This can be instrumental in analyzing strengths and weaknesses of current IT. The same is true of an object approach which identifies:

- The applications programs for each of the databases available in the system, and
- All programs which have the right to access a given database.

Information elements, databases, and programs are all objects. Once the necessary mapping into computer storage of these objects and their connectivity has been achieved, it is possible to examine a host of other issues relating to usage of available resources. As Figure 2.8 suggests, we can take each specific function, examine whether or not its definition is satisfactory, and then evaluate the adequacy of IT supports addressed to it.

For any given level of IT solution we can reevaluate the adequacy of implementation, both by studying the objects and by experimenting on different implementation scenarios. Subsequently, always through the use of objects, we can study return on investment through an interactive examination of:

- Obtained practical results
- Cost incurred in function execution
- Profit and Loss by function

Figure 2.8 can be brought down to the detail of *atomic elements and function*. Once this detail is established, an object-oriented solution permits reverting to Figure 2.7 using *inverse multiple inheritance.*

Apart the *functional inheritance*, atomic functions can be handled along a *structural inheritance* dependency. The latter is essentially a process mapping the current organizational chart—but it is flexible and can be restructured interactively. Typically, this is done:

- If and when the organization changes, or
- There is a need to effectively redistribute the functions.

Computational procedures are simple enough since the objects in the database are atomic. This avoids the shock of major reprogramming jobs after significant organizational changes.

The low level of investment that this imaginative project has required is impressive. Capitalizing on already existing know-how with the shell (Ptech), the whole effort took 3.5 man-years, which is very reasonable given the obtained results.

Not only with new technology we can do things which were unfeasible with old technology, but we can as well significantly speed the execution of what might have been doable. A company which prefers not to be identified started a similar ambitious project in 1986. Ten systems experts participated but 6 years later—after having spent 60 man-years—the major goals were abandoned. What is now functioning is roughly 10 percent of what Ciba-Geigy did in 3.5 man-years.

The difference in cost effectiveness is 3.5 to 600—and is that of new technology versus the mentality and paleolithic tools of mainframers. The new, object-oriented technology required just 5.8 percent (per thousand) of the money that old technology demanded for half-baked results.

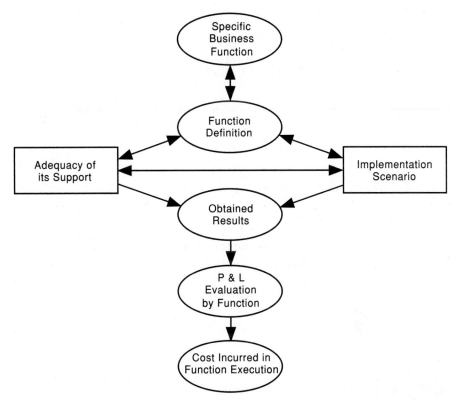

Figure 2.8   Further detail on the interaction between business functions and supports.

3

The Contribution of Fuzzy Engineering

3–1 INTRODUCTION

Money can be made by those companies whose cost structure does not depend on selling millions of copies of a given product. This is well understood by niche players who look for opportunity in small numbers—but big companies often forget the wisdom of having and maintaining very low production and distribution costs.

The problem with many companies is that their management somehow has lost contact with the underlying efficiency criteria. For others, cost effectiveness constitutes the sort of decision they are unable to make. In a similar manner, while senior management wants its company's business to prosper, it fails to pay attention to ongoing technological changes and does not appropriately adapt to them.

Typically, the management of companies which are not so well off seems to believe that because of large size and other characteristics of their firm, both the company and its executives are safe. Nothing can be further from the truth. No one is safe in this world.

Contrary to this steoreotyped attitude, open minds see the point that blending the information technology already in house with the peak of new developments helps in creating competitive avenues. One of the high grounds in the competitive landscape can be reached through *fuzzy engineering* of which we spoke in Chapter 1.

The present chapter explains in practical, comprehensive terms the role of fuzzy engineering. Even if it emphasizes only the fundamentals, such discussion helps in providing the reader with needed background. As such, it assists in:

- Understanding and appreciating the real-life cases which can be successfully exploited
- Explaining the role played by fuzzy- versus rule-based systems

The introduction of fuzzy engineering in business and industry is just starting, but "Pity the business that falls in love with the status quo." This statement, made by a senior executive of a large British company, summarizes the view of many forward-looking firms that are keen in implementing new concepts.

Another executive view offered in the research project which led to this book is: "Today we have at our disposal technology we would not have dreamed of 10 years ago, and yet people take 300 percent more time to complete a data processing job." These two quotations are very much related, defining what is wrong with the majority of current systems.

In business and industry, companies that wish to change the status quo and better their performance are *architecturing* their solutions through the use of high technology. They lead themselves towards flexible integration where close collaboration with the endusers—an advance on traditional practice—plays a vital role.

With the advent of practical knowledge engineering implementations, data processing and computer specialists became concerned that they might be replaced by expert systems. Now it is clear that IT professionals will not be replaced by expert systems, but by colleagues who know how to capitalize on a variety of new technologies to create systems that will ensure their corporation's future success—and fuzzy engineering is one of the basic tools along this frame of reference.

3-2 CONCEPTS UNDERLYING FUZZY ENGINEERING

The notions of *crisp* and *fuzzy* have been briefly introduced in Chapter 1, at least at the reference level. But since the aim of this book is to be comprehensive to the reader who, up to this point, had no precise knowledge of such issues, we will start by repeating the basic notion of fuzziness to assure its understanding.

Starting with a paradigm, contrary to Data Processing which, as the name implies, centers on the processing of numerical information (data) without consideration of how *crisp* of *fuzzy* this data* is, Fuzzy Engineering addresses both numerical and logical issues and distinguishes *shades of gray.*

---

*In Latin, data is noun, plural. In English language IT technology, it is *noun, singular.* It has no plural.

The *degree of fuzziness* is based on these shades of gray on which we reflect and manipulate.

A query is crisp if it asks: *"Yes"* or *"No."* An answer is crisp if indeed it gives a "Yes" or "No" response. An answer is fuzzy if it has at least three alternatives: Yes, Maybe, or No.

Most likely the "Maybe" response would have different tonalities or hues: "I don't really know, but probably yes," "Rather yes," "50–50 chance for yes and no," "Rather no," "Most probably no."

Close parallels exist between these concepts and real-life situations. An example is that of investment decisions. The question every investor asks himself or herself and his or her banker is: "Will the market go up or will it go down?"

There are no crisp answers to this query. Even within a bull market there may be downs, or in a bear market there may be ups—momentary recoveries. Asked by the son of one of his best customers: "Dr. Morgan, do you think the market will go up or will it go down?" the great banker responded: "It will fluctuate young man, it will fluctuate."

> This is one of the best practical examples of vagueness and uncertainty that can be expressed through fuzzy engineering.
>
> Nobody ever succeeded in writing J.P. Morgan's dictum in a crisp form through COBOL, PL/1, FORTRAN, or any other of the data processing languages. But it can be written by means of fuzzy sets.

With the exception of direct measurement which, within a margin of error, stands a chance of being crisp, all other information tends by its nature to be fuzzy. This is particularly true in management, and in finance.

Even simple cases like the time for driving from one city to another may involve a fuzzy answer.[*] An example is given in Figure 3.1, which presents a time plan for driving from Monte Carlo to Zurich based on 15 years of experience.

> There is no evidence that this drive will take less than 5.4 hours. This is the minimum of the minima (minmin).
>
> The maximum of the minima (maxmin) is 5.6 hours.
>
> It is just as likely that the drive will take from 5.6 to 6.0 hours (equal possibility).
>
> The minimum of the maxima (minmax) is indeed 6.0 hours.
>
> There is no evidence that the drive from Monte Carlo to Zurich will take more than 6.3 hours (maxmax).

---

[*]We will see another example with fast, medium, and slow driving in Section 3–6.

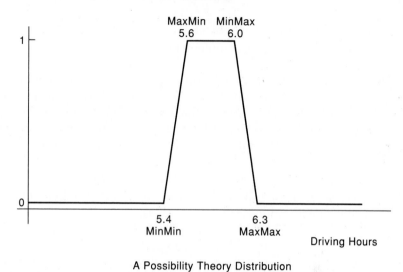

A Possibility Theory Distribution

Figure 3.1   Time plan for driving from Monte Carlo to Zurich.

Notice the increasing possibility in the range from 5.4 to 5.6 hours and the decreasing possibility from 6.0 to 6.3 hours. This distribution curve is *not* symmetric and contrary to a probability distribution (bell shaped curve) it has no single central value.

Typically, in most fields of human endeavor *our knowledge* for answering queries is imprecise, and by being so it resembles the distribution curve of Figure 3.1. That's why deterministic approaches followed by data processing cannot address the majority of managerial problems, no matter how much the bunch of mainframers talk of "Management Information Systems," "Executive Information Systems," "Info Centers," "Information Warehouses," and other irrelevancies.

If crisp approaches would not do, then the predicates being used should offer the user different possibilities than "Yes" or "No," "1" or "0," "black" or "white." They also should be able to express tonalities of gray between the stated two black-white boundary values.

Predicates are the motor of the fuzzy engineering system. In logic, a *predicate* is something affirmed or denied in connection with the subject of a proposition. In grammar, a predicate is a statement about the subject of a cause or sentence. It may be:

- A *verb* of complete meaning
- A verb and its adverbial modifier

- A transitive verb and its object
- A linking verb and its complement

A predicate can also be an appellation or title that *asserts* something. With fuzzy predicates this affirmation has embedded in itself a degree of vagueness and uncertainty, the same degree which prevails in the real world.

It is important, however, to take notice that the different vague and imprecise predicate possibilities take place within a *real domain*.

> In the general case, in mathematics, a real domain is one *nonimaginary*.
> In *Possibility Theory* the real domain consists of numbers, quantities, or logical expressions (see Section 3–4).

It is fundamental to realize that logical expressions can be real but not crisp. Their existence helps define a realistic *workspace* which integrates with the philosophical notions underpinning the world in which we live—and at the same time it expands them.

A workspace reflecting possibilistic concepts helps in reducing the representation process to its essence, while keeping it in a model structure. This simplifies the task of mapping it into computer memory.

Mapping a process and its information elements into the computer is a prerequisite for handling by computers. It is opening up new possibilities, but also implies constraints that alter some of the concepts of computer processing to which we have been accustomed in the past.

3–3 USING INTELLIGENCE TO EXPLOIT DATABASE RESOURCES

Predicates operate on *information elements* (IE) which are typically stored in databases. A database is an organized collection of information elements that serves as infrastructure in transaction processing, and is accessed by endusers through a query language.

As a repository of information elements which can be *multimedia* (text, graphics, image, voice, animated image, data, and compound electronic documents), the database is structured according to a *model*. Into the database(s) is mapped the business cycle of a company, its products, processes, and the relations it has with its clients, suppliers, employees, and shareholders.

Because of this very reason, the database is a corporate resource whose able exploitation can provide a road map to corporate activites, from product design to marketing action. Database users exploit its contents according to a *schema* in their mind, using a set of *methods*:

A *schema* is the framework that defines the components of a database and their relationships.

Methods are the codes that determine the information elements behavior, such as the calculation of an object's cost or price.

In essence, methods help in creating the new predicates by acting upon the appropriate information elements and old predicates which can be found anywhere in a distributed database.

Since, in an environment of growing competitive pressures, methods, schemata, and information elements change, databases have been the foundation technology for managing corporate *knowledge resources*. It is through database management techniques and products that organizations seize the opportunities offered to them by the marketplace.

Prior to computer-based solutions, this was done through paper records, which are bulky, clumsy, often incomplete, and labor-intensive. Hence databasing through computers is an improvement over older methods, the problem being that the large majority of companies use computer-based approaches as a sort of paper record—they do not have the necessary *cultural* change to get more mileage out of them.

The online exploitation of databases started in the late 1960s and is connected to advances in computer processing as well as in communications. These include:

- Real-time transactional applications
- Trading operations
- Decision support
- Experimentation on a growing range of issues from product design to market drives and conditions

Successful organizations have always capitalized on the management of data resources and they have done so in the context of migrating from classical, slow, and cumbersome offline data processing to more sophisticated applications domains. But quite recently,

Stepwise refinements can no more satisfy the fast growing needs.
The whole issue of computer memory and its usage has to be revisited and revamped.

A meeting held with investment banks in Wall Street, during the research that led to this book, was to reveal that *less than 5 percent* of applications on mainframes have a management orientation. Yet managers and professionals account for about 66 percent of a company's payroll.

For over half a century, since the advent of the first programmable calculators, *computer memory* has been seen as one logical level which may be stored at different layers of physical devices. Hence the distinction between cache, main memory, auxiliary storage, and so on.

While the physical distinction remains, and in a way it is addressed through paging, the use of Artificial Intelligence (AI) in connection to Information Technology (IT) has radically altered the single logical level. Indeed, it has changed the whole concept of computer-generated memory space, creating different reference levels.

3—4   INTENTIONAL AND EXTENSIONAL REFERENCE LEVELS*

Whether they are fuzzy or crisp, the events that interest business and industry take place at two levels of reference. If properly exploited, these levels assist in creating a new architectural structure which underpins the computer-generated domains:

1. An *upper* one which is *intentional*, hence commanded through knowledge constructs, and is forming an *object-oriented* idea database
2. A *lower* one which is *extensional*, and therefore consists of memory locations which contain data and may be organized in a hierarchical, networking, relational, or object manner

At both levels of reference, the architecture to be used in object mapping and manipulation should be flexible and enriched with tools which permit changing the existing representations, converting from crisp to fuzzy or vice versa.

The first is the process of *fuzzification* (see Section 3-7).
The second is the process of *defuzzification*.

Fuzzification and defuzzification can be effected both at the intentional and at the extensional level of reference. Information processing concepts reside in both layers. The *intentional predicates* are logical entities which have broken free of their physical origins but not necessarily of their conceptual spacial limitations. Within these constraints, they command and manipulate information elements.

---

*In Part Three, we will build on this notion to develop the solution of intentional (deductive) and extensional databases.

Enriched with the appropriate tools, the *intentional* concept leads us into the spacial handling of *objects*.

The *extensional objects* are self-standing entities, callable through commands and supervised through demons.[*]

Extensional objects are essentially facts such as measurements. A *fact* is true in a given state, within which it can have values. *States* present boundaries for facts, within a specified domain.

Predicates relate facts to a given state. Rules commanding a given system fire if symptoms are present. The catalysts of change are *events*. An event can be practically anything:

- Something taking place
- The state or value of another event
- A hypothesis (tentative statement)
- The result of the test of hypothesis
- A yes/no or fuzzy response

Essentially, events trigger rules leading to conclusions. The trigger by a given event can be intentional.

Intentional events have *rule* characteristics.

As predicates they reside in a *knowledgebank*,[†] which is a logic database.

The reason for an intentional event may be to assure global database access, guarantee compound electronic document administration, collect the information elements necessary to compute the risk taken in a financial transaction, or see through other complex tasks.

In all likelihood, during the coming years this concept too will change as we understand the power of the intentional layer and move toward intelligent database management systems. These will typically be widely distributed, operating in a global sense and based both on AI and on object manipulation.

Intentional predicates able to facilitate the handling of long transaction and complex queries will be both fuzzy and crisp, often offering alternative paths for action. Hitachi and Nissan Motors, for example, developed a knowledge-based system which exploits large inventories of auto parts through fuzzy engineering when the user is not sure what he or she is

---

[*]A demon is a supervisory process. Most employees see their boss as a demon.

[†]We will talk of the development of a knowledgebank in connection with prototyping in Section 3–6.

looking for, and through a crisp fast track when the user knows what he or she is searching for and how to find it.

3—5 ALTERNATIVE WAYS OF INSTRUCTING THE MACHINE

Fuzzy engineering is altogether a new ball game but it is based on established theory. Quite often in literature, the terms Fuzzy Set Theory and Possibility Theory are used interchangeably. This is not precise. Possibility Theory is one of the two best structured ways to express Fuzzy Sets—the other being Bayesian (conditional) probabilities.

Possibility Theory should not be confused with *Probability Theory*, even if the latter is much better known.

> Probability Theory treats in a stochastic manner crisp predicates, based on 1 or 0. Something exists or does not exist.

> These are boundary conditions for Probability Theory which, as stated, also includes in-between values (0.1, 0.2, ... 0.7, etc.) to describe the vagueness and uncertainty of a response.

In a way, it may seem that we are altering to our advantage the science of mathematics, raping it in the process. This is of course an illusion which, like so many other illusions, has its believers. The latter are typically the one-track minds unable to change their way of thinking and open up to the changing environment.

"Mathematics," one of my professors at UCLA taught me 40 years ago, "is a game of signs and rules." We can construct any mathematical system we please, as long as:

1. We clearly establish the signs which we use, without homonyms and synonyms, and
2. See to it that the rules of the game are complete and noncontradictory.

If one of the new and different mathematical systems is fuzzy engineering, others exist as well, like non-Euclidean geometry and chaos theory.

The reason why it has been necessary to institute a new mathematical system is to be able to both accommodate and handle the concepts of vagueness and uncertainty. Fuzzy Engineering permits us to use uncertainty in an analytical sense, and in so doing it does not contradict the mathematical rules of *its* system.

With Possibility Theory, the rules are close to those prevailing in the manager's mind and within the notion of a real domain, the way they are expressed not only in mathematics but also in philosophy. In both cases, the real domain means:

- Existing,
- Actual (not merely ideal),
- Essential, and
- Ultimate (not derivative or phenomenal).

Operating within a real domain is a matter not only of practicality but of principle. Rules have to be explained to the computer. Classically, this has been done through programming.

Processing functions are modules of instructions to the computer to do something.

These instrictions are real domain artifacts.

Since the invention of the programmable calculator in the immediate pre-World War II years, *programming approaches* explored ways of increasing the extensibility of the programming language, so that it can be used for more purposes than its designers projected. Successive evolutionary steps led, in the early 1980s, to the knowledge engineering *prototyping* shells, but evolutionary developments did not stop with "this" or "that" breakthrough.

While the mass of technologically illiterate EDPers[*] continues laboring with COBOL and other ossified programming languages of the 1950s and 1960s, the advanced elements of the IT community have combined the best features in existing tools with the new evolutionary concepts characterizing our epoch.

An example is that of bringing together, for software development, the *knowledge engineering* of the 1980s with *object-oriented programming* of the late 1960s. Prototyping shells have added object capabilities to themselves by including multiple inheritance and method combination, as well as hiding the details of underlying hardware.

An advantage of high-level abstractions supported by the new programming languages is that it is easier to write portable software and the resulting programs are really flexible. The disadvantage is that execution cost of some of the abstractions may be high, but the price of hardware is steadily dropping and quite rapidly so—while the cost of human labor increases.

---

[*]Many people ask what EDPers means. They are the disciples of EDP which in the 1950s stood for "Electronic Data Processing," but now—as some Wall Street banks suggest—it rather identifies "Emotionally Disturbed Persons"; creatures of the Cretaceous Period (65 million years ago) who, like the dinosaurs, are going to be extinct.

After all, what are our alternatives? There is a fast growing amount of programming work to be done and this can be accomplished either:

- By *brute force* throwing a large number of expensive human programmers at the problem, and getting substandard results, or
- By using *intelligent programming systems* which employ machine power for 1.000 percent or better gains in human programmer productivity.

Through knowledge engineering and object orientation we are aiming at high-level functions that can be used to automatically operate on programs as well as on data. The system is using its knowledgebank for intentional reasons; hence it is using intelligence.

3—6 INTRODUCTION TO CONCEPT OF KNOWLEDGEBANKS*

Computer programs can operate on other programs and on themselves just as they operate on information elements. This can happen at runtime through interpreters of the shell's high level commands, or offline by means of precompilers and generators.

In both cases, we typically start with a prototype which is a working model of the real world. The prototype is very easy to *visualize*, simplifying the comprehension necessary by the enduser. Quite importantly, *changes* to the prototype are simple as well as rapid.

The power of the prototype can be expressed in these simple sentences. The motor behind it is the knowledgebank of the shell.

Figure 3.2 explains how this approach works. It also identifies in a comprehensive manner the development and use of a knowledgebank. Starting with the concept of a new project,

The first milestone is that of developing an Epistemological† model, and most particularly the conceptual level of it.

This is followed by a dual emphasis on the Grand Design Model (including the databasing and networking infrastructure) and the Prototyping Shell.

---

*The challenges raised by this introductory text will be elaborated in Chapter 8 on Distributed Deductive Databases.

†Epistemological means scientifically based at the conceptual, mapping, and usage levels.

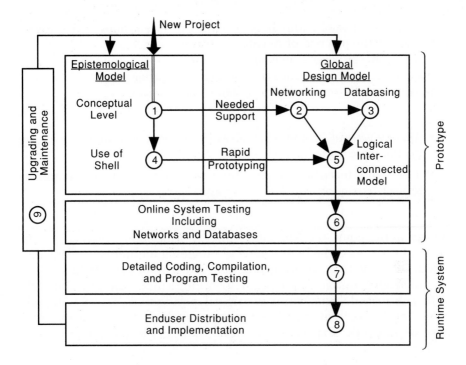

Figure 3.2   Development of a knowledgebank.

The *knowledgebank* is intentional, while the database is extentional. The contents of the knowledgebank are the rules—whether crisp, fuzzy, or both. Knowledgebanks do have to be managed, hence the need for a knowledgebank management system (KBMS).

Whether the model that we are building is fuzzy or crisp, all the work being done must be computer-based. The same is true of *testing* the artifact that we develop.

Compilation is simple mechanics, and should also be fully automated. The same is true of *diagnostics* simplifying by so much the *maintenance* job, which is itself being radically revamped.

As we have seen with the discussion on the intentional and extentional layers, the concepts of knowledgebanks and databases are not conflicting. If anything, they are complementary and we can make the best use of both.

There are as well a number of important workspace issues to be discussed. They extend beyond knowledge engineering and object-oriented solutions, while utilizing the facilities provided by them. There is, for instance, the need for a steady policy of *reuse*—from the sharing of collections of software components between diverse groups of developers and users, to the practice of reusable software.

The concept behind such sharing came up in the mid- to late 1980s because of the need to advance the *concurrent engineering* practice. Any work done concurrently on interactive systems makes necessary:

- *Multiple usage* of a common database by different professionals working on the same project, and
- The ability to *visualize* in real time all changes made to a common project by any one of the team players.

Further to the point, the reusability concept brings up interesting systems aspects, for instance, the requirement of providing for functional flexibility and, at the same time, assuring structural integrity of the system.

Managing *reusable software* means managing a mix of old code (typically with inadequate documentation of original specifications, as well as modifications made over time), and new programs which rarely integrate well with the old code. Experience, however, indicates that within a defined workspace:

Object-oriented solutions can make existing programs effectively work together and with databases.

To achieve this goal we need to store, select, combine and disseminate such objects—including the concept of *class management.*[*]

Class management is the mechanism needed to handle object classes among software communities. One of its prerequisites is the ability to model software information. Another is the means to navigate through object class collections.

Hypertext approaches, for instance, can deal with versions of interrelated software objects and information elements. This is important in terms of managing software *building structures* within the logical space of our work.

Class management, incidently, may involve both crisp and fuzzy characteristics. The same is true of the content of the building structures in reference, where crisp and fuzzy software components can coexist. One of the key contributions by fuzzy engineering is precisely this possibility of coexistence, since crisp conditions are a special case of the fuzzy universe.

---

[*]See also D.N. Chorafas and H. Steinmann, *Object-Oriented Databases*, Prentice-Hall, Englewood Cliffs, NJ, 1993.

3—7 INTRODUCTION TO THE MATHEMATICS OF FUZZY ENGINEERING

Every knowledgeable engineering designer will appreciate that a good system is one simple to conceive and easy to understand. The mathematics of possibility theory, as we will briefly see in the following paragraphs, are rather simple. They have neither the long development history nor the rigorous aspects of probability theory and this can be an advantage.

The rules are often redundant, yet powerful enough to enable us draw up the first models.

There is more than one way of *fuzzifying* a certain situation, contrary to what prevails with other branches of mathematics.

This flexibility and nonexclusivity in terms of model structuring fits well the type problems encountered with management applications. It also makes it feasible to develop initially simple expert system structures which can become more sophisticated.

In principle, when we experiment with the implementation of fuzzy set theory we will be well advised to distinguish among two alternatives:

1. The predicate being developed represents the idea we make of a vague class of objects.

The fuzzy characteristics typically prevail as we move from ideas and concepts to the model, in a rule-oriented form. But there is as well an alternative approach:

2. The predicates are deduced from statistical references.

These may be crisp or fuzzy. In the past, in the large majority of cases they were taken as being crisp—which is an approximation—because no tools were available for the handling of fuzzy data. But this has changed.

An example of class 2 regarding fuzzy data is a histogram constructed on the basis of opinion polls. Research points out that opinion-based statistics fall under possibility rather than probability theory, and should be handled in a possibilistic manner.

To help in explaining the domains in which the implementation of possibility theory extends, Japan's Laboratory for International Fuzzy

Engineering (LIFE) has developed the chart in Figure 3.3. It presents in a nutshell the many aspects and applications areas of the new field, ranging from:

- A mathematical infrastructure (the basics)
- To computer architectures
- And the rich domains of its possible implementation

One of the common elements among the implementation domains in reference is that they are characterized by a system concept, where each component and subsystem:

- Receives an input,
- Features its own processing rules, and
- Gives an output.

This sounds like general *cybernetic* theory and to a substantial measure it is so. But there are as well important differences from already existing cybernetic concepts. For instance,

1. The inputs to a given processing module are not independent, but directly concerned with each other.

Hence, to simplify a system we should strive to reduce the number of inputs to each processing element, or *Predicate Box*, though this tends to increase the number of the processing elements themselves.

Figure 3.4 shows a Predicate Box. It has inputs and outputs. Three inputs have been used as an example:

- Gear
- Velocity
- Acceleration

This is a real-life application in the automotive industry where a fuzzy engineering artifact correlates these three inputs in order to detect a pattern: The driver's way of running his or her car on the road. The driver's profile is the output, as he or she is cruising through a database.

2. The fuzzy conditions characterizing each input should be defined quite carefully in terms of the necessity (or belief) value of each variable.

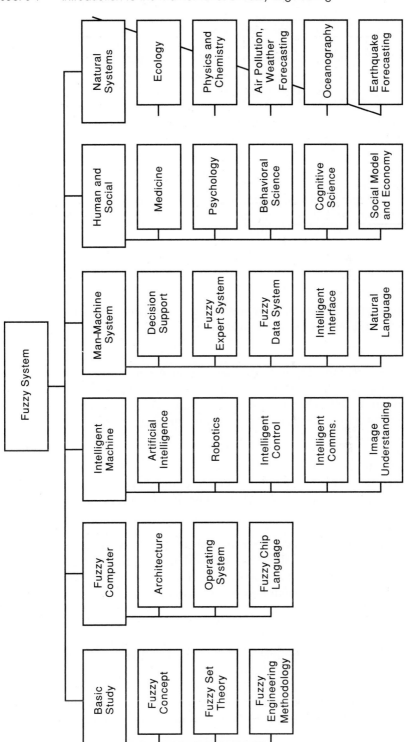

Figure 3.3 Expected fields of fuzzy engineering implementation, as seen by LIFE.

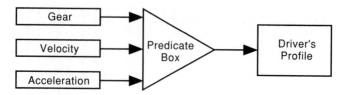

Figure 3.4   A fuzzy engineering artifact with three inputs and the driver's profile as an output.

In the example in the following paragraphs, the behavior of three drivers (fast, median, and slow) is characterized by the appropriate curve which defines in how many hours they can cover a distance from A to B. Figure 3.5 contrasts the fuzzy representation to a crisp way of description. This leads to rule 3:

3. In principle, the curves representing a given behavior should overlap, just because the system is fuzzy.

Once the fast, median, and slow driving curves have been defined in an overlapping way, they bring forward truth values that might not be really fulfilled in a 100 percent sense by anybody. A given driver may be 30 percent fast and 60 percent of a medium speed driving habit.

4. Due to the impact of vagueness and uncertainty, the sum of partial qualities being expressed may be less than 100 percent (as in the above example), or more than 100 percent. It does not need to square out.

This sets possibility theory apart from probability theory and the deterministic models. It is one of the basic issues that need to be understood. As stated, fuzzification of an uncertain situation is not an exact process, precisely because there is vagueness in the system.

5. While in some cases we may have only two inputs to the Predicate Box, in others there may be three or more inputs.

When this happens, it is wise to sort these inputs out into homogeneous groups, classifying them in terms of importance and/or precedence. Bringing the inputs into homogeneous sets has the advantage that we can simplify the system by treating two or three inputs to the Predicate Box, at each time.

6. Once the inputs to a processing element (Predicate Box) have been defined, we must address the output coming out of that box.

This is done in a way similar to that used for the inputs, with the added requirement that the appropriate matrix must be established, combining

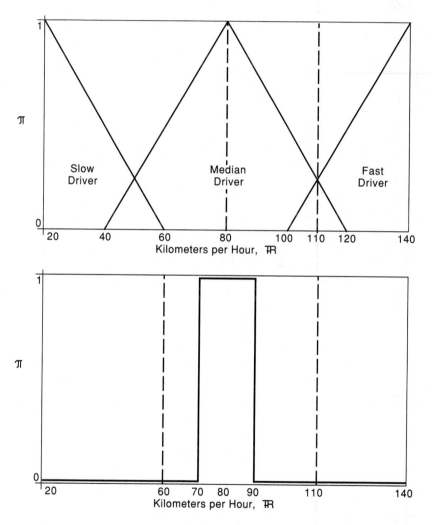

Figure 3.5   Fuzzy representation and the crisp alternative. $\mathbb{R}$ stands for real domain.

the inputs to create the output. Essentially this matrix defines the predicates that characterize the processing node.

7. Any valid solution to fuzzy engineering will have a limiting case, which is essentially the crisp alternative with values that are either 0 or 1—hence probability theory.

Figure 3.5 explains this concept. The upper graph represents the driver's speed curves based on the notion of fuzziness. This is expressed through a membership function to three alternative populations: slow drivers, median drivers, and fast drivers.

Any driver belongs to one of the three sets by a specific value. A person driving at the speed of 20 to 60 km/hour is slow; 40 to 120 is median; 100 to 140 is fast. A driver who keeps 110 km/hour is by 30 percent a member of the median set and 30 percent of the fast driver set. He or she belongs to both but only a little.

If a 70 to 90 km/hour driving speed is strictly enforced,* then the situation becomes rather crisp as shown in the lower half of Figure 3.5. It is a yes/no case: respecting the rules or not respecting them.

A driver who runs at 110 km/hour is outside the speed limit. He or she does not observe the rules. The same incidently is true of a driver who runs at 60 km/hour. Indeed, anybody outside the 70 to 90 km/hour speed range is breaking the rule, whether he or she is a fast or a slow driver.

These are the basic concepts underlying the new wave of information technology. They are applicable all the way from automotive engineering and home appliances to the senior management level. This is essentially an enabling technology which permits us to handle an impressive number of situations, reduces undue complexity, and serves managers and professionals well beyond what has been possible so far.

---

*The lower limit helps to keep the car flow fluid, as was some years ago the rule in Switzerland.

4

Applying New Transactional Technology in Business

4-1 INTRODUCTION

As we have seen in Chapters 1 to 3, the conceptual, mathematical, and software developments of the 1970s and 1980s, which in their time dominated a good deal of information technology, are by now a thing of the past. Solutions for the 1990s increasingly require the able handling of fuzzy engineering and intelligent database concepts.

A good example is offered through *long transactions* which involve a fiat of processes accessing in parallel a number of dynamically restructured databases. A long transaction takes time to execute; addresses itself to diverse, heterogeneous but networked databases; and may involve 1,000 or more disk accesses versus 8 to 10 for a short, classical transaction of the debit/credit type.

It is at times possible to decompose long transactions into subtransactions, each one of them atomic or at least fairly simple. What groups together diverse short transactions into one common body is the online execution of a *metalevel*, for instance, a complex customer order, which has not only to be followed through in detail but also its execution reported in real time to the client.

The online execution of a long transaction is part and parcel of customer order facilitation and a contributor to good business practice. It is as well a matter of survival in a market that is more demanding than ever, where competitiveness is judged by quality of service.

The execution by a broker of conditional buy/sell orders given by institutional investors provides a good example on the type of transactions that are of growing importance in the business environment.

Institutional investors typically constitute the sophisticated part of a broker's clientele.

They are also the more lucrative clients whose relationship management is a focal point for any broker.

Many financial institutions, as well as industrial organizations, tend to look at their client base in strata, as shown in Figure 4.1. Dai-Ichi Kangyo Bank, for instance, has 1,000,000 business customers. Of these, 20,000 are in the top "A" list which benefits from very advanced database supports and sophisticated information services.

Long transactions and complex queries are executed in response to customer orders which originate in the upper A and B layers of the market. Short transactions address themselves to the lower, C layer of the stratified client population as shown in Figure 4.1.

Although the C population typically represents some 80 percent of clients, it contributes less than 20 percent of a company's profits, as Pareto's Law suggests.

The two top layers, A and B, consist of the *more sophisticated* and also *more demanding* clients who contribute the 80 percent of the bottom line.

The concepts, tools, and solutions that we discussed in the first three chapters are used in connection to the A and B populations for innovation,

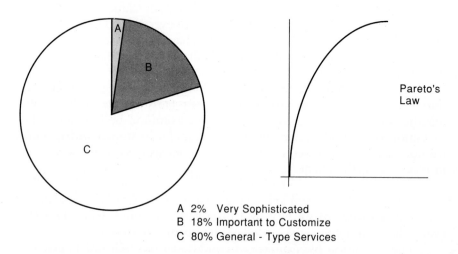

A 2%   Very Sophisticated
B 18% Important to Customize
C 80% General - Type Services

Figure 4.1   Stratification of the client population in terms of requirements for services.

market penetration, and greater profits. By contrast, in the C population they are employed to swamp costs.

4–2 OVERRIDING NEED FOR ANALYTICAL CAPABILITY

Following up on the example which was presented in the introduction, during the mid-to-late 1980s, the financial industry has seen a revolution in its analytical capability which it developed in response to the challenges of deregulation and of growing client needs. As the market evolved and grew, advanced analytical tools, simulators, and supercomputers have been used to:

- Assess rapidly developing market effects on client portfolios
- Experiment on alternative financial products, their costs and benefits
- Develop new products and services in compressed time scales (time to market)
- Optimize the financial decisions made in the trading day and evaluate the results

In the case of the broker whom we have taken as the background example, clients usually communicate by telephone to enter orders and obtain quotations. For the most part, the trader gets his or her quotations from other dealers and buys or sells for the customer without taking risk or committing the bank's capital to the transaction. He or she just charges a fee.

Such fee, however, has to be justified. The client will judge the quality of service that he or she is getting through the minute attention paid to the given order which may be quite complex. This service might:

- Involve different types of securities, including alternative and complementary purchases or sales
- Deal in different currencies, on treasury availability or other criteria
- Imply price limits which may vary by security, by currency, and by market
- Consider currency risk, country risk, company risk, and other risks

These are in a nutshell the background reasons of complex transactions whose able execution calls for new advanced concepts and for powerful tools. Known as *rocket scientists** on Wall Street and *financial engineers* in the City of London, the people able to execute these transactions are highly valued. But what about the tools?

New dimensions of computing have been explored in order to sharpen the tools that we are using. This becomes a "Do it or die" issue as client demands grow, because of the availability of higher caliber individuals and, steadily improved analytical services offered by competitor brokerage firms.

The use of modern mathematical tools has moved from science to finance. Option Adjusted Spreads (OAS) for mortgage-backed securities, for example, use Monte Carlo techniques developed during World War II for the Manhattan Project, the American effort to produce a nuclear bomb.

Through analytics, instead of using just a few scenarios to characterize a given financial instrument and its behavior, investment banks can emulate thousands of paths to determine interest rate sensitivities and/or evaluate latent risk factors. With supercomputers, this can be done in a few seconds.

Interactive computational finance has been characterized as a surgical application of computers and communications technology to an old profession. Long transactions are the result of this surgical operation. Banks try to capture a multidimensional perspective with subsecond response time, which enables them to participate in the race to buy low and sell high without being caught with deadwood. The more progressive financial institutions know that without the appropriate tools at their disposition they will either be frozen at the switch or jump in with incomplete knowledge and get burned.

A similar reference is applicable to manufacturing firms, an example being *Just in Time* inventory management. Quite simply, it cannot be achieved by means of the old, worn-out tools of information technology—the mainframes, COBOL programs, nonintelligent terminals, 3270 protocols, IMS, and DB2.

4—3 NETWORKS, DATABASES, AND WORKSTATIONS

Even simpler transactions than those considered in Section 4-2 need analytics as their application perspectives expand and more factors come into the equation. For instance, the bank acts in the market on behalf of its clients—but in the case of some large transactions it may also use its own capital. This means that:

---

*Rocket scientists are experts in mathematical modeling from the aerospace industry and nuclear engineering, now applying their skills in financial phenomena.

Its dealer(s) would have to take the side of the investor, opening a long currency position to accommodate a customer who wishes to sell or buy currencies.

Having filled the customer's order, the dealer would normally trade to eliminate the position or at least to neutralize risk.

This is an example of a financial long transaction, since the different trading events of which we just spoke are related. It is as well an example of a networked transactional environment where each operation depends on many others for its execution.

Networks interconnecting database resources and online access to databases are two of the pillars for a successful execution of transactions in the described environment. Selected information elements of these distributed resources must virtually converge toward the trader's workstation, as suggested in Figure 4.2.

The kernel around which this service revolves is the intelligent communications network.

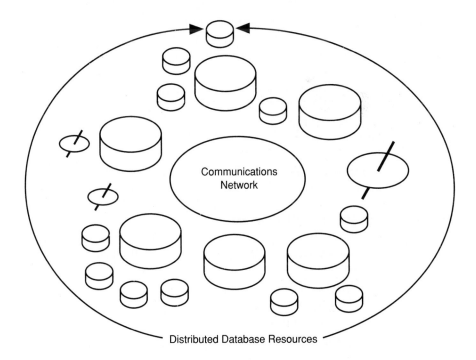

Figure 4.2   The communications network is the kernel of distributed databases.

By all likelihood, the information elements have been stored in magnetic as well as optical disks, under heterogeneous DBMS and incompatible formats.

No matter how great might be the incompatibility, for the enduser
access to these data resources should be absolutely *seamless*, easy,
friendly, and forgiving of his or her errors.[*]

Finance is not the only domain where long transactions and complex
queries distinguish the advanced institution from the outdated one. Many
examples are present also in manufacturing, merchandizing, and the transport industry. When online airline reservations started, more than 30 years
ago, they were concerned mainly with short transactions: Checking
whether seats were available on a given flight (read) and, if yes, reserving
one seat for the new customer (write). This has been the transport industry's
counterpart to debit/credit. But times have changed.

As we will see in the American Airlines case study, business clients
today constitute the most profitable population for air carriers, and business
clients have complex requirements that must be answered in real time.
Sophisticated passengers will be rarely interested in just one flight leg, the
debit/credit approach to airline reservations.

Business clients like to know about correspondences and continuation,
ask for hotel reservations in a given category, want to benefit from discounts,
require a rented car service available upon arrival, and so on.

Databases for reservations and accounting data as well as frequent flier
credits have to be accessed—and these typically are distributed.

All types of reservations have to be made through subtransactions,
then rolled back if for any reason the global transaction aborts.

This is another way of saying that the requirements posed by long
transactions are never static. They evolve all the time and change as a result
of new services, competitor actions, market developments, regulation or
deregulation, tariffs, and other factors.

Many long transactions pose visualization challenges. As such, they
are excellent candidates for intelligent graphics and pattern recognition
applications. More likely than not, they will demand:

- Multimedia communications,
- Knowledge engineering solutions,
- Access to heterogeneous databases,

---

[*]See also D.N. Chorafas and H. Steinmann, *Solutions for Networked Databases*, Academic
Press, San Diego, CA, 1993.

- Different types of conditional updates, and
- Significant discipline in execution.

As these examples help document, due to their complexity, transactions contrast to short transactions, which are atomic. But they are as well long-lived and may keep the database in an inconsistent status for minutes or hours.

Since they are particularly important in computer-aided design (CAD), computer-aided manufacturing (CAM), and computer-integrated manufacturing (CIM)—but also in banking and finance (forex, securities, treasury)—one may wonder how fuzziness in update can be reconciled with a sound, dependable practice. The answer is that a successful commercial environment often depends on sophisticated tools to access, manipulate, and protect information elements. This can be done more accurately through fuzzy engineering than in a crisp manner.

4—4   INFORMATION TECHNOLOGY AND MARKETING STRATEGY

Successful information technology implementations are always subservient to marketing strategy. In the case of the financial industry, for instance, transactions are a building block of the intermediary's business—therefore of the bank—and they have to be handled in a manner serving this function, not just in any way.

Long transactions complement the process of *Relationship Banking*, which is a *customer-centered* business strategy. This contrasts to only product-centered or only market-centered approaches, both *complementing* them and *restructuring* them, but also

> Brings emphasis and attention on the need for *deductive distributed databases* (read: intelligent databases),
>
> Makes able *database mining*[*] a key word in continuing the customer relationship, and
>
> Improves quality of service through the reliable handling of *long transactions*.

Both the appropriate methodology and sophisticated software are a "must." Yet in the majority of cases institutions let their technology drift, staying instead with the tools of yesterday. Only the *leaders* are able to keep up with the new requirements. The laggers have nothing really available in a

---

[*]Discussed in Section 4-6.

technology-oriented sense to satisfy their top-level clients. This hurts their market standing as well as their profits.

The raison d'être of any business is to make money, and this can best be done through innovation. But when important software and hardware projects are put on hold while the trivial ones are given priority, the company only gets backwater technology for which it pays big money.

Because of backwater, a company risks losing control of the most lucrative sector of the market, and once control is lost, it is very difficult to recover it again. Falling behind is very easy and it happens when:

The company's computer people are still resting on past laurels,

Both management and the systems expert do nothing new that will differentiate their company from others, and

No competitive advantages are forthcoming in the sense of advanced technological support to satisfy the requirements of the most important clients.

These conditions spell disaster in terms of relationship management. Market share, new product development, and able technological support go hand in hand. Solutions with *market impact* and *low cost*—in short, with *competitiveness*—can only be found in the frame of reference shown in Figure 4.3, which revolves around a solid and steadily upkept client base.

Important clients today are demanding *quick response* programs. This is a totally alien concept to many of the people who manage technology operations.

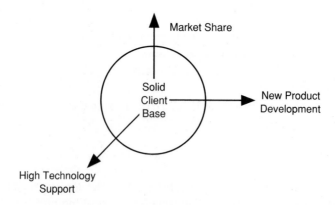

Figure 4.3 Market share, new product development, and technological support constitute the frame of reference of competitiveness.

Do-nothing conditions in data processing operations are so widespread that it would take a book to describe them in detail. But two examples stand well above the others:

1. The unreasonably long time it takes to develop new computer applications, and
2. The inability to provide seamless access to the corporate databases.

Each one of these issues, and evidently both in unison, strangles the efforts of the company's product divisions to keep the market under control, and to better the market share as well as the overall profitability.

We are what we do. Most often, even able people do nothing when they discover the perpetual motion machine of automatic budget renewal. After they get hold of it to their profit, they will not let it go that easily.

Resistance to change comes from those who *stand to lose* significant advantages from *the inefficiencies* of the current system. But in industries whose customers are accustomed to shopping for value, failure to change condemns a company to decay.

A recent study has shown that to survive a computer technology company must *reinvent itself* every 2½ years. The same is true of financial institutions and other service industries whose survival rests on steady innovation through imaginative moves and high technology.

4—5 KEEPING AHEAD OR BEHIND COMPETITION?

A recent study which I did in America and Western Europe documented that the No. 1 reason for the inability to face the challenging demands posed by the most important customers has its roots in the stagnant information technology mentality. This is well exemplified by an *awkward* mainframe-and-COBOL*-oriented culture which keeps the company *behind* competition.

New financial products are highly dependent on advanced technology. For instance, in foreign exchange, futures, and options it is not always possible to determine the maturity of a forward transaction at the time the deal is done. But,

If we decide on a forward transaction with a fixed maturity date for hedging purposes,

---

*Also 3270 protocol, hierarchical DBMS, and other nonsense.

Then a foreign exchange swap transaction offers the opportunity to change the maturity to the desired date.

Financial engineering provides the necessary tools so that this can be done in an able manner, while remaining covered against currency risk.

Continuing with the same financial example, a swap transaction in forex usually takes one of two forms. One is a combination of a *spot* and a *forward* transaction, according to the algorithm:

Spot purchase + *forward* sale
Forward sale + *forward* purchase

It is important that spot update and forward sale are concluded at the same time. If they are not, it is not possible to hedge the foreign exchange risk. If they are, then our institution is ahead of those segments of the market that are not yet able to master new technology.

The algorithms, "spot + forward" and "forward + forward," are examples of long transactions. Increasingly, they characterize sophisticated dealing by financial institutions and treasury operations. But they also call for a fair amount of interactively exploiting the contents of the databases to unearth hidden factors or values at any time and anywhere in the world. This is known as *database mining* and is best served through distributed intelligent databases, which we will examine in Part Two.

Long transactions and database mining go hand in hand. The one needs the other. Forward transaction, for example, can be shortened or lengthened by means of a swap, provided we have instantaneously available the information to make this operation meaningful. They are shortened when they are advanced[*] and lengthened when they are renewed.

Since a swap transaction of this kind may involve a combination of spot and forward, the calculation of *swap income* and *swap costs* is based on computing forward discounts and premiums.

Rushing into commitment does not help. Able decisions need experimentation, which involves both simulators and information. More than that, real-time experimentation calls for the analysis of patterns—to be unearthed through database mining.

Swap costs represent the interest rate differential in the markets between currencies involved for the swap period. Their calculation is synonymous with executing the customer order in an able manner. The able handling of such transactions:

Demands the best of our knowledge in information technology as well as in financial dealing

---

[*]In which case, the original due date is changed to a later date.

Involves an execution process that spans over time and over different marketplaces

Has to be multifunctional as well as be able to operate in a distributed execution sense

Another example of a long transaction is an order placed with, say, the London stock exchange but at the same time involving transactions in New York, Zurich, and Tokyo. These transactions:

1. May need to be in five different moneys: dollars, pounds, German marks, Swiss francs, and yen.
2. The money may have to be debited to different client accounts held with branches abroad.
3. Portfolio Update, too, will have to be executed on-line to update assets.
4. Reporting has be consolidated for the treasurer who gave the order, but also distributed by account, type of money used, and status of portfolio.

These are examples of long transaction execution by financial institutions. But clearinghouses and stock exchanges, too, have to face similar challenges as transnational companies today are quoted in more than one bourse.

Update consistency and *database integrity* are the issues, so that the databases in each and every one of the exchanges are properly synchronized at all times. Short of this, the "solutions" that the information technologists provide will be poor in results and rich in entropy.

In order to assure database integrity while avoiding the any-to-any network which would have been the neater solution, the now defunct project PIPE/Euroquote brought up an irrational 13th database fed by the other 12.* This number corresponds to the participating stock exchanges of the European Community. The software was to take care of:

- Translating the received transactions,
- Queuing up for updates, and
- Broadcasting transactional information.

This seemed to be a simpler solution than any-to-any connectivity, however, as it was found out the hard way, it posed severe problems, for instance, synchronization of switching in a network-wide sense; assurance of consis-

---

*The databases of the stock exchanges of the 12 member states of the European Community. See also D.N. Chorafas and H. Steinmann, *Do IT or Die*, Lafferty Publications, London and Dublin, 1992.

tent image through 13 heterogeneous databases; and dependability of satellite broadcasting in spite of weather interferences. The project crashed.

As far as the communications discipline is concerned, sequencing was found to be a tough nut to crack, particularly in view of message exchanges concerning market trends. Other challenges have been:

- The handling of corrupt messages,
- The dynamics of the refresh channel, and
- The use of the re-request channel.

The lesson is that the execution of long transactions poses many challenges, and solutions to the majority of them have to be custom-made. This is compounded by the fact that experience in handling them is still thin and computer vendors, as well as third parties, are way behind in producing needed sofwtare.

4–6 ENTERPRISE INFORMATION AND DATABASE MINING

Some of the computer vendors, particularly those who in the past enjoyed near monopoly, use the term *Enterprise Information System* for an all-encompassing commercial product. Such an approach could not be further from the real requirements of a user organization.

Today, user requirements are not only advanced but also focused. The issue of long transactions was not invented to make system designers unhappy or frustrated. It grew out of daily practice:

Once the basics have been satisfied, customer requirements expand, and

New solutions become necessary both to respond to evolving needs and to exploit the latest advances of technology.

The cost-effective exploitation of such advances is not made just to keep at a state-of-the-art level, but rather for reasons of building a new, more effective enterprise information system that enhances the company's *competitive position* while it helps in *reducing costs*.

In one way or another long transactions have been handled during the 1980s, but *manually.* This had disastrous effects on the bottom line. Consequently, some organizations thought of improving the processing picture by creating another incompatible database which, acting on bad advice, they plugged into their network. This was supposed to help integrate all information elements necessary for a long transaction. In reality, it ended by having discontinuity as a result, which in many cases ranged from uncertainty to chaos.

Those who projected (and still preach) the database recentralization approach lacked the background and/or the vision to understand that the distributed environment grew out of necessity. Neither did they realize that it is not possible to turn back the clock.

The errors that sneaked into this recentralized approach, wherever it was tried, have been legion. Lack of dependability of the contents turned off potential users. The updating mechanism remained weak. The experience has been costly, and finally it was found out that nothing was gained by creating another overlapping 13th database. Progressive organizations have realized that creating another database ends by adding to the confusion, rather than solving any problems. What is needed is *Database Mining* of the existing resources, done in a seamless, any-to-any manner.

Database mining is executed through heuristics and algorithms. It is flexible, able to answer ad hoc queries on information and patterns of information in the database, and capitalizes on *seamless access* to existing resources. Hence it works without changing the existing data structures or investing in unnecessary projects like the 13th database.

To support Relationship Management, for instance, since the early 1980s Dai-Ichi Kangyo Bank has operated the Group Information System (GIS) which works fully on-line. GIS analyzes and manages the profit and loss and balances of the

- Domestic banking,
- Overseas banking, and
- Securities transactions.

This includes everything concerning each major client of the bank. Some 20,000 companies are on GIS out of 1,000,000 corporate customers—or roughly the 2 percent of clients which contributes a big chunk of the profits.[*] Long transactions are the result of the requirements of these top customers.

Some technical characteristics are worth noting that set long transactions connected to enterprise information apart from the more classical queries and transactions. Foreign exchange provides an example. The exact determination of the foreign exchange spot rate has to be in line with the prevailing spot rate or around a level defined by the client:

Hedging costs may, however, be incurred, for instance, in obtaining a currency with a higher interest rate at a later date than originally expected, and

---

[*]See also what has been written in Section 4-2 relative to the "A" class of customers shown in Figure 4.1.

When the exact determination of the forex spot rate becomes available, this will have an impact on cash positions. Hence, real-time experimentation must precede commitment.

Given that currency markets have locality (dollars in New York, pounds in London, deutsche marks in Frankfurt, Swiss francs in Zurich, yen in Tokyo), *real-space* information is vital. Real-space systems are real-time systems of a global nature which:

- Operate 24 hours per day,
- Cover all contintents, and
- Consolidate real-time information for decision and commitment reasons.

These are operational characteristics which escape classical data processing chores, but which a true enterprise information system should include. The demands being posed have little to do with the trivial data handling chores, but a great deal with survival in the fiercely competitive market of the 1990s.

4–7 MARKET COMPETITIVENESS AND TRANSACTION HANDLING

The able handling of long updates through on-line operations provides a superior setting for creating advanced database applications. We already know from short transactions that teleprocessing requires the services of a transaction processing monitor (TPM) which:

Allows multiple resource managers to work together in order to assure the integrity of a transaction, and

Through an appropriate commitment protocol makes sure that a transaction either completes or has no effect on any database involved in its execution.

The reliability of database management rests on the way information is handled between the steps of a transaction. The right solution must provide the basic mechanism for queued transaction processing, but interactive environment queues may also be counterproductive.

The apparent contradiction in this statement is due to the fact that modern business challenges are not being solved by yesterday's technology. Any dynamic company operates in an ever-changing environment and has to take advantage of emerging markets—which means changing and simultaneously protecting its current computers and communications investments.

As customer demands evolute and market requirements change, new transaction processing systems have to be introduced, substituting old models without upsetting existing applications.

A rich, integrated, easy-to-use technological infrastructure opens new doors for business, looking for custom-designed solutions able to meet unique needs.

Distributed, scalable, multidimensional growth permits to more appropriately allocate processing and databasing power. It makes feasible adding system software incrementally anywhere in the world, affording higher performance without sacrificing database integrity. Solutions have to be based on:

- Business stream requirements
- The exact nature of *our* long transactions
- Update and query frequency
- Geographic relevance
- Remote access and task invocation

As we saw in Chapter 1, the foremost organizations now study the wisdom of using object-oriented solutions. Problems relating to updates are not disappearing through object views, but object approaches are more flexible, although one has to remember that an uncharted territory can be dangerous.

Learning to use new technology is a foremost need, because next-generation real-time and real-space systems are expected to become very sophisticated featuring multiple time-constraint levels. As long transactions evolute, their requirements can be answered only through:

A dynamic and adaptive behavior towards systems solutions, with change as a permanent rule.

The observance of logical timing constraints, including an efficient method of handling priorities of events.

For instance, netting and settlement systems demand the representation of complex entities with several levels of transaction handling. The same is true of Just-in-Time inventory management. We need to model a real-space approach for the representation of entities of the environment, capturing the semantics dynamic behavior of real-world entities.

The dynamic behavior of an object can be represented by operations that specify the manipulation of complex interactions. The integration of *inference rules* into the distributed heterogeneous database system will look after integrity and consistency constraints to be enforced.

Inference rules will assist in transaction handling and query processing, helping to extend the semantics of the schema.

The expertise acquired by the database system through these rules will help in maintaining integrity and in enhancing performance.

Any organization will be well advised to take a strategic view of its technological investments and this suggests that an AI-enriched approach should be taken, to answer in an able manner many issues connected to long, complex transactions, for instance, authorization and authentication for security purposes, fast response time for effective interactivity, protocol conversion, and traffic management for seamless networking.

4–8 PRODUCT DEVELOPMENT AND MARKET SENSITIVITY

From the automotive industry to banking, the long length of time needed to develop new products and processes is definitely a thing of the past. Not only does market sensitivity have to be acute (otherwise the organization loses contact with the ground), but also the product offering must be presented quickly and be value differentiated, and cost effective.

Successful new products can never be unidimensional and they practically never stand alone. They have to be studied, developed, marketed, and connected to other existing products, as well as to specific references concerning customers and market focus. Figure 4.4 has been drawn along this line of reference, based on an example from a loans environment.

Once the product has been defined, marketing should allocate profit targets by customer, but this can be effective only if the appropriate software support is available and it works online.

For the top 20% of customers follow-up must be done in a very timely manner, incluidng exposure.

Evaluation by market and currency in which top customers operate is feasible through models, computers, and networks.

Profit and loss follow-up by product should be databased, actuated, and visualized by means of expert systems.

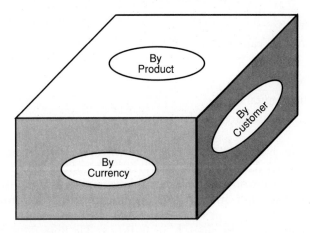

Figure 4.4   Loan management, deposit management, and other follow-ups.

This triple approach is an excellent implementation from which management can greatly benefit—particularly so if all elements in accounting and marketing are detailed and integrated. The level of the interactive presentation should depend on management's ad hoc needs.

As we will see in considerable detail in Part Two, particular attention must be paid to *interactive graphics*. That is why mainframe-based operations reaching the enduser through nonintelligent terminals, or workstations using dumb protocols like 3270, are a very unsatisfactory approach.

There are, as well, other prerequisites to be fulfilled. For instance, in its Treasury and Forex applications, Barclays Bank in London demonstrated that up to 20 sensitivities may be required in order to evaluate correctly a proposed transaction.

To gain a fast response, this financial institution said that it has to use either a $5 million mainframe dedicated to the sensitivity job, or low-cost, high technology such as supercomputing. The learned reader could easily guess what Barclays Bank has chosen.

Sensitivities are issues crucial to the evaluation of any transaction. What makes processing complex is that all sensitivities should be properly analyzed and accounted for in real time in relation to one another. For instance, sensitivity factors affecting a loan include:

- Nature of business
- Integrity of borrower
- Rating of directors
- Turnover

- Margins
- Outstanding capital
- Finance costs
- Overhead
- Working capital
- Capital expenditures, and so on

The able handling of sensitivities involves long transactions and requires access to databases which are rich in content. This is a subject which goes well beyond the classical Management Information Systems (MIS) perspectives and other "executive information" nonproducts some vendors want to unload on their customers.

In conclusion, technology is an indispensable ingredient but it is *not* everything. Successful manufacturing companies and financial institutions are those able to shake up the conservative, self-satisfied old culture—insisting that every person is able to innovate in the way his or her work is being performed.

The need for innovation must be thoroughly appreciated in order to gain from the technology investment that *our* company is making in networks, databases, workstations, software, or anywhere else.

An *research and development spirit* should be applied selectively, but, where it is applied, it should be implemented well.

Innovation should be seen as an opportunity giving more people at more levels the possibility to develop and lead projects, altering the organization's culture in the process.

Every *professional* should feel that the management of change is part of his or her job, and should not depend only on the lucky break of a given innovation's spontaneity.

The organization as a whole should create channels to speed the flow of new ideas, turning them into saleable products. Because many contributions are necessary to any transformation, everybody is an integral part of such an effort.

But while absolutely necessary, the innovation effort should not be given carte blanche. Prior to starting a project on a new product, really any project, there should be:

- A down-to-earth profit and loss estimate
- A factual, realistic business opportunity analysis
- A well-documented projection on costs—including development and marketing

- An equally well-documented and controllable budget

Yet, many product efforts and marketing projects are authorized without the benefit of a break-even study, not even a simulation on product pricing and costs. Such simulation is important in all cases, but the more competitive the product or the market is, the more vital the simulation becomes—and the higher the technology that should be used.[*]

---

[*]See also D.N. Chorafas, *Beyond LANs-Client Server Computing*, McGraw-Hill, New York, 1994.

5

Promoting Innovation
in Database Operations

5–1 INTRODUCTION

Chapter 4 has explained why long transactions alter the way in which user organizations look at databases. Therefore, the virtual integration of databases becomes a "must." Short of this, we can not handle in an able manner the complex requirements that long transactions pose—and the same is true of long queries and database mining operations.

Few information technology executives would argue that database applications done today should be of an innovative nature. But in which ways is a given database application innovative?

- Does it need to demonstrate new concepts or only a different technology?
- Does it have to apply an existing technology to a new domain? Or to an old domain in an innovative way?
- Should the application show a novel integration of different solutions into a much more effective setting?

Innovative database applications must be able to demonstrate departures from the old beaten path in order to answer in the best possible manner current and coming requirements. A first-class example is the IMKA project which is discussed in this chapter.

But innovation is not done just for its own sake. Closely associated to the innovation drive is the vital issue of cost effectiveness. We know that a new database structure has costs associated with it, but:

- What are the development and deployment costs?
- Can we quantify the corresponding benefits?
- What is the real nature of the payoff?
- How is the payoff measured in terms of money and time saved or earned?
- How long will it take for the integrative database solution to be deployed?

Speed of action is essential. Database applications should be done on a fast-track timetable. How long does the application take to develop and deploy? How well is the timetable observed? How is the development effort justified? How is the design validated before deployment?Which are the provisions made for steady maintenance after implementation?

Maintenance is a crucial issue in database deployment. One of the key questions to be answered is who maintains the innovative database: original developers, domain specialists, less-experienced "maintenance only" personnel? There are no unique answers to these issues, but a valid response to a couple more questions can help in finding the way:

Is the subject of our study in a domain where database requirements are expected to change over time?

Has anything been done to automate different phases of the maintenance problem?

As the exploitation of databases gets enriched with rules and heuristics, questions relevant to integrative database design, implementation, and maintenance tend to increase. They become more demanding in terms of required accuracy in the answers.

A great deal of attention has to be paid to database practices, including attention to problems inherent in the integration of distributed heterogeneous resources. Applications perspectives have to be brought into the picture, such as the conceptual work of the engineering designer and the analytical models using the corporate memory facility.

5—2 APPLICATIONS-DEPENDENT AND APPLICATIONS-INDEPENDENT DATABASES

Some books suggest, and it is advised as well by a number of consultants, that modern databases should be designed in an applications-independent way. Practical reasons make this statement only half-true.

Starting with the fundamentals, in the 1990s any organization of a certain size finds itself with a number of incompatible databases which it needs to integrate in order to handle in an able manner the developing information technology environment. This is a result of the so-called *legacy* applications:

> A recent research I did in America, Japan, and Western Europe has shown that the typical larger financial institution and manufacturing company has between 15 and 25 incompatible database structures.
>
> Smaller companies have fewer incompatible databases, but the problem is not radically different. Take the case of VSAM and IMS on mainframes, DB2 for InfoCenter, Oracle on minis, and dBase III on PC—and there you are.

On each one of these incompatible databases run applications, some of which tend to cluster under the same system. Hence a number of companies have chosen to attack incompatibilities by clustering reference, with the application perspective as the pivot point.

Even within this admittedly more limited approach to database integration, there are technological challenges to surmount. A good example is that of engineering databases, where incompatibilities create major problems in the exchange of computer-aided design (CAD) outputs, and their transmission from one CAD system to another.[*]

User organizations try to respond to this problem by setting virtual standards. STEP/PDES is an upcoming international standard for representing digital product databases, including shape/size data and three-dimensional CAD geometry, and tolerances, materials, assemblies, and configurations.

STEP will be used to exchange data among various vendors of CAD and computer-aided manufacturing (CAM) systems. It specifies a conceptual data model able to define the structure of product information. An object-oriented data modeling language called *Express* is complementing that model.

---

[*]See also D.N. Chorafas and S. Legg, *The Engineering Database*, Butterworths, London, 1988.

PDES is the American version of the proposed STEP international standard adopted by the U.S. Department of Defense (DOD). This is seen as the cornerstone to the Computer-Aided Logistics System (CALS) of DOD. CALS Phase Two, which is now in effect:

Requires contractors to deliver product information to the government in STEP/PDES Level 1 file format, and

Mandates Level 3 database implementations, with considerable consequences to database evolution, particularly for multimedia.

It is foreseen that coming implementations will make it easier to write STEP translators, while applications will directly access Level 3 databases, eliminating the need for translation. In fact, such databases are an essential component of the STEP program, needed to develop the coming generation of concurrent engineering and logistics applications.

A British development, the CADDEC system[*] automatically converts the STEP model from *Express* to C++. The C++ code is used to implement directly the STEP data model in Ontos, the object-oriented DBMS.[†]

In terms of mechanics, CADDETC takes product data in STEP Level 1 file format loading into the object database of Ontos. This approach:

- Provides the needed Level 3 STEP common database reference, and
- Offers a path between Level 1 and Level 3 formats.

Object orientation has been chosen for efficient Level 3 databases because it can implement the STEP data model directly. It also has the high performance required in modern CAD/CAM applications. In contrast, relational databases and older programming tools are not well suited for this job.

The reason for this statement can best be appreciated by taking a look at Figure 5.1. At least a dozen different databases can be involved in a CAM application, many of them being incompatible to one another. It follows that more rigorous solutions than those already available are necessary for integration purposes, and this is what the object orientation is expected to provide.

By going beyond relational database models, object classes can be represented in a more efficient form, along with the introduction and inclusion constraints.

---

[*]By the CAD/CAM Data Exchange Centre (CADDEC) affiliated with the University of Leeds.

[†]Described in D.N. Chorafas and H. Steinmann, *Object-Oriented Databases*, Prentice-Hall, Englewood Cliffs, NJ, 1993.

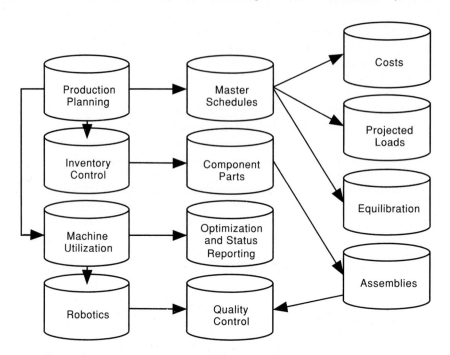

Figure 5.1 At least a dozen different databases are involved in computer-aided manufacturing. Many of them incompatible.

The views that are defined through an object approach are join queries over the primary keys of the underlying tables, and they are rather easy to update.

This method has several attractive features. It is relatively simple to implement, requires minimal but high-level changes to existing database structures, and uses a knowledge-enriched mechanism to provide the user with an integral view of objects.* It also assures automatic enforcement of the constraints for most of the functions that insert, delete, and update operations perform.

Such application emphasizes the provision of an integral view of the database and its objects, as well as the services that can be provided by heuristic approaches. Being an evolutionary process, it can work in synergy with existing applications.

These references highlight the direction recent standardization efforts are taking in order to assure the able execution of critical applications. But

---

*As will be explained in Part Two, through the presentation of deductive and intentional databases.

it will take years to implement the new evolving standards. Therefore, other projects focus on solutions that can assure a virtual database integration with immediate implementation.

Some of the virtual database integration projects use knowledge engineering and take an application–independent design approach. This, too, has significant merits as we will see in Section 5-4 when we discuss IMKA.

5–3 INTEGRATING LOGICAL AND NUMERIC COMPUTING PROBLEMS

One of the risks of application-dependent approaches to the challenge of database integration is the creation of different closed user groups, blocking further cross-database access efforts. This risk should be studied at the outset. Future problems could be removed by accounting for federated solutions which go well beyond any given applications domain.

Another particularly important issue in database integration studies is the association of the logical and numeric computing problems. This has three aspects:

1. The integration of languages primarily designed for either symbolic or numeric computation, but not both.

Until recently, solution to the problems behind the symbiosis of languages with two different orientations has not been recognized as a goal. In engineering design, however, the incorporation of existing analysis programs, which most likely are written in FORTRAN, with Bill of Materials (BOM) lists and knowledge engineering constructs is now becoming the norm.

2. The need that the reasoner in the logical world must understand what is going on in the numeric routines.

Frequently, it is not sufficient to treat an engineering analysis program as simply a black box that returns results, since results may be incorrect for a variety of reasons or reflect incompatible assumptions. Additionally, error conditions may arise which have to be taken care of in an integrative manner.

3. The growing demand that a multimedia engineering database incorporates past drawings with present drawings and with steadily upkept Bills of Material.

Past drawings, particularly those done prior to the mid-1970s when computer-aided design came into practice, will be on paper in all probability.

Even with high-resolution scanners it is not easy to carry them into the engineering database. The job is doable only through artificial intelligence interpreters, and even this does not offer 100 percent assurance.

At the same time, an engineering database which is split between magnetic disks, optical disks, paper records, and aperture cards will be highly ineffectual. Companies that have gone that way for a number of years have found through experience that they end up by paying for computer costs which are high, while getting paper-based efficiency which is low.

The able exploitation of an engineering database calls for the provision of a fairly homogeneous environment, whether the implementation is central or distributed. It also requires that knowledge engineering artifacts play a vital role, as we will see in Section 5-4.

When Hughes Aircraft Company recently designed a new chip, its engineers wanted to built a microcode emulator. They estimated that this would require more than one man-year (52 weeks) if done through the classical approach. Through the use of an expert system shell, it took 11 weeks, a 1:5 ratio. Note that the product of the shell was not an expert system as such, but a simulator.

A similar statement in terms of savings through the use of conceptual innovation and new technologies is valid in the financial industry. Payment documents are still on paper; only some of the information they contain goes on computer. This makes it necessary to handle both the paper and the database references, but as a result:

The cost of the combined operation is increasing,

While, correspondingly, the relative efficiency is decreasing.

By contrast, an innovative solution would take an integrative view of the problem, starting with the document which interfaces to the payments system environment and doing away altogether with its paper base, substituting it through data communications.

When the substitution of paper through online transmission is not feasible, because the business partners are not ready for such approach, then progressive banks store the incoming paper document on optical media (imaging) which still permits them to eliminate the paper. Figure 5.2 shows an approach to problem solution that has been successfully applied. It combines:

- Imaging solutions, and
- Knowledge engineering.

Imaging provides the support. Knowledge engineering is necessary for document understanding and assistance in signature recognition, as well

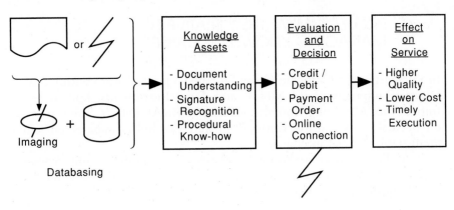

Figure 5.2   An innovative solution to document handling.

as for other functions. These are two costly jobs which, in the large majority of cases, are still manually done.

A different way of looking at the same issue is that classical programs access a database that is largely numeric and exploited in a procedural manner—but this is just one of the three basic actions needed for document handling. The result is that the other two have to be done by people shuffling paper, which means:

- Costs,
- Delays, and
- Errors.

Also, there is a very low return on the investments. Compare this to the exploitation of an imaging database through knowledge engineering. It is done automatically through a *semantic* data model, hence the handling of the meaning involved in the operation.

A semantic data model can operate on top of a relational DBMS, allowing object attributes to range over object classes. One approach:

Stores all the attributes of a hierarchy in one base table, and
Uses internal codes to distinguish object and subclasses.

Such implementation requires a comprehensive database design methodology based on semantics, concentrating on modeling and involving the translation of behavior aspects in a manner seamless to the user. This is one of the main goals that Project IMKA undertook, as we will see in the next section.

5—4 PROJECT IMKA, THE INITIATIVE FOR MANAGING KNOWLEDGE ASSETS

In Pittsburgh, the Carnegie Group* formed a joint venture with USWest, Digital Equipment, Ford Motor, and Texas Instruments, known as the Initiative for Managing Knowledge Assets (IMKA). IMKA's aim is to make intellectual assets available through software that links databases, enriching them with artificial intelligence.

At Ford, IMKA software keeps track of equipment and processes, used to make intellectual assets available through software that links databases enriching them with artificial intelligence.

Knowledge-oriented approaches provide efficient support for market-driven applications that were not well served through classical data processing.

This makes feasible solutions to difficult problems that traditional software techniques have not been able to address.

Traditional software is no longer sufficient because the computational tasks that surround market-driven manufacturing are not simply numerical and repetitive as they used to be. As we have seen in Section 5-3, the new challenges present in engineering and in other production-oriented environments involve logical processes. Hence they cannot be served through classical routines alone.

As project IMKA, among other similar efforts, has demonstrated, knowledge engineering can be instrumental in generating a good plant schedule that maintains efficient use of resources, assuring:

- Product quality,
- Low cost, and
- Customer satisfaction.

Knowledge-enriched solutions allow one to handle new, tough problems that are too costly or even impossible to do with conventional programming techniques. The following implementation example explains why.

At Ford, IMKA software helps in automating the manufacturing of electronic components at every one of the company's plants around the globe. It contains such details as how solder flows across a circuitboard and acts as a repository of manufacturing know-how.

---

*A knowledge engineering firm founded by the faculty of Carnegie-Mellon University (CMU).

Figure 5.3 presents a networked view of how this approach works. Knowledge engineering constructs interface to a SQL–type database; knowledgebanks can be accessed by applications either by being directly associated with them or through networking.

Online access to knowledge resources matters a great deal. When some time ago employees in a Ford plant in Brazil tried to speed up production by rotating the boards made there by 90 degrees, the failure rate jumped.

> Flowing at a new angle, the solder shorted out the circuits, as different changes can have adverse effects.

> But many of these adverse effects were already known in other Ford plants, and knowledge-based IMKA software could tell what might happen before time and money was wasted.

Such solutions can be powerful because they enable the developer to have available all the knowledge and relationships pertaining to a problem, prior to making a decision. In essence, they permit exploitation of community intelligence.

Automation is not the only way to capture intellectual capital. Often ordinary story telling has significant results. A study by the Palo Alto Research Center of Xerox revealed that repairmen learn most about fixing copiers not from company manuals but from swapping stories.

However, while story telling may not necessarily be a waste of time, it benefits only the small group engaging in that discussion—not the rest of the firm. No wonder then that Xerox turned to knowledge engineering.

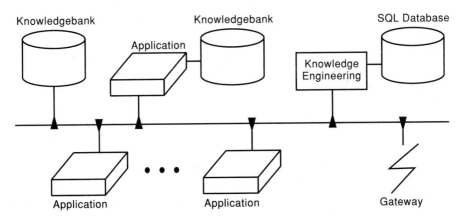

Figure 5.3   Networked applications and knowledgebanks in an IMKA environment.

The corporate memory facility makes feasible knowledge-sharing through a simple, straightforward procedure:

1. When a repairman finds a part that failed, he or she logs the fact into a database.
2. Assisted through expert systems, other repairmen have access to these facts.
3. Accumulated knowledge guides maintenance engineers to problems.
4. But online assistance goes well beyond troubleshooting, helping design engineers when they project a new copier.

As the Xerox and the IMKA examples help demonstrate, progressive companies look at the knowledge-enriched database technology to address the challenge of building corporate memory facility applications. These exploit the company's assets in know-how.

The aim of these and similar projects is to make available the mechanisms for integrating knowledge applications with data management systems. To reach such a goal, we need a combination of characteristics that will enable us to address today's challenges:

- A powerful knowledge representation system, and
- The ability to integrate applications delivery in a heterogeneous, distributed environment.

One of the high points is of course the integration of incompatible databases, and IMKA is addressing this problem only in part—within a more limited relational DBMS environment.* But what has been achieved in the first phase does allow users to build components that fit naturally with existing:

- Corporate data,
- Applications,
- Knowledge, and
- Problem solving methods.

It also permits engineering of new applications, integrating them with existing systems. This, as we said in the beginning of the present chapter, is one of the foremost challenges for the 1990s.

---

*The first supported database is Oracle.

The importantance of the management of the knowledge assets embedded in the corporate memory facility can be documented through a reference to USWest, a $10 billion Regional Bell operating company.

> Management estimates that 50 percent of the corporate assets are knowledge assets.
>
> *Knowledge Assets* essentially means the collective experience and expertise of the company's managers, professionals, and other employees.

Not only does the knowledge relate to the corporation in the conduct of business, but it also constitutes one of the most important competitive advantages of the firm, hence the need to have a mechanism in place to store and protect the knowledge assets.

In terms of exploitation, a corporate memory facility can help put the right level of skill at the right place at the right time. The IMKA project did not suddenly appear. USWest looked at the different types of technology to help streamline operations, and the conclusion was that knowledge-based systems could help reduce the decision making process *from years to months*, and in some cases from months to days.

5-5 INTERACTIVE IMPLEMENTATION PROCEDURES THROUGH IMKA

The interactive handling of knowledge and information assets stored in distributed heterogeneous databases is particularly critical when we consider that market windows are becoming smaller all the time. The key word is efficiency in exploiting business opportunity.

The example of a corporate memory facility which was described in Section 5-4 blends well with the *intentional* and extentional aspects of databases which were discussed in Chapter 3—and which will be analyzed at much greater length in Part Two.

> The knowledge-based structure is the intentional component of the system.
>
> The IMKA developers see relational databases as a source of relatively simple data, an extentional contribution to applications.

The relational database connection helps provide the user with the extentional source of information. For this purpose, the interface is designed to facilitate the use of existing data in a knowledge management sense— hence bringing intentional aspects into the picture.

An IMKA application retrieves data from relational databases, and Includes it seamlessly as part of the application's knowledgebank.

Embedded in IMKA are functions for opening and closing a connection to a distributed database structure, verifying the mapping between the database class and the frame, and compiling it into an internal representation.

There is functionality for setting a read or write lock for a specified relational database table and corresponding class, downloading records and converting them in instances of a database class, updating information elements to reflect changes made to database instance by the IMKA application, and also for removing database instances form memory and retrieving the table definitions.

Database records are represented as instance frames in the knowledgebank, with columns handled as attribute slots. A direct relationship between database tables and knowledgebank classes is also supported.

For consistency purposes, locking is provided for read and write operations.

IMKA applications can specify either no locking, read-only locking, shared update, or exclusive locking.

Transaction support is also on hand to assure database consistency.

Select, commit, and rollback operations are among the featured services.

IMKA's Phase 2 will provide support for integrating Oracle and Ingres databases. The network and database driver interfaces are designed in a way to permit extension to additional databases and networks over time.

Phase 2 will also feature an Integrated Frame Base (IFB) for permanent knowledgebank storage. The purpose of IFB is to address the knowledge management needs of applications in the same manner that data is handled through a database management system.

IFB will allow several applications to share the same knowledgebank, using available facilities in different ways if necessary, storing know-how within the application's memory, and assuring the consistency and integrity of the knowledgebank.

With IFB, knowledgebanks can be maintained independently from the applications that use them.

For greater flexibility, IFB will support multiple simultaneous reads from different applications.

Facilities will also be provided to create, delete, backup, and restore the IFB contents.

In terms of user control over value copying, Phase 2 aims to make available to users the ability to define whether string and other defined type values are copied when storing or retrieving objects, or when mapping a frame into a subcontext.

A networked client-server model will be integrated in Phase 2, enabling one application built with IMKA technology to communicate with another IMKA application. With this model, an IMKA knowledgebank and an IMKA application could reside on different machines in a network. To communicate:

1. The server process accepts a request for service, performs the requested service, and returns the result to the requester.

2. The client process, which is the requester, asks for the services from a server process which can support multiple clients.

A client-server approach is vital to the capture and storage of knowledge assets, which in spite of 40 years of computer usage no one records. This is a process important to forward-looking companies that understand the business interest in capturing knowledge and creating a system out of it.

5–6 DEVELOPING SYSTEMS SUPPORT FOR THE IMKA PROJECT

The type of system development done today by the foremost organizations is changing. The makers of tools and platforms, as well as the managers of important information systems projects, have to take notice of this fact.

The Carnegie-Mellon Group did so. In Phase 2 the IMKA project will extend the programmer interface built in Phase 1 and deliver SQL integration capabilities, a shareable knowledgebank, and extensions to knowledge representation. IMKA will not be directly supporting fourth- or fifth-generation languages, but:

Applications could be built which would make use of fourth- and fifth-generation language capabilities.

As a C++-based technology, IMKA applications can be integrated with a variety of existing and newly developed software and associate tools.

A modernized SQL interface will provide for connections to compatible relational databases across a TCP/IP network.

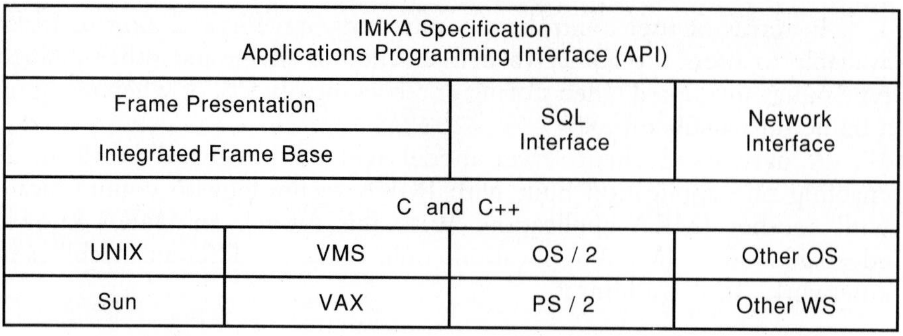

IMKA Specification Applications Programming Interface (API)			
Frame Presentation		SQL Interface	Network Interface
Integrated Frame Base			
C and C++			
UNIX	VMS	OS / 2	Other OS
Sun	VAX	PS / 2	Other WS

Figure 5.4   A layered view of facilities supported by IMKA.

IMKA Phase 2 assures an integrated support for using user-defined C++ objects as values on slots.* This enables better integration with C++'s object-oriented programming capabilities. It will also permit the user to save and restore portions of the knowledgebank.

The ability to handle the knowledgebank in an efficient manner gives the application developer better control over the loading of frames, which can be especially important at runtime. This fits well with the layered applications programming interface and linguistic facilities of IMKA shown in Figure 5.4.

Within the IMKA specification, an API helps the software developer to built client-server–oriented implementations.

IMKA-based applications can function as a client process, a server process, or both.

An IMKA application opens either a relational (extentional) database or a knowledgebank (intentional) storage facility by acting as a client process requesting information. Server processes able to handle multiple clients with incoming requests follow a first-in, first-out (FIFO) protocol.

Network drivers manage connection, registration, and message passing, being represented as C++ classes. All network-specific functions are concentrated in specific drivers, enabling the systems developer to add support for additional constructs.

The SQL interface provides access to external data sources. In this way, an IMKA application retrieves information elements from databases and includes them seamlessly as part of the application's knowledgebank. The adopted solution provides functions for:

---

*They may include, for example, encapsulated graphics or complex algorithmic functions.

- Opening and closing a connection to a relational database,
- Verifying the mapping between the database class and the frame, and
- Compiling into an internal representation.

As we discussed in Section 5-4, software sets a read-or-write lock for a specified relational DBMS table, downloading records but also updating the table to reflect changes made by the IMKA application.

Typically, database records are represented as instance frames in the knowledgebank, with columns as attribute slots. New records can be created and existing records retrieved or modified. There is support for direct relationship between database tables and knowledgebank classes.

This architectural approach has been chosen to help in capturing the general understanding of a problem, as well as the specific expertise needed to solve it. The aim is one of enabling the user to employ all available knowledge and information to generate a solution.

For instance, a knowledge-based troubleshooting system for computers might contain information about problems that occur in software and hardware. Expert systems assistance facilitates man–machine communication in answering queries such as:

- What causes the failure?
- How does one test for it?
- How does one repair it?

As it cannot be repeated too often, the power of a knowledge-based system over classical programming lies in its ability to represent all the information about a problem, together with the associated knowledge. This helps to control directly the effectiveness of a given solution.

The tools that we use for system development should enable representation of complex relationships that often characterize business problems, such as the interaction between orders, due dates, and machine scheduling—the example shown in Figure 5.1. The language available for expressing these relations should be both flexible and able to handle logical as well as numeric information.

These are practically the principles that we have discussed in Sections 5-2 and 5-3. Subsequently in Sections 5-4 and 5-5 we saw that IMKA is one of the projects which brings these principles into practical application.

The approach which has been elaborated captures the broad scope of available knowledge and information, extending valuable expertise, making critical know-how more broadly available, and enabling better decisions more quickly. These are the characteristics for success of the information systems in this decade—and they are applicable not only in manufacturing but also in banking and the service industry at large.

5–7 GIVING RISK MANAGEMENT AND SECURITY THE ATTENTION THAT THEY DESERVE

Just like the manufacturing industry cases discussed in this chapter, the power of any financial organization resembles, in at least one aspect, the power of the military. Survival lies in its ability to *continue to deliver*. Both knowledge and information are vital to this process, for more than one reason.

For instance, it would be wrong to keep on delivering at any cost—and hidden costs, like the *risks* being taken, can far exceed the more classical and visible costs. That is why the lack of an integrative global risk management system can destroy a company.

Examples taken in the financial industry usually focus on loans. The handling of integrative global risk taken with loans requires long, complex transactions as well as database mining. But loans are not the only example in the risk domain. Another lesser known, but even more risky case is netting, settlement, and affirmation:

The *affirmation* part of the trade is open to a number of major risks, since the intermediary guarantees something for which it has no firm assurance.

When affirmation is done, it becomes a commitment which can topple the clearer because of leverage at the depository side.

There is as well the problem that all rules and regulations have not yet been defined by country and cross-country. Worldwide, there is a wide gap in needed legislation, although since the depression of 1929–1932 the United States has guarantees of Federal Insurance—and above this many brokers are offering a $10 million extra insurance coverage to the client.

While alien markets hold many surprises, what particularly preoccupies the management of a clearer is the staying power over the longer term in a complex operation involving different product lines and a widely scattered topology. Risks are further magnified by information handling failure rates.

Figure 5.5 shows a tremendous cross-border failure rate due to very complex dataflows. These statistics are really surprising, particularly for countries like Switzerland, Germany, and Sweden—which are all export oriented and internationally minded. However, these are:

- Contractually bound deals that fail, with all the accompanying consequences.

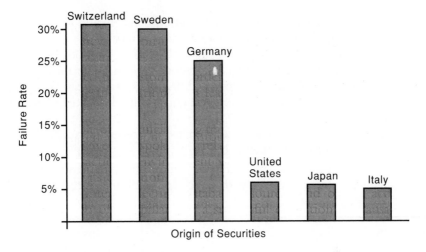

Figure 5.5   Average failure rate for cross-border deals because of lack of appropriate infrastructure.

- The most likely reason for such high rates is lack of infrastructure for cross-border dealing.
- The failure calls for last-minute fixing—which costs money and entails risks.

Through a support similar to the one IMKA aims to provide, a corporate memory facility can help in bringing such information-handling failure rates under control by capitalizing on knowledge acquisition and its exploitation.

Risks and exposures that are not faced in time result in legal, financial, marketing, customer-related, and finally managerial liabilities. These may include:

- Fraudulent transfers or settlements,
- Loss of confidentiality and damage to custody,
- Inaccurate information about customers, their financial assets, and the firm's property,
- Errors and operational failures which can have both legal and financial aftermaths.

Citicorp, for example, experienced a computer error that could have cost the group as much as $2 billion.* This happened when one of the

---

*Information Security Monitor, November 1989, p. 12.

bank's computer programs for the clearinghouse automated payments system (CHAPS) initiated a duplicate series of transfers.

While not a computer crime as such, this is a good example of how classical software problems can potentially lead to serious financial losses—and we should all learn from it. DP-type software can be a source of major troubles, particularly when legal constraints clearly define liability:

> CHAPS-initiated payments are normally *irrevocable*, except with the permission of the recipient, but
>
> Through good luck, in Citicorp's case, almost all of the duplicate payments were recovered with the cooperation of the receiving organizations.

The following is another example where legacy applications could not deliver control action. Apparently due to a lack of sufficient controls (though there may as well exist other reasons) by Headquarters over the funding and lending operations of its affiliate in the United States, the Atlanta branch of Banca Nazionale del Lavoro was able to hide $3 billion—or according to some estimates I heard in Rome $5 billion—of "unauthorized" loans to Iraq.

These examples should be instrumental in bringing management's attention to the need for effective systems and procedures regarding risk and security. In this regard, the knowledge-enriched corporate memory facility is a good solution.

Attention is further warranted by the fact that increasingly, laws and regulators are holding senior management liable for the adequacy of protection of financial information. Therefore, in order to respond to the threat with which it is faced, management must:

1. Understand the major aspects of the risks being taken.
2. Undertake all necessary precautions through rules and bylaws.
3. Provide effective system solutions, automating such rules and bylaws by means of knowledge engineering.
4. Steadily audit computers and communications, permitting no sacred cows.

Advanced technology is an instrument, not a goal. But it is an instrument that permits us to face the increasingly international political, social, and economic challenges. If we do not use high technology and know-how to our advantage, we will suffer the consequences of major failures in our businesses.

6

Getting a Better
Understanding of Available
Database Resources

6–1 INTRODUCTION

The need to understand better the database resources that we have available has been highlighted all the way, from the computer-aided design and computer-aided manufacturing cases which we discussed in Sections 5-2 and 5-3 of Chapter 5, to the risk management references of Section 5-7. Understanding of the knowledge and information assets available in our company is the first basic step to their able usage.

This is precisely what the Agro Division of Ciga-Geigy* decided to do. A carefully done project brought to top management's attention the idea that while the macroscopic view sets the boundaries, the microscopic view establishes the inventory of what is to be found within their perimetry. Subsequently, we need to:

Analytically examine each one of the component parts of the global database system.

Focus our attention on the definition of form and function, as well as on interconnectivity.

---

*Switzerland's largest chemical conglomerate, Ciba-Geigy has been selected as the best example of database reorganization, within the framework of a research type of implementation, among 70 companies in America, Japan, and Europe.

To get a better understanding of available resources and their nature, and to examine how they may support or constrain one another, are the reasons advanced by the Agro Division of Ciba–Geigy for choosing and using an object-oriented shell. This work helped in developing a model of the division's information technology operations, a multiple goal best expressed in six phases:

1. A global definition of business done by the Agro Division
2. Development of a metamodel concept and methodology leading to a Strategic Information Plan (SIP)
3. Inventory of all information technology components in software and hardware
4. Inventory of supports, from databases to programming languages and applications
5. A dictionary of metadata and its updating methodology
6. Consolidation of systems findings through metamodels.

This is the chosen perspective in the case of the specific implementation under discussion. Step 1 was done by a consulting firm assisting in the establishment of a Strategic Information Plan. Step 2 started at the end of 1989 by setting up a metamodel concept and associated methodology. We will see how the different steps were executed in Section 6-2.

6–2 ESTABLISHING AND FOLLOWING A STRATEGIC INFORMATION PLAN

As explained in the Introduction, among the priorities has been the foundation of the Strategic Information Plan. Subsequently, the Agro Division of Ciba-Geigy elaborated the basic parts of the SIP using Ptech.[*] This led to the metamodel which, in November 1990, was followed by step 3.

Next to the inventory of all information components (in hardware and software) steps 4 and 5 were executed, followed by step 6. The global model for the Agro Division has been worked out by organizational unit and it includes:

- Data types,[†]
- Applications languages, and

---

[*]An Entity-Relationship–oriented analysis and design tool, by ADT, which the company chose to create its CASE environment.

[†]At the prototyping phase it contained 600 data types. The company estimates the total to be over 10,000.

• Development tools.

Given the complexity of the environment, particular attention has been paid to the interactive definition of all information technology resources. This effort addressed itself both to applications and the infrastructure at the Agro Division (Swiss operations) as well as those at the parent company Ciba-Geigy which are used by the Agrobusiness. This work:

Mapped organizational departments and sections employing the different systems and components of information technology operations.

Produced an inventory of supports focused on databases, DBMS, database computers,* other hardware, operating systems, office automation shells, and programming languages.

Developed a clear picture of the very important links that exist between the different components of the information system.

Emphasized both physical and logical databases as well as their tools, and also covered different types of analytical queries.

Some of these queries concerned technical issues. Others are management-oriented, for instance, What about phasing out IMS? Which of the current processing systems are using it? What would a replacement policy involve in reprogramming?

Mapping the data flow is one of the examples of further developments made possible through the infrastructure which was constructed. The work done on metadata responded to the question: "Which data types are used in which applications?" This query has been addressed to a number of data types and their classes: customer, product, supplier, account, bill, and so on.

Solutions have been elaborated and represented in a visual manner. The result is a coherent mapping of the information resources of the Ciba-Geigy Agro division, presented to the Board of Management in a way easy to understand and act upon.

How well the project has been received is exemplified by the fact that after the macroscopic view had been dealt with, the Board asked for a consolidation proposal. Within this work, problem domain concepts determined the object types, as the macroscopic model permitted experimentation.

Results have been positive. The recent integration of three operating units of the Agro Division, made for organization reasons, has been studied interactively through the model in reference. Restructuring of the database—as a consequence of reorganization—took two days rather than months that might have been required otherwise.

---

*Teradata DBC 1012.

This is an application designed for leading-edge technologists and database specialists interested in the implementation of advanced concepts in database administration. As such, the application demonstrates the contributions to be offered by object-oriented solutions and the benefit derived by the organization.

The Agro Division project demonstratetd how well new developments in database tools can present opportunities and reveal constraints of which the organization might not have been aware. These are benefits obtained through new technology which legacy-type applications cannot deliver.

In this and other similar advanced examples, emphasis has been placed on the domains in which the evolving high-power tools can be used. The reference is particularly true in terms of an efficient management of distributed databases for:

- Better service quality,
- Reduced costs, and
- Greater productivity.

The contributions of object-type orientation, the usage to which the resulting knowledge-enriched database systems can be put, and the able administration of new technologies are highly related subjects that have to be examined in unison. The key to obtaining tangible results is to emphasize not theories but *solutions*.

6–3 OBSERVING A FAST DEVELOPMENT TIMETABLE

When we talk of development timetables we should appreciate that there is a learning curve and associated setup cost. Productivity derived from new tools and methods pays dividends after the learning effects have been assimilated and applications become a matter of course.

In the Agro Division case, phases 1 to 5[*] required *two calendar years* of work, including the interview of 130 people, the top of the Division, mainly central directors and department managers.

How did they see the business and their future needs?
What was most important for them in support terms?

The background reason behind these interviews was to get the knowledge of the people who use information systems services. The research

---

[*]Detailed in the Introduction.

revealed the need for powerful tools to promote and facilitate the developing *enduser* requirements. Three pilot projects were part of the CASE-tool evaluation.

1. A coarse-grain analysis of functions, data types, and relations regarding future information systems implementations

The obtained results were discussed with a number of software companies in terms of offering quotations for realizing the goals company executives put forward.

2. Interactive work with users focusing on the design of a small database

Ptech helped to improve the system analysis timetable, but most importantly it provided solutions that are factual, easy to demonstrate, and easy to prove.

What impressed the endusers is the fact that a small database design interactively done and immediately visualized is far more comprehensive than paper documents. Furthermore, in terms of design it proved to be much more factual than manual work on information elements and structures which had been used previously.

3. Integrative database design involving larger database perspectives

Quite important is the timeframe within which step 3 materialized. An impressive amount of work took just *one* month for the company analyst to do, with an outside consultant contributing one week.* A by-product of this project enhanced the results already obtained in step 1.

Of the 15 users who actually participated in these three projects, 13 loved the way in which the work was done. Quite significantly, they were endusers with little previous experience in information technology—while both the reactionary people in the team were well-experienced EDPers.

One of the major challenges encountered during the work in reference has been the *synonym* problem—sorting out equal terms as well as contradictions and different incompatibilities. Using knowledgebank principles, this part of the project expects to catch an estimated 80 to 90 percent of synonyms using existing Ptech functions and the defined metamodel.

Many companies have found the problem of synonyms and homonyms a tough nut to crack. Its origins lie in data anchored in legacy programs

---

*Interestingly enough, these 5½ weeks represented only a small part of the time and effort invested in the same project done in parallel with a more classical tool.

and associated functions that are hard to remove. It takes both advanced tools and dedicated effort to overcome this problem.

Without a particular relation to the Agro Division of Ciba-Geigy, Figure 6.1 identifies the complex interaction that exists between computer-based processes and information elements. As such, it helps explain what the sorting out of incompatibilities involves by way of system work.

Although the flowchart in Figure 6.1 is based on input from one industrial sector, with only minor transformation, it can address itself to other domains of industry as well, both in manufacturing and in finance. Few companies so far have given to the issue of synonyms and homonyms existing in their databases the attention which it deserves.

When considering ways and means to improve database quality in a company, sorting out inconsistencies and incompatibilities must be a prime consideration. It takes both highly motivated and dedicated systems specialists and powerful tools to get results—but once this has been achieved, technology transfer can be successful.

A basic premise is that there exists a significant degree of communality between solutions, even if these may seem to be of different orientation and they are not necessarily interdependent. Two examples that look like they are different yet they have much in common are:

- Computer-integrated manufacturing (CIM)
- Computer-integrated banking (CIB)

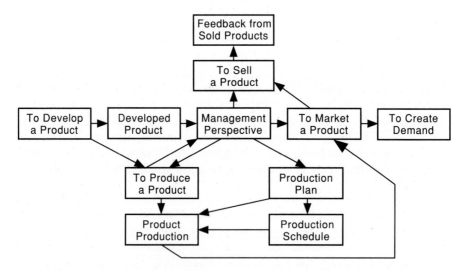

Figure 6.1   Synonym problems come from data anchored to the function.

Part and parcel of their common ground in terms of database stream-lining is a valid approach to the problem of synonyms and homonyms. A solution to the *synonym* problem is a microscopic issue. At Ciba-Geigy, by using the shell at their disposal, the analysts applied different queries to each data type, as for example:

Tell me all the relations which are relevant to this information element.
Tell me all information elements used by a given process.
Tell me all data types related to this one and its subclasses, and so on.

Both *relations* and *related data types* have been handled as *objects* in a fully interactive manner. Visualization was assisted by the fact that the chosen shell uses different colors per class of queries. The identifiers of databases used in a departmental sense were blue for marketing, green for design, and red for finance.

Distinct colors greatly help in visualizing overlaps and substitutions. Much of the tool's power also came from the principle of inheritance.

Even the fact that synonyms existed in the database was used to advantage: The *classification* and descriptor jobs have been enormously assisted through proper identification.* A similar reference applies to *homonyms*, where the same identifier was employed for information elements in a variety of data repositories.

Instrumental was as well the fact that the chosen tool permits a reminder operation connected to a hard delete. This keeps the information elements in dotted form representation diagrams, with relations in the background. Reminder services can be quite important to subsequent work.

6-4 AN INTEGRATIVE APPROACH IN HANDLING INFORMATION RESOURCES

From a macroscopic viewpoint, the object-oriented solution provided the company with an integrative view of its resources, and with the ability to access online, in all instances, logically restructured:

- Information elements,

---

*On classification and identification, see D.N. Chorafas, *Handbook of Relational Databases and DBMS*, McGraw-Hill/TAB Books, New York, 1989.

- Distributed databases,
- Database management systems,
- Analysis and programming tools,
- Applications modules,
- Operating systems, and
- Hardware components.

The chosen process of classification and identification was extended to all programming languages in the library: COBOL, PL/1, office automation shells. Here again, color has been used to identify different types and therefore to help in visually discriminating between heterogeneous items that must be grouped together. In a pragmatic and orderly manner, all:

Organizational units within the Agro division have been classified and identified.

Information elements, databases, and DBMS employed by each unit have been handled with discipline.

Applications programs and their modules, whether they help one or more organizational units, have been mapped into the system.

Links have been effectively provided between different applications modules and the databases they access—therefore between databases and programs that work with them.

As a result, any change to an information element or alternatively to a command, immediately flashes out its partners (databases and/or applications programs) which can be affected by this change. Such bridges are dynamically upkept and they are visible at the user's request.

Ptech also provided the possibility of establishing a *time sequence* flow-chart in the way shown in Figure 6.2. The established process specifications help in enhancing security clauses throughout the network of interconnected information elements and other data resources.

We can effectively compare what IMKA has been offering (which was discussed in Chapter 5), with what the Agro Division of Ciba-Geigy obtained through its work with a powerful Entity-Relationship shell. IMKA laid a different infrastructure, distinguishing intentional and extensional aspects.

It placed in the knowledgebank information contained in rules and commands.

It left in the database values (data) accessible in computer storage.

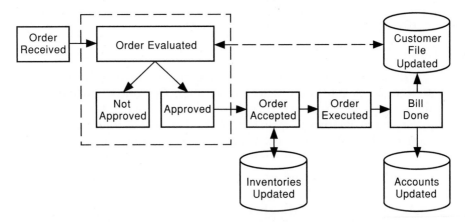

Figure 6.2   Order evaluation and time-stamping of operation sequence.

The corporate memory facility of an IMKA implementation includes decisions and rules, linking observed data to diagnostic hypotheses, combining certainty factors, and focusing on maintenance procedures (in the case of the automotive application example).

By contrast, the study done by the Agro Division of Ciba-Geigy oriented itself toward the concept of a *global database* which includes extentional information stored in distributed databases. The aim of the project has been to identify how this distribution has taken place, in order to provide better supports for global database management.

In the Ford example with IMKA, the developed construct contains in its database facts about the particular circuit being analyzed. By contrast, in its corporate memory facility it stores:

- Conclusions reached thus far, and
- Rules justifying such conclusions.

The latter are represented as assertions. There is as well the history of design solutions which have been employed, conclusions dependent upon them, and problem status.

The global database orientation at Ciba-Geigy is somewhat different. It may, for example, include customer orders, current shipments, accounts receivable, and so on. At the same time, nothing excludes that in the global database are stored plausibility concepts and decisions.

As companies with experience in knowledgebanks and databases would appreciate, the lines dividing the two of them are not immutable. Yet, there is a significant difference between:

- *Knowledge*-type queries, and
- *Data*-type queries.

Whether global or local, the database implies quantitative references and we more or less know what we are after. By contrast, when we are using a knowledgebank we only have an *idea* of what we *might* want. This may be qualitative or quantitative. As IMKA and other projects help document, the system will use its know-how to provide us with answers by exploiting its intentional component.

6–5 SEAMLESS AND EFFECTIVE MANAGEMENT OF CLIENT ACCOUNTS

The implementation examples from Ford, USWest, and Ciba-Geigy may have industrial background but also constitute an excellent reference for other sectors, such as banking. A case in point is the seamless and effective management of client accounts which is of critical importance to any business.

As it has been shown by means of the case studies, the integrative approach which has been adopted with these projects permits us to restructure online the customer account without having to reshuffle the distributed databases and their information elements. This has a great impact on competitiveness, because it permits both:

- Accuracy, and
- Speed of response.

In all of the cases that we have seen, the goal of a global information model is meta information. This permits more homogeneous dealing with different instances, as well as control through cross-checking purposes for special application purposes.

> The resulting dynamic procedure can overcome limitations and incompatibilities which exist due to different file and data structures.
>
> Interactive data access in a heterogeneous environment has a tremendous commercial potential as all companies, from banks to manufacturing, now focus on *account integration*.

Account integration is at the heart of a customer-centered approach to market handling. The management of leading companies recognizes that the emphasis on customer account handling is of fundamental importance in business competitiveness, thus underlining the need for:

- Real-time customer profiles
- Pattern recognition of market trends
- Induction and deduction based on customer operations

Among financial institutions, for example, patterning and forecasting of client behavior is the basis on which rests *relationship banking*. This in turn requires seamless and effective management of databased customer accounts.

But in the larger number of cases, easy, flexible, dynamic relationship management is not typical among industrial firms and financial institutions. File structures and applications programs were oriented over the years to a discrete approach and is not that simple to convert old software to an integrative view. Yet this is an absolute need for the 1990s.

Based on an object-oriented approach, the enduser should be able to pose a query to the system about a given client account as instance of *client class*.

The system should respond by showing the effective linkages and security considerations in connection to database elements and applications programs.

We will look in greater detail into the impact this can have on seamless account management in Section 6-6, but let us underline at this point that effective interconnection between information elements and application programs is one of the main problems in software technology. There is a great benefit to be gained by having on hand the knowledge necessary to interconnect, without manual intervention, processing routines to storage devices, accessing online the results.

In one of the implementation examples that has been studied,[*] once the enduser has identified a process, the system will present to him or her a tree structure which connects the applications routines of his or her choice to:

- Organizational units,
- Lines of business,
- Accessed data types,
- Tools that were used in programming,
- Operating system(s) under which the programs run, and

---

[*]The user organization prefers not to be identified.

• Hardware specifics as well as locations.

The query might as well have included the resources available to a certain department. Then in its visualization the object–oriented system will show in color: data types, DBMS, OS, applications programs, and tools by department. At the user's request, such presentation can be:

• *Macroscopic*, along the major lines of reference, or
• *Microscopic*, by means of zooming in on details.[*]

In both cases, pointers link the applications modules to the database(s) and their DBMS. The system can answer queries on objects—from data types to processes, business functions, critical success factors, and beyond. Responses are not only applicable to the prevailing conditions at that moment, but are also dynamically upkept.

Queries can address both the whole knowledgebank of the system and subsets of it, as well as instances of the classes included in this multimedia resource, intermediate results, clusters and subsets thereof—as well as nested queries. This helps to exploit the full power of an object orientation.

Other facilities, too, contribute to the user-friendliness of the results. In a macroscopic presentation, for instance, color permits us to clearly identify the relevant variety as well as possible incompatibilities in resources. But reading the fine print needs zooming, which is available.[†]

6–6 BENEFITS OBTAINED THROUGH AN OBJECT STRUCTURE

Section 6-5 indicated that the integrative approach that an object orientation makes feasible assures the ability of restructuring online the customer relationship and its accounts. Component parts of the customer account or accounts may:

Find themselves in different databases.

Use a variety of application programs.

Even depend on different organizational departments in regard to "this" or "that" function.

---

[*]The University of Tokyo developed a different terminology in connection to its virtual reality projects. Macroscopic approaches are called *programming-in-the-large*, and microscopic approaches are called *programming-in-the-small*.

[†]See also the discussion in Chapter 14 on graphical user interfaces and visualization.

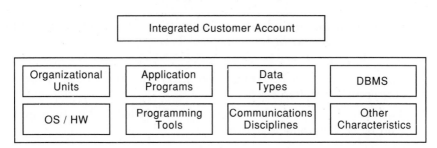

Figure 6.3   Integration of a customer account and its visualization.

Seamless and effective management of client accounts requires an integrative response. This is precisely what the object–oriented solution offers. Figure 6.3 shows the map that is automatically visualized* through a shell command to integrate a given customer account. System response:

> Is bringing online to the user's attention a customer account's component elements, and
>
> Is identifying their current location and content, in answer to an ad hoc query.

As it can be appreciated through Figure 6.3, this is an excellent approach to interlinking in an ad hoc manner information elements in databases and types of applications. The reference was made by Ciba–Geigy, for example, that in the case of just one application module some 150 different data types were identified.

The able online handling of customer accounts means *competitiveness*. The system that we are building must present the best possible approach to consolidation. The object structure should permit flexible responses to an impressive range of ad hoc queries.

> Zooming to greater details means two-way layering—general to specific and specific to general.
>
> Layering permits to see the next level of detail, doing so node-by-node.
>
> This process can be repeated through different layers, each successive one of a still finer grain.

Through a system solution each node can be anchored to corresponding detailed nodes by means of networking. This approach to visualization

---

*In a project undertaken in this domain.

opens new horizons in enduser interactivity. As Professor Terano aptly suggested in the context of his own projects[*]:

> The metalayer will be based on macroscopic knowledge, which is conceptual and often fuzzy.
>
> The lower layer will reflect microscopic knowledge. The finer grains tend to be crisp and analytical.

Several finer grains at the microscopic layer will correspond to a coarser grain at the metalayer. Both the lower level components and the metastructures need to be networked—among themselves and trans-layer.

This is precisely what past, discrete island approaches have been missing and in any way cannot support. Examples of distinct but interrelated frames of reference that should have been networked are: billing, inventories, customer files, general ledger accounts, and so on. As every organization knows, all of them deal with the same information elements, hence the need of networking the microscopic views.

This relatively simple concept rests at the basis of any integrative procedure. It is as well the cornerstone to relationship banking and to able customer account management at large.

An object-oriented prototype used in an able manner allows us to discover that this approach is as well most efficient in flushing out possible duplications of effort. The reference is valid for both information elements and programming modules—which exist in duplicates and triplicates in all organizations, though to a greater degree in some than in others.

Just to enrich this last example, let me add the case made in a recent conference regarding the very careful analysis carried out by a big, well-known American company. A thorough study documented that one and the same process was programmed in more than 1000 different programs, while each time it came up it was programmed anew.

Computer-literate management does appreciate that a good methodology to screen out duplicates and get rid of wasteful practices through software reusability is most valuable, and the more dynamic the firm is, the more such a policy is necessary.

"Twenty years ago I told the user 'I know what you need'," said a cognizant information technology executive. "Today the user tells me what he needs because he is computer literate." But the level of computer literacy which we have and share is highly related to the technology we use:

> People who are literate at the level of COBOL and PL/1 are grossly illiterate when it comes to using relational databases.

---

[*]See the references to LIFE made in Chapter 1.

People who are literate at the relational database level can be illiterate in what concerns the study and implementation of object-oriented solutions.

People who can build a DP system should appreciate that they are not necessarily able to support the business of their company through legacy-type approaches. They should as well understand that data processing exists because of the existence of the company, and a good business can be destroyed because of poor information technology support.

6–7 USING INFORMATION TECHNOLOGY TO GET RESULTS

To say that the solution that we examined in the first four sections of this chapter is valuable to Ciba-Geigy would be to state the obvious. A similar reference is, however, applicable to all dynamic firms where steady client demands and an unrelenting pace of technology is forcing us into constant migrations.

"We use IT either because we must or because of the competitive advantages it offers," says Stefan Janovjak.[*] "But we cannot obtain competitive advantages as long as we don't know what we have in terms of information resources—or we fail to recognize the relations and links existing among the different components of our corporate resources."

This is almost a self-evident truth, yet many data processing people today find it difficult to understand what the leading information technology user organizations have found when they tried to integrate heterogeneous databases running under incompatible DBMS; for instance, that left to themselves relational language capabilities are insufficient to provide interoperability.

There is a reason for this gap. The images provided by the aged and obsolescent legacy applications, which by majority run on mainframes, are distorted, and therefore their effectiveness is low. That is how some generals fight a new war with the weapons of the last one, which is irrevocably past.

This basic reference has a number of aftermaths. Most of the people currently working in software development lack clear knowledge of existing new data structures and efficient applications tools. As a result, system migration has typically become a migraine. Moreover,

Throughout the larger organizations alert workstation users are requesting access to the corporate data for business reasons.

---

[*]Divisional information manager, Agro Division, Ciba-Geigy.

But response to their demands is slow, deficient, or both, tending to increase the proverbial computer center–management gap.

Closing such gap calls for the wisdom of comprehensively capturing interdependencies of available technological resources, exploiting all of them to the fullest possible extent. The reference is applicable through a wide spectrum of information technology and includes:

- Human windows,
- Processes,
- Applications,
- Databases,
- Networks,
- Software, and
- Hardware.

All this forms a system that should be able to support at any time, anywhere, an interoperable business viewpoint. Solutions should aim to use the cutting edge of technology to gain market advantage, otherwise they are not worth their salt.

We can take as an example global object management for transactions, messages and queries along the line of the approach discussed in Section 6-6. Global object management will typically address itself to multiple nodes:

- Accounting for all events (global, local), and
- Handling the aggregation of changes.

This can be effectively worked out if the solution to be provided is agile enough to bring the objects to the user node rather than process the request at distant node(s) and bring the result(s) to the user node with all the delays resulting from queuing up.

To be effectively implemented, such strategy calls for supervisory interpreters (demons) and generally seeks to implement an intentional database structure. One of the best-known money center banks in New York which experimented along this frame of client-server reference documented a 1000 percent increase in analysis and programming productivity.

An order of magnitude improvement in productivity is no minor effect of chance. Significantly, the tools are now available and the most advanced professionals are using them already.

Top management has to realize that it is not enough to make major investments in this or in that computer and communications domain. It is important as well to manage these investments in an able manner: Their links to business users have to be properly established and thereafter upkept. This cannot be done through worn-out tools, methods, and concepts.

Solutions like those provided in Chapter 5 and in the present one also call for intelligent migration, which minimizes the negative consequences of change on business functions and on endusers. This is doable provided we appreciate:

- Who are the users today and tomorrow,
- Which business functions and processes are performed by each one of them,
- What they incrementally need in their work,
- Which information elements are being accessed,
- Where such information elements reside and of which type they are.

Top management policies in fostering renewal in information technology are evidently fundamental. They must underpin the efforts put forth by the technologists.

Within the organization, business strategy should define the macroscopic top management vision of the type of company its owners want it to be. Information technology must always operate under this vision and correspondingly serve in an able manner the microscopic views.

To develop an application in a right way is important, but to develop the right application in an efficient manner is even more important to corporate survival.

7

Global and Local Issues in Database Management

7–1 INTRODUCTION

One of the reasons why the IMKA and Ciba-Geigy case studies are so important is that they address a *distributed database* (DDB) structure, and do so after that structure has been in place, not as a precondition to its deployment. At Ford, USWest, DEC, Texas Instruments, and the Agro Division, the databases have grown over the years and, as anywhere else, they have been heterogeneous. Therefore,

> It became important to use knowledge engineering and object-oriented methods, to virtually integrate these incompatible structures.
>
> Without such integration, a sprawling database gets out of control. It becomes unaccessible to the users and as a result the company can find it difficult to operate.

The distributed aspect of information processing is not a new concept. The term distributed data processing (DDP) has been used for two decades to describe a mangerial and technical decentralization of computer resources. But over the years the definition of DDP has meant different things to different people confronted with a wide range of products representing a variety of views. This led to major disappointments.

As a result, there have been successive redefinitions of the DDP concept. Technology played a major role in this development. Originally, the phrase "distributed data processing" was used to describe some sort of interconnection among independently managed microcomputers; then it applied to workstations cooperating with hosts acting as servers.

The dynamics and problems of each of these types of solutions are essentially different, but in the bottom line the reasons are common: Rapid drops in the cost per cycle of computing resource coupled with significant increases in functional capability. Distributed implementation references and cost factors apply just as well in terms of memory devices.

The concept of distributed databases came around in the mid-1970s promoted by the:

- Decentralization of computer resources at the DP end
- Increasing use of database management systems and data dictionaries
- Growing implementation of peer-to-peer networks
- Availability of pass-through software which made it possible to manage databases in a network-wide sense
- The accelerated drop in cost of storage per bit of information

Since the beginning, however, distributed processing and distributed databases have been subject to major constraints. A clear precondition for the development of DDP and DDB—not properly appreciated at the time—has been the availability of software that would provide for the distribution of functions, facilities, and data across interconnected computers. Such software has developed slowly and piecemeal, without much thought given to integrated services and without support for cross-vendor interoperability.

It comes, therefore, as no surprise that heterogeneity dominated all the way, from data structures to DBMS and other basic software. Applications programs were not exempt from this reference, making it very difficult to determine exactly what is available at every database site, and what sort of inconsistencies exist between various databases.

Just as difficult has been the task of rationalizing the distribution of information elements across different machine architectures, operating systems, DBMS, data structures, and network protocols. Systems heterogeneity has represented a special set of constraints, even as some database management aspects have matured.

Therefore, the hope that object-oriented distributed database solutions can help overcome this hurdle has created a great amount of interest in the information systems community. This is particularly true of the larger installations which have been faced with an almost chaotic repertoire of parochial database solutions, each with differing capabilities, obscure limitations, and fuzzy boundaries. Can object-oriented approaches help in getting out of this impossible situation?

7–2 CONCEPT OF A GLOBAL DATABASE

Modular structure, predicates regulating distributed processing, and global database management are a better way of approaching large scale system challenges than the haphazard ways and means we have had so far. The solutions that we adopt should be semantics-oriented, support a polyvalence in conceptual schemata, and admit powerful extension.

We now begin to appreciate that such extensions should include dynamic object classification and, therefore, event analysis. Our methodology must:

1. Have a formal object-oriented foundation, with semantic meaning.
2. Be modifiable and extensible, for instance towards multimedia.
3. Be expressed in terms of fundamental concepts, in an application-independent manner.
4. Render the distributed components usable within the framework of any-to-any interconnection.

We can achieve these goals by supporting a layered architectural approach which helps integrate the hardware and software components in our network. Up to a point, distributed system resources can live with diversity, provided a mechanism is put in place which permits us to assure at least *virtual homogeneity*.

One of the critical design features of a distributed database is the approach we take in providing access to and from objects made resident in a wider topology. This requires the:

• Careful avoidance of unwanted redundancy,
• A system-wide coordination, and
• The assurance that a consistent global database image is being maintained.

Given the growing size of present-day databases, a totally redundant solution with all users having all multimedia IE nearby is not an option. *Partitioning* the database among specified nodes is the solution, providing access to all authorized users through the proper distributed mechanism.

Such policy calls, first of all, for a system-wide view, to be followed by organizational perspectives. Organizational issues involve classification and identification of all objects in the *global repository*.

The concept of a global repository must definitely reflect the fact that we do not start building the database from scratch, but we have to integrate and account for past commitments and existing local solutions. These integrate with one another and into the global concept, within the three axes of reference shown in Figure 7.1. The key issues are:

- To use our past (both positive and negative) experiences in database management
- To list the failures we did in the past and we wish to avoid
- To project not only on how to meet our goals but also on how to steer clear of serious pitfalls

The use of a simulator of the distributed database facility will facilitate as well as document the organizational and technical decisions to be taken. Experimentation can help define optimization steps necessary in handling an object-oriented environment, for instance, channeling update transactions (including derived transactions) to where their target objects reside.

Instead of using brute force in reaching for objects in remote locations, updating them, and then sending them back to these locations, an object-oriented optimization makes the difference between:

- A distributed object-based application, and
- A distributed record management.

Such a difference can be highly significant. Properly established object orientation minimizes communications between nodes in a network, for a given task. Moreover, when a sent transaction creates derived transactions having targets in the same node where the sent transaction is executed, no further communication is required.

The latter is *not* the situation with an updating program reading multimedia information elements from a remote node and sending the

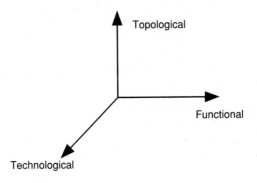

Figure 7.1   Three main axes of reference in global database design.

updated version back to the remote node. In this record-oriented case, different references have to be read and updated in multiple requests; hence the efficiency is low—but this approach is quite popular in current practice.

The foremost organizations have come to appreciate that failure in using object-oriented solutions in distributed databases has unacceptable drawbacks.

A developer working for one node must know all the rules related to application data in other nodes.

He or she must also be extra careful when he or she needs to update data in these other nodes as a consequence of an activity in his or her node.

Secondary effects that are unaccounted for at the design stage result in loss of consistent image in a global database sense.

Normalization within the perspective of networked databases can be promoted through the appropriate *data dictionary* facilities. The data dictionary is the repository containing the standard definitions of the objects in the global database and providing:

1. *Directory* services that define where each object is located in the distributed environment
2. *Quick index* to help identify redundant names, overlaps, and possible discrepencies
3. *Multimedia definitions* for all objects in the database, including their names, aliases, attributes, and usage
4. *Concept and schema classification* featuring all relevant distribution including a general thesaurus
5. *Semantic description* containing the meaning, definition, and semantics for dynamic binding and other missions
6. *Constraints*, therefore metadata and metarules including facilitators for internal and external schemata
7. *Controls*, such as allowable range of values of different values by code, lock managers for synchronization, but also information on volume for dimensioning reasons
8. *Links* to programming modules as well as in an any-to-any object sense, including logical and contextual relationships
9. *Security* characteristics of each object, including access, read/write, add/delete, authorization, and authentication
10. *Metalevel structure* which should have a dual perspective: one by object,

the other covering end-to-end the global database, its administration, maintenance, and integrity control

As Figure 7.2 indicates, the directory is at the kernel of this object-oriented 10-fold approach which is a far cry from the much simpler data dictionaries of the 1970s and 1980s. The latter practically consisted of a directory, data definitions, links, and controls.

There is no data dictionary software available today with such sophistication. This is one of the problems to be faced by the user organization which (contrary to rationality) would need to provide the missing software by itself. The task can be eased, however, through the use of knowledge engineering.

Because of differences in user functions with respect to the distributed database environment, the inevitability of involving communications linkages, and the probability of using incompatible database management sys-

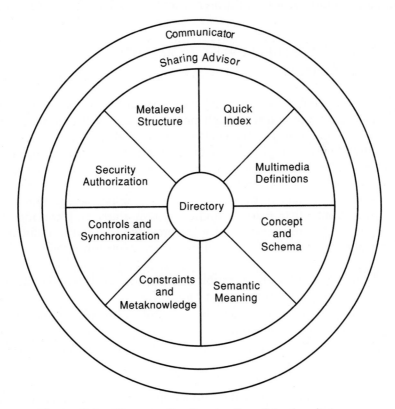

Figure 7.2   The expanding functionality of the data dictionary.

tems, the proper architectural design will require significant forethought and experimentation. No architectural plan will be valid without online networking.

From the open-ended perspective of a networking system, we can add, remove, and redistribute resources as required.

Global database components can evolve towards new technologies through gradual introduction and/or substitution of network components.

Different data handling and processing techniques must be developed and implemented without interrupting ongoing operations.

The observance of these important points adds a considerable amount of flexibility. Let us always recall that no matter how big a system we buy, we end up saturating it. Databasing engines never finish growing; they are constantly evolving and getting bigger. Why not adopt from the beginning a modular solution to answer the user-oriented problems in an able manner?

7–3 A DISTRIBUTED OBJECT-ORIENTED SOLUTION

A distributed database software is characterized by its ability to support *one logical* database placed at multiple physical locations. When it is properly integrated, this logical system reflects a single logical environment, although it may involve different physical media; it is independent of the equipment on which each database runs; and it represents an orderly collection of objects accessible by user entities: people, programs, and terminals.

Whether we talk of functionally or geographically distributed databases, we should first make a unified system study and consider both the topology and the services that are provided. Typically, a distributed information system will be divided into three main subsystems:

1. Remotely and locally accessible distributed objects whether active or passive, of the form shown in Figure 7.3
2. A transport mechanism which assures object-to-object and process-to-object communications
3. Object handling actions performed through distributed computer resources

This system should provide a built-in mechanism for object classification as well as for integrity control. More sophisticated structures will incorporate a knowledgebank management system based on a high-level

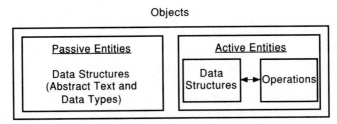

Figure 7.3   Passive and active entities in an object environment.

multimedia data model. Such approach not only makes the development, administration, and maintenance of the global database easier, but also enables support of object evolution with the ability to accommodate polyvalence at the level of the kernel.

The approach that has just been described can be instrumental in structuring a network-wide *attribute space*, with each object-oriented attribute having the following features.

1. *An attribute name*—This identifies the attribute and makes it feasible to call on it. An attribute name must be unique network-wide with respect to the set of all attribute names. This reference is applicable to the classes, the subclasses, the objects, and it is necessary to support the attribute inheritance rules. As with class names, multiple synonym attribute names (aliases) may be permitted but have to be stored in the data dictionary, as we saw in Section 7-2.

2. *Value of an attribute*—Such value is either an entity in the database or a collection of such entities. The value of an attribute is typically selected from its underlying value class, which contains the permissible values. But it may also be the special value *null*.

3. *Applicability of the attribute*—This is specified by indicating that the attribute in reference is either a member attribute, which applies to each member of the class, or a class attribute, referring to a class as a whole. In the latter case there will be only one value for the class.

Names, attributes, and their values should be valid in a global database sense through physical nodes, their interconnections, gateways, and higher level communication facilities. Account should be taken of the fact that due to their growing size, distributed databases are often managed independently from one another yet they must provide a global, network-wide image.

In the sense we have defined it in the preceding section, a distributed database environment consists of several cooperating components running on different physical nodes. Cooperation is realized by the communications mechanism which is established between the databases in the network, served through nodes and gateways.

A steady requirement within such an environment is *dynamic change*. However, due to the relatively large size of current and future distributed databases, independent modifications can lead to loss of consistency and unique image—yet such type of modification is a prerequisite for adequate flexibility.

Knowledge engineering can provide the missing link in this connection. For a practical example, consider a branch office network, with the environment in each branch consisting of workstations, file servers, a departmental number crunching computer, and gateways.

These elements can be implemented in a networked sense by configured objects with associated references. These objects:

- Receive requests via proper interfaces,
- Gather transaction data from input notes,
- Execute the transaction operation, and
- Store results on a file server.

A local monitor analyzes all activities taking place within the branch. A global monitor does the same in a network sense. A system model is necessary for administration and maintenance reasons. Every component should be included in this model: workstations, file servers, node types, communications facilities.

Correspondingly, an application model will consist of the various kinds of application components (logical entities) and their interconnections including message passing. Important references are:

- The process commands effected by the application modules
- Encapsulated objects in the distributed database of the branch and network-wide
- Names and attributes of objects in other nodes within the global database network
- The online contribution of the data dictionary, in regard to the basic functions we have defined.

Full distribution transparency must be provided with the mechanisms for communication between application components mapped into the model. This should reflect message passing between objects but also among operating system processes. It should as well include concurrency and consistency facilities.

7-4   MODELING THE DISTRIBUTED SUPPORT STRUCTURE

As with all information systems activities, distributed databases require a great deal of preparation and the documented answer to questions such as: What functions should be distributed? Where should they be distributed? How and where should we control the hierarchy of functions? How can we assure database integrity? How should we enhance consistency, reliability, and security? What is the contribution of object-oriented approaches?

While decisions on where and how to distribute the objects in the database are organizational, the answer to many other queries is technological. A great deal depends on the configuration language to be used and the same is true of the code generation language.

The database configuration language should be able to describe structural and allocation aspects, helping to handle the distributed database resources at large. It should as well feature a dynamic change notation to specify alterations of the:

- Object distribution,
- Development standards, and
- Application structure.

In other terms, a distributed programming language must be able to specify the information elements and their associated computational and communications aspects. Such facilities should be fully integrated into the object-oriented implementation.

With connection to code, in an object-oriented solution C++ can be directly generated from process descriptions provided there is an expressive amplifier for written statements able to produce:

- Class libraries with methods for all of the basic operators and functions, assuring integrity as prescribed by system design
- Efficient implementation of logical and implication constraints
- Disciplined modules enabling the incorporation of existing code and facilitating hand-crafted work by software engineers
- Optimization, achieving high performance for generated applications

While these requirements may exist also in a record-based implementation of distributed databases, an object orientation increases the associated demands for accuracy. For instance, it calls for compile-time checks of semantic restrictions.

Specific, object-dependent problems must be handled, one of them being mobility control of database components in distributed approaches.

In general, this requires the incorporation of configuration facilities in the programming language.

Linguistic solutions addressed to a global database will use semantic information about applications, exploiting this to manage structural, object-oriented, and computational aspects. There may, for example, be:

A mobility control manager deciding about adequate object migrations in the distributed system

A dynamic allocator to handle independencies, given allocation changes and components interactions

Demons to observe object exchanges, applications, and progress, generating semantic information about them

Syntactial tools able to modify and structure objects and applications interactively

Auxiliary media such as housekeeping routines and interface adaptation facilities

Extensions to the object structure permit progressing towards global objects. However, local objects that are not invoked remotely can be implemented more efficiently in a more limited topological sense.

Within this growing object utilization perspective, it is necessary to have available active threads of control, assuring that all distributed elements can be adequately represented. Particular attention should be paid to the object-addressing mechanism.

In a distributed database environment, object addressing must be performed in a decentralized manner.

Special solutions are required to achieve location independence of object addresses when objects migrate.

All of these references are part and parcel of information modeling within a distributed database environment. The process identifies and describes the control action required to operate the system, determining what types of objects exist and what facts are known about them. The facts we need about these entities are of two kinds.

1. Those necessary to define the types of relationships that exist between objects, and
2. Those pertinent to dynamic objects being described, providing some measurement of each entity and its behavior.

A relatively critical component is the ability to assure a generic representation of the objects and their partnership descriptors. The use of information structure diagrams supports modeling premises and quickly focuses on the identified class types and their context within the real world.

Always in a distributed database sense, inversion and matching are further mechanisms for establishing the equivalence of different ways of viewing the same essential relationships among objects. The system must also provide the ability to define an attribute whose value is calculated from other information in the database: This is the case of a derived item, and specification of its computation must be associated to the derivation.

The approach often taken to defining derived attributes is to provide a data dictionary section of high-level attribute derivation primitives that directly model the most common types of derived information. Each of these primitives provides a way of specifying one method of computing a derived attribute.

More general facilities should also be available for describing attributes that do not match known cases: A complex derived attribute may be defined by first describing other attributes that are used as building blocks in its definition, then applying one of the primitives to these building blocks. Such a procedure can be repeated for attributes of the building blocks themselves.

7–5 OBJECTS AND MESSAGE PASSING FACILITIES

As we saw in Chapter 1, object-oriented solutions offer advantages, new concepts, and better tools. One of them is effective message exchange. The execution of message-based communication facilities rests on system primitives. The need to exchange messages is generic to all object-type systems, and this underlines the importance of the primitives in reference.

Starting with the fundamentals, between objects, message exchange takes the form of direct or indirect communication.

Direct message exchange is based on explicit naming of communication partners (objects).

Indirect communication rests on intermediate ports serving as messages queues.

The key advantage of indirect communication is the ability for broadcasting, as well as the ease of change in logical interconnections. In addition, fault tolerance can be achieved when two or more redundant servers are attached to one logical port.

However, in what regards return and reply facilities, basic message passing is unidirectional. This simple paradigm makes feasible the direct return of a response from the recipient to the sender, though three-way handshake protocols can also be implemented.

Extensions to the basic message-passing mechanisms permit the transfer of references to remote objects. Other extensions help provide controlled access to servers in accordance with authentication and authorization requirements.

Such solutions are particularly important to re-engineering projects aiming at coexistence of old and new database structures as well as to incremental deployment. To do so in an able manner, we have to:

Conceptualize the existing system, particularly emphasizing its prevailing characteristics

Generate appropriate data dictionary entries for the old and new concepts

Replace old file calls with new object-oriented calls

Build the application system on new structures, incrementally switching out old approaches

Applications that cut across the departmental lines characterizing organizations during the last decade are a good example on the domain which can benefit from the evolutionary activity suggested by the foregoing four points. Corporate-wide cost control that transcends functions, departments, and affiliates is an example on this reference. Another example is global risk management.

Figure 7.4 can be examined under this light. The goal is the provision of a computational infrastructure for global risk management. Three main classes of objects are defined:

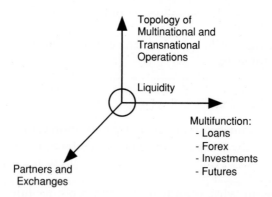

Figure 7.4   An object-oriented view of global risk management.

1. Topological
2. Multifunctional
3. Partner-oriented

The kernel common to all is *liquidity*. Typically, liquidity-type information is distributed throughout a global database, along geographical and functional frames of reference. The functional line itself is composed of distributed databases, including those of loans, foreign exchange, investments, options, and futures.

The message-passing mechanism must operate along this dual global sense. Enduser access has to be strictly controlled, whether the users are persons, programs, or terminals. Acknowledgment and reply facilities should be provided in a way transparent to the user, but the latter must have the ability to actuate narrowcasting operations.

This is a good example to use for function modeling purposes, employing an object-oriented solution. Liquidity information gathering, as well as other object domains, may, however, need to combine manual (paper based) and automated functions within the bank. This will split the functional model into two parts:

> Some of the communications paths will need to be implemented using the manual transfer of messages, for example, liquidity evaluation reports.
>
> Other communications transfers will be made fully online, exploiting information elements in databases.

While the manual part is a negation to the procedure we have described in connection to the object-based approach, it provides excellent material to study function modeling and introduces the subject of designing an object-oriented subsystem. This can be done without the hinderance of existing solutions and record-based database contents.

The parallelism between the two processes, manual and automatic, can help identify the infrastructure necessary to create information supports covering transactions and their risk evaluation. The period of time may be coarse (for instance, hours or a day), or fine grain (minutes, seconds, subsecond intervals)—as the global risk management objectives warrant.

The solution to be selected should permit entity storage and retrieval as well as composite representation of compound electronic documents,[*] in contrast to a tabular data presentation which is the usual case. It should make feasible:

---

[*]See also the discussion on multimedia in Part Three.

- Prechoice of visualization criteria
- Use of an inheritance mechanism
- Metalevel-type structures
- Classes and instances

It should also be possible to evaluate the breadth of the functional modeling and its capability to comprehend and control risk-related information in the distributed database system.

Based on a real-life situation, such study may well indicate that there is need for data translation. While in principle the objects to be transmitted should be transparent to the message-passing mechanism, diversity in data structures and DBMS heterogeneity may make it necessary to support explicit data translation between nonhomogeneous representations. For this, data descriptions have to be provided as well as knowledge-based translation mechanisms, enabling an open system communication between incompatible computers.

7–6 MOBILITY CONTROL IN AN OBJECT ENVIRONMENT

While object mobility is welcome, we also need the means for exercising supervision and control over mobility in a distributed database system. This requires specific distribution-related language primitives, such as the *move* primitive, which transfers a given object to the location of:

- A given target object, or
- A certain target node.

Network and database primitives must assure the ability to fix an object dynamically (for instance, by a *fix* operation), while another primitive makes it possible to *cancel* the action in reference.

In reality these are extensions of concepts that have existed with local environments, but distributed database solutions require fully explicit control of object migrations. The latter could be done by the application programmer, although this may be quite difficult when developing large distributed applications.

The message is that more rigorous primitives are necessary to support a higher level, goal-directed mobility control approach. In design and in implementation, our goal should be to locate communicating objects dynamically through a common reference, as well as to provide location definitions.

On instantiation of a given location, its objects must be automatically identified by a distributed protocol which decides about their migration to a common reference and the node at which this shall be instituted. Alternatively, the destination of the migration could be decided by the programmer, but this is not an efficient solution. Protocols should settle issues such as:

- Expected, network-wide interobject communication intensity
- Actual object types and their dynamic fixing or binding
- Specific modifiers that can operate in the nodes of the location structure
- Conflict resolution heuristics, when an object is involved in more than one collocation (nodes) at a time.
- The moving of objects back to their original location, once an operation is completed.

Ideally the associated rules must be automatically generated through software monitoring, which performs an analysis of invocations, with definitions and links available through the data dictionary.

This becomes more complex in the case of polyvalent communications support, for instance, a multiparty approach involving more than two object interactions or complex exchanges between communication partners. Distributed multicast activities commit operations and should be given their due weight.

An example of this type of application is an object-oriented system for university administration, designed to support the student, course, class, and faculty components through databases spread in many campuses. The University of California provides a realistic scenario along this reference frame.

The construction of a semantic network showing property inheritance and classification, such as the one shown in Figure 7.5, would make a useful contribution. For information modeling purposes, we have to involve

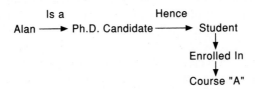

Figure 7.5   Semantic network showing property inheritance and classification.

entity types, relationship types, and attributes on campuses as widespread as Berkeley, Los Angeles, Santa Barbara, Davis, and Irvin. The objects are:

- *Resources*: Courses, faculty, clerical assistance, classrooms, supplies
- Entities identifying *demand* for knowledge and facilities, posed by the registered student
- *Constraints* which can be both temporal and spatial as contention is generated for the available resources by the demand agents

Course attributes, content specification, course assembly structure, planning, and scheduling involve multiuser requirements. The automation of course programming using an object orientation involves relationships that are:

- One-to-one,
- One-to-many,
- Conjunctive,
- Disjunctive, and in cases
- Stochastic.

At the same time, the organizational structure of a university raises the interesting question of whether to consider the different operating units, campus, college, division, and department, as being distinct entity types or just different in their attributes.

Both homogeneous and heterogeneous hierarchies must be studied as possibilities. The examination of the underlying curriculum will indicate at least a four-dimensional network focusing on: subject of study, time, classroom, and lecturer.

Since the campuses of the University of California are distinct from one another, each with its administration, a distributed office planning and user interface software will be necessary. It should cover the major object classes identified in Figure 7.6. Within this environment, object mobility control should be instituted conversing towards one of the office systems to be considered as *basic*.

This example provides as well an opportunity to examine the concepts of dimensionality and classification. Each attribute of an object must be categorized according to the value space to which it belongs. Some value spaces, such as time, length, and classroom, are physical in nature; others are logical, for instance, names, social security numbers, course titles, and course contents.

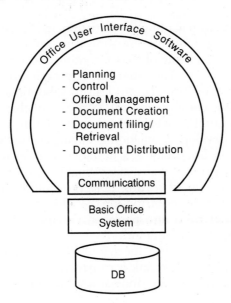

Figure 7.6   Organizational structure within an object environment.

7-7 RECONFIGURING THE GLOBAL DATABASE ARCHITECTURE

The solution to be adopted in the planning study for the University Curriculum should enable the representation and management of communication between an arbitrary number of processes. It should be based on a scenario construct, which through a self-contained notation describes the feasible course schedules and associated prerequisites.

Any pertinent runtime process will participate in the scenario and perform its implied communication roles. Basic communication can be realized by different mechanisms, including message passing, with runtime management divided into:

- *Initiation* phase, which implies participation of objects and processes in the scenario
- *Computation* phase, involving the calculation of feasible alternative course schedules
- *Optimization* phase, where one of these alternatives will be selected subject to given criteria
- *Termination* phase, with the end of the performance of optimization chores

Different options regarding the initiation and termination process are possible. For instance, blocking initiation if not all participating processes are already present, or sorting objects according to their pertinence to local computational processes. The latter strategy capitalizes on the fact that though local schedule computations lead to suboptima, the optimization phase which follows computation can take care of that.

Either way, a number of tools based on communications and schedules will need to be developed, including debuggers with inspection level functionality. Just as important is a deadlock analysis tool which detects deadly embrace situations by analyzing synchronization conditions.

The initiation step of sorting objects according to their pertinent location—and therefore contribution to the construction of schedules—brings another need into perspective. This concerns a mechanism for distributed object configuration.

Distributed configuration mechanisms should focus on the global database at large. Their major task is to structure support for coarse-grain allocation, the fine grain being done at a subsystem level:

> Local level allocation and optimization are necessary inasmuch as we currently do not have the know-how and the tools for global level fine-tuning when confronted with heterogeneous environments.
>
> Yet, a top objective of resource allocation in an object-oriented solution is heterogeneity support. To develop even a coarse-level solution, it is absolutely necessary to provide data translation facilities between heterogeneous databases.

The hope is that this approach can be facilitated through object-based multifunctional layout descriptions. The reason for the word "hope" should be found in the fact that this type of software module currently exists as an experimental prototype at universities and industrial research laboratories, but is not used yet in practical applications. Such programs involve:

- Object-oriented consolidated product databases
- Integration of distributed databases using a knowledgebank
- Authoring systems for purposes of analysis and planning
- Modeling of logistics solutions for wide-ranging support reasons

An example of an application is the ARPA Initiative in Concurrent Engineering (DICE), which we have already discussed. This program addresses itself to engineering contracts farmed out to high-technology companies by the U.S. Department of Defense, which have to be executed in a concurrent manner.

Object-oriented approaches are being used in connection to DICE, with the goal being to permit weapon systems designers working for different firms to create, manipulate, archive, and manage real-life engineering projects, without additional programming effort for design coordination purposes. This is expected to improve in a significant way industry competitiveness, cut costs, reduce the lead time, and improve the resulting product quality.

Applications can be projected in the financial industry with similar goals and expected results. Apart the object-type orientation, any approach towards reconfiguring the database architecture will require a configuration language which may be:

- Declarative, or
- Operational.

The declarative version describes the target configuration, and is easier to understand and use, but is more difficult to design and implement. The operational alternative focuses on the actions needed to generate the configuration we seek.

Prerequisites exist with both approaches. It is necessary to provide full configuration management support, and for this reason specific tools are required.

The initial configuration notation has to be transformed into an internal representation.

Such effect can be obtained through a compiler, provided the configuration language assures the needed references to allocation issues and their definition. A configuration supervisor may, for example, handle allocations heuristically, also updating internal representation(s).

The model must be able to interconnect system elements through a distributed database.

Within this infrastructure takes place the actual communication between configured elements, with the internal representation itself being distributed. Runtime configuration changes must be specified through a change notation and interpreted by the configuration supervisor.

Semantic representation can help in managing objects, both current and archived, within a networked environment.

Such a concept should be supported through tools able to handle the underlying network data management chores both for objects and for user-developed applications. With the explosion of code creation capabilities in today's networked environments of high-performance workstations, the need to organize and manage objects is most critical.

Tools should be in place for an automated workflow control within every subsystem, and network-wide, assuring that only users with proper access clearance can gain reach to objects and use their attributes.

This access may need to be further restricted based on the current status of a given object, as well as for reasons of configuration consistency. In addition, a dynamic change notation mechanism should be available to specify configuration changes.

Particular attention should be paid as well to the way in which the node structure of the underlying distributed system is described and defined. To permit the able handling of heterogeneous nodes, their protocols should be known along with all pertinent specifications.

Tools should also be available to handle heterogeneous nodes that result from different software and associated data structures.

A valid solution would provide an integrated object management and distribution perspective by supporting a broad range of functions, including check-in/check-out access and import/export of objects. Software must as well facilitate retrieval of objects by standard or user-defined attributes, object location, and access tracking within the global database.

A similar statement can be made regarding the network-wide promotion of compound electronic documents through user-defined approval cycles, integrated backup, and security features. A data dictionary should maintain the central repository about objects we have seen at the beginning of this chapter, allowing them to be stored at any location in the distributed database network.

8

Distributed Deductive Databases

8–1 INTRODUCTION

Databases are built to be used. The objects stored in a distributed database system will be retrieved, viewed, manipulated, and stored again by persons, programs, workstations, hosts, and other databases. Many of these accesses will be done for query reasons, others will be transactional.

Query optimization, concurrency control, and recovery are, with variations, issues common and important to all distributed databases. But there is no homogeneity and no general agreement on how to handle them. Solutions diverge when it comes to:

- Utilizing query algorithms or heuristics
- Featuring ad hoc query capabilities
- Using natural language interfaces
- Supporting replicated information elements
- Providing the database system itself with *deductive* facilities

During the 1957 to 1969 time frame, there was active research on precursors to deductive databases conducted at several locations in America, including the Rand Corporation, MIT, and Stanford University. One artifact known as relational data file (RDF) had an inferential capability and was implemented at the Rand Corporation.

In the course of the same chronological reference, the resolution principle was dicovered by J.A. Robinson for theorem-proving reasons. At about that time, other researchers at Stanford Research Institute (SRI) worked on the application of resolution to deductive processes in connection to databases.

In the decade of the 1970s, the concept of logic programming was advanced to a significant degree. In England and in France, work on Prolog established the equivalence of declarative and procedural semantics.

By the late 1970s, there were several research centers applying logic to databases with significant results. In the early 1980s, formal theories of databases were proposed that reinterpreted the conventional notions, with the implementation of recursion becoming an important topic.

The handling of negation in rules was worked out with the introduction of stratified databases and the handling of disjunctive information. Eventually, this led to the work done by ICOT* in Japan on a two-layered structure: the *intentional* and *extensional* database (in the late 1980s).

We have spoken of intentions and extensions in Chapter 3, when knowledge engineering was introduced. We will return to this topic in Chapters 11 to 13, where the architectural perspectives of intentional and extensional databases will be explained.

8–2 DEDUCTIVE AND OBJECT-ORIENTED DATABASES

There are a number of applications concerned with the use of logic in databases. Examples are semantic query optimization, update and validation, the generation of cooperative answers, and so on. The reason behind the interest expressed in this topic is that it helps enhance the applications perspectives. Solutions are far from being uniform.

Layered database structures, therefore stratified databases, allow negation in the body of a statement but not recursion through negation. Disjunctive databases are able to handle disjunctive facts and conclusions.

Object-oriented databases extend well beyond abstract data types into database semantics, inheritance, polymorphism, dynamic binding, and the *meta* concept.

Deductive databases and object-oriented databases are at the forefront of research in terms of next-generation intelligent database systems. Hence they master a premium over other projects.

The deductive database has the capability of rule-based deduction through first-order logic, but exhibits a rather restricted modeling ability.

---

*New Generation Computer Project.

The object database has a strong ability of data modeling, such as complex structure of object and inheritance among attribute values of objects, but is less equipped in intentional rules.

Aiming at providing a powerful single framework for intelligent database systems, researchers labor to integrate the object-oriented paradigm with the advantages of rule-based deduction. Some of the research projects in this domain are based on frame theory. A frame graph is a structure graph describing relationships among defined events as well as between events and actions. Individual topics are thought of as frame-like entities, each slot adopting a value within a range.

At the same time, logic programming has contributed to understanding the semantics of database contents and management. It has helped as well to extend the concept of relational databases, introducing new techniques as well as tools for database users. Deductive, object-oriented databases contain:

- Logical extensions
- Data modeling aspects, and
- Computational modeling.

Among logical extensions are certainty factors, null values, negation, membership functions, and so on. Data modeling extensions include identity-based aspects but also other issues, such as:

- *Structural*—like nested relations and complex objects
- *Behavioral*—for instance, databases with procedures and abstract data types

Among computational modeling extensions are the *constraint paradigm*, which operates like query processing based on constraint solving, and the object orientation paradigm, including active objects, autonomy, late binding, and transactions as well as query processing based on message passing.

Embedded in a deductive database, the object concept addresses a whole range of issues from agile user interfaces (human windows), to knowledgebanks and the extentional database itself. In the background of Figure 8.1 is the effect of this integrative issue and its component parts.

The data types in the distributed extensional database can be integers, strings, or other structures, for instance, graphics, text, and image—hence multimedia. The data model may be nested, including complex objects, their inheritance characteristics, and their semantics.

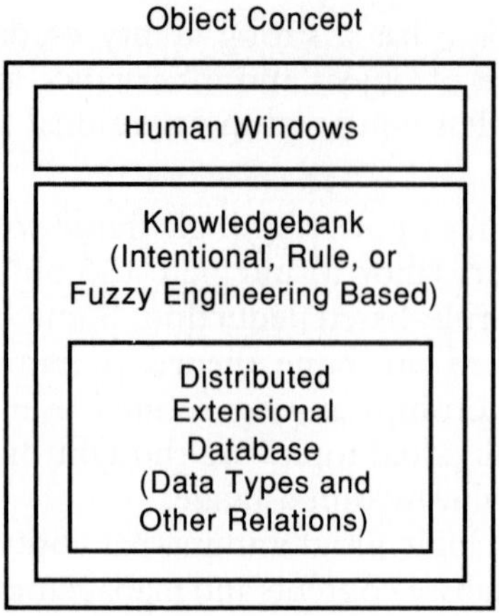

Object Concept

Figure 8.1   Enriched with object orientation, deductive databases address themselves to several domains.

Deductive database rules can enhance the power of relational databases by providing a unified high-level interface and a mechanism for handling recursion.

The integration of object orientation and knowledge engineering can augment the deductive capability with semantic data modeling characteritics.

Such model's functionality is propelled through knowledge organization which induces many researchers to think of a deductive database as a deductive extension to a relational database. To be sure, deduction provides a powerful tool for:

• The definition and manipulation of rules,
• Integrity constraints, and
• Generalization hierarchies.

However, we also need an organizational tool for database design, going beyond the simply relational language interface by providing the power of the specification of constraints, recursions, and the like.

The linguistic support underpinning this reference should provide specification capabilities, as well as means for the manipulation of real, virtual, and hybrid components. The handling of complex data objects is important, including set-, tuple-, list-, and text-valued. The same statement is true in connection with the manipulation of global and local constraints.

8–3 DISCOURSE KNOWLEDGE AND WORLD KNOWLEDGE

We have seen a number of references where an object approach can be instrumental in terms of providing deductive facilities, which may be of two types. *Discourse knowledge* concerns the way clues from current context are used to help interpret a sentence—which may be part of a text in the database, a message, a meaning, or a context. *World (global) knowledge* is concerned with:

- Information about how the whole system and its environment are currently configured
- Expertise regarding physical and logical facilities, facts, states, values, and constraints

Objects may be mapping into themselves the decomposition of functions into subfunctions and sub-subfunctions, as the logic of a given system is detailed. World knowledge functions help to construct a model which is chosen because, say, it represents the establishment of communication paths, or there may be need for deductively accessing information storage, market behavior, customer accounts, or profit center returns.

Knowledge obtained through deductive processes helps in comprehending goals, as well as in understanding the acts of other participants in a message dialogue. Hence deductive databases can play a key role in real-life performance of an information aggregate.

Two strategies are available for query processing in connection with object-oriented distributed deductive databases:

1. A *bottom-up* evaluation of queries is done from already known facts towards new facts.
2. *Top-down* evaluation moves from queries to known facts, and in cases helps provide a better performance.

Top-down evaluation essentially instantiates custom-made hierarchical object structures, which are ephemeral. However, given the size and distribution of the database, there is the risk of entering infinite loops unless knowledge engineering assures the necessary metalayer—and, therefore, the associated constraints to the search which needs to be done in a database-wide sense.

This goal is served through the layered approach to which reference has already been made. In a top-down manner we distinguish:

- The intentional database (IDB), which most likely will include in itself integrity constraints
- The extensional database (EDB), which essentially is a set of facts stored in the distributed database structure

Among the deductive database features are capabilities of definition and manipulation of extensional database components, intensional database aspects (including virtual entities, relationships, and attributes), generalization hierarchies, integrity constraints, and recursive definitions. We have already spoken of these themes.

As will be discussed in greater detail from Chapter 11 onward, the EDB part is a conventional relational database consisting of entities, relationships among entities, and plain information elements. In the context of our discussion, these are handled as independent objects in the database.

Each object is represented by a set of attributes, which may have complex structures but their relationships have similar definitions. They also have properties associated with them defined by a set of permitted values constituting the domain.

The IDB part consists of the specifications and deductive rules which, as stated, can as well be fuzzy. Integrity constraints are associated with entities, relationships, and their attributes.

8–4 THE DEDUCTIVE FACILITIES OF A QUERY

A DBMS stores, updates, processes, and accesses objects. Stored objects are partitioned into collections or classes with the same structure. Queries are used to select subsets from the aggregate of objects in a distributed database. As such, they provide a high-level declarative style of programming.

While since the beginning of real-time operations and online database access there have been query facilities of sorts, the more elegant linguistic interfaces were introduced rather recently in connection with relational systems. Object-oriented databases tend to improve upon this performance by providing capability for:

- Querying collections,
- Assuring class extensions, and
- Manipulating classes of objects.

For instance, both Ontos and Open ODB feature a query language that is an object-oriented extension of SQL. But also both provide better

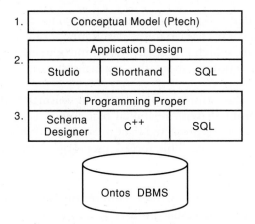

Figure 8.2   The programming environment of Ontos.

alternatives than SQL's extension. Figure 8.2 presents the case of Ontos as an example of what the programming environment of an object DBMS involves. As noted, there are three layers:

1. *Conceptual modeling,* which is done with Ptech[*]
2. *Applications design,* for which three artifacts are available by the Ontos vendor
3. *Programming/Coding,* where the center point is C++

SQL is featured in the last two layers. However, SQL is by no means an ideal tool for casual endusers, despite the fact that it became an ANSI standard of sorts. Most importantly SQL is still short of the fundamentals that characterize:

• An object-oriented query language[†]
• A distributed database query manipulator
• A linguistic construct able to handle database-wide deductive facilities

Japan's Electrotechnical Laboratory (ETL) calls the different versions (ANSI SQL 1986, 1989, 1992) "naive SQL," as none includes intentional rules. Even if the deductive features are for a moment left out of the equation, which should not be the case, the syntax for ad hoc queries addressed to distributed databases has become quite complex, particularly when dynamic joins are involved.

---

[*]See the reference to Ptech in Chapter 6, in connection to the Ciba-Geigy case study.
[†]Which will be most likely supported with ANSI SQL 95 (or SQL 3).

The fact is that a 15-year-old artifact cannot face the new requirements in an able manner. This has led to the development of various incompatible frontends for SQL, which practically means introducing nonstandard components. That is enough about the normalization efforts by ANSI and how far they can go.*

Aside from the complexity presented by mismatched tools and missions, a major problem with relational technology is that, to date, it has not performed as well as projected in connection with high-volume online transaction environments. This forced user organizations into a *multiple DBMS* strategy. They:

> Employ one solution for high volume online transaction work and another to provide casual enduser access, and
>
> Face the steady need of extracting and transferring information between incompatible sets of file structures.

The better alternative, of course, is to improve the performance of a distributed database by planning access strategies that minimize the amount of communications for query response.

Companies that have been proceeding along this path, with or without vendor assistance, have found through experience that the best strategy is the use of knowledge engineering artifacts to automatically optimize queries by:

> Choosing a valid and efficient data path in the distributed database landscape
>
> Allocating work to different nodes in a way that reduces the number and size of communicated messages

Query optimization issues arise because there are many ways to perform the steps necessary for responding to requests for information. To optimize a query, the software must be available to decompose it and find a sequence of steps that minimizes *cost*, where cost is a function of communications, processing, and memory accesses, not only of one factor.

A valid optimization strategy is based on the exploitation of statistical information. The software must record and then determine about:

- The number of tuples in the underlying tables
- The distributed storage accesses

---

*It would be superfluous to emphasize that SQL under DB2/MVS and SQL/DS/VM is not fully compatible, though coming from the same vendor. The same is true of OS/400 SQL and OS/2 SQL. Neither is the other SQL version truly compatible with another version.

- Expected amount of object communications

In other terms, distributed database management systems must not only contain quantitative information, but must also work in tandem with a data analysis construct which can benefit from knowledge engineering.

The able use of knowledge engineering can provide the necessary synergy, reversing the past trend of having database management software, statistical packages for data analysis, and flow control routines work independently from one another. The difficulty of optimizing under noncoordinated conditions underlines the need for:

- DBMS able to support dataflow routines working online with the more classical database management components
- Statistical and communications management packages able to assist the databases in a networked sense

As a result of this dual drive, some early versions of statistical database management systems have been able to model, store, and manipulate IE in a manner suitable for the needs of distributed database users. Such constructs aim to apply both expert system approaches and statistical analysis techniques to the management of distributed resources.

The concept underlying these premises is that as they become increasingly necessary, *deductive capabilities* bring together a number of disciplines so far handled in a self-standing manner. These include object orientation, agile ad hoc query facilities, idea databases,[*] and statistical and dataflow evaluation techniques.

8–5 KNOWLEDGEBANKS AND DEDUCTIVE DATABASES

The intelligence embedded in deductive databases can be constructed as a knowledgebank mechanism within the framework of object-oriented solutions. This statement is valid whether we talk of smaller or larger networked systems.

Optimally, the artifacts in reference[†] will be distributed in a way reflecting both their users' and the network's requirements. Both are increasingly based on more complex and higher level information and knowledge models.

---

[*]See also, D.N. Chorafas and H. Steinmann, *Supercomputers*, Chap. 13, McGraw-Hill, New York, 1990.

[†]For a specific example, see Sections 15-5 and 15-6 in Chapter 15 on *knowbots*.

The management of expanding database systems generally needs convenient solutions with a growing amount of intelligence.
This distinguishes the suggested approach from that of naive databases, but so far deductive solutions tend to address specific domains.

As explained in Chapters 11 and 12, a system's knowledgebank can be seen as an extended form of database intelligence. Typically, it supports deductive algorithms and/or heuristics addressed. It also permits fairly complex data models to be constructed.

A deductive approach can first be taken as a subclass of knowledge-enriched objects, considered in terms of classification hierarchies. Current intentional database approaches are, however, restricted since we are still gaining knowledge on how to handle their extensions. An example is the introduction of group semantics and the creation of an attribute system that can compose attribute names. The core effort should work toward system integration in a distributed environment regarding:

- Efficient performance,
- Modeling power,
- Formal semantics,
- Abstraction capabilities,
- Parallel processing, and
- Deductive mechanisms.

This approach can lead to direct or declarative representation of objects in each domain with the main goal being their efficient processing with only automatic translation into lower level language. Three issues top the list of themes to be studied carefully:

1. *System-type* logical extensions to intelligence-enriched approaches including certainty factors, best enforced through a *fuzzy engineering* implementation

2. *Data modeling* extensions able to incorporate structural aspects, behavioral aspects, and identity-based references

3. *Computational modeling*, with extensions addressing query processing based on constraints as well as object-oriented paradigms (autonomy, late binding, active objects, message passing)

In a deductive database environment, knowledgebanks are the higher-up layer which, as is shown in Figure 8.1, should be considered as the databases' extension. It is in this particular sense that in the deductive databases' solution adopted by ICOT, the system consists of three layers bottom-up:

- Databases
- Knowledgebanks
- Enduser interfaces

Users can define each interface of the layer addressed to them for their own applications and also access different resources. The enduser interface layer should effectively provide operational solutions, all the way to the handling of noncrisp queries, graphics, electronic messaging, and other interactive implementations, as well as experimental features such as flexible editors for multimedia.

Under current implementation perspectives, the top layer typically consists of knowledge representation languages[*] and various kinds of experimental modules based on them. Another feature is deductive mechanism(s) and an object management framework to create a structure of a distributed, deductive object-oriented framework.

Deductive and inference mechanisms are provided which correspond to each knowledge representation language.

The deductive database is architectured as an extension of the relational database, leading to the latter's reconstruction.

Knowledgebanks have an artificial intelligence kernel. They may be rule based or, in more sophisticated versions, heuristics oriented. We have spoken of the fuzzy engineering alternative in Chapter 3, which is able to handle vagueness, uncertainty, and more generally noncrisp environments.

As Figure 8.3 demonstrates, there exist two alternatives in addressing the distributed database layer: One is to have an object-oriented DBMS; the other is by means of a relational DBMS.

Today, the more common way of approaching the lower layer is to look at it as composed of relational structures. But, increasingly, object solutions will be necessary to address multimedia applications and other domains where object structures are the more efficient alternative.

In this way, Japanese researchers suggest, we might get the best of both worlds. The underlying data model of the database layer will be at the same time:

- A nested relational model, and

---

[*]Like the American Airlines example discussed in Chapter 9.

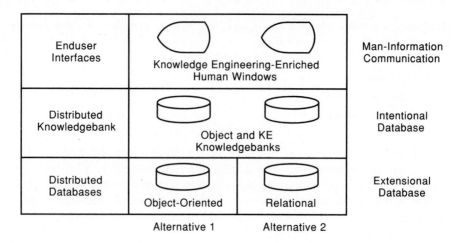

Figure 8.3   Successive layers of deductive database constructs.

- Some structured model such as semantic network with classification hierarchy.

In turn, semantic networks and classification hierarchies may be supported on nested relations. Terms expressing rules or structured information elements should be treated as a data type and be retrieved by unification and pattern matching. Prototyping may help in projecting and implementing the strategy that has been just described.

$8-6$ ROLE PLAYED BY PROTOTYPES

To appreciate the role played by a knowledgebank in modern information technology we should start by examining why we really need them and what they can contribute. Prototypes work by *analogy* and analogy is a powerful paradigm we often wish to exploit. It helps:

- The accuracy of software development, and
- The work done within program specifications.

Classical program development approaches can meet neither the sophisticated requirements nor the massive dimensions of present-day computer-based jobs. But if instead of working the old way by paper and pencil we prototype the finding of system analysis and the initial stages of system design on a computer, we gain a great deal in productivity.

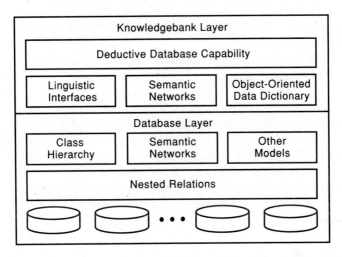

Figure 8.4   Knowledgebank and database layers of the ICOT project.

For software development, for example, ICOT employs a prototyping approach with database objects, relation objects, tuple objects, and a schema object. This is quite different from conventional designs supported by classical DBMS and is reflected in the diagram in Figure 8.4.

Contrary to the slow, costly, and error-prone approach of software development through COBOL, PL/1, FORTRAN, and other languages occasionally beefed-up by pseudo-CASE,[*] prototyping permits the exploitation of *dynamic knowledge* which describes generic types of systems as well as the tolerances of specific applications.

Beyond the applications perspectives, the analytical reasoning made possible through prototyping is most suitable for the experimental design of intentional databases and the mapping of the rules that they employ. This approach permits us to evaluate integrity constraints and whether or not information elements in the distributed extensional database satisfy these constraints.

Other types of experimentation can be quite vital as well. At least in the database layer, the ability to process also known as *database bandwidth*, a large quantity of data is necessary to provide effective operations environments. But performance optimization requires studies; it does not come automatically by implementing traditional DBMS approaches.

Prototyping can be effectively used as well to help evaluate different types of constraints. For instance, a given constraint, once enforced in a query, may substantially reduce the search space in the deductive database.

---

[*]Computer-aided software engineering.

Optimization constraints may be compiled together with the rule definition.

Other constraints, such as integrity constraints, can play an important role in the evaluation or termination of deductive rules.

One of the key reasons why experimentation is so important is that we are increasingly dealing with large systems that involve many unknowns. Large systems are not small systems that have grown over a period of time. They have totally different requirements in terms of conceptual definition, design, implementation, and maintenance.

Critics may say that not everything is very clear in this new domain of technology. From some people's point of view, it is very difficult to discriminate between

- Data, and
- Knowledge.

If this is the case, and it may, then it is even more important to use analogical reasoning and prototypes. During the 1990s, this will increasingly be true of many applications, as prototyping can be of help in evaluating different hypotheses, to obtain a documented result. Section 10-5 in Chapter 10 presents a practical application of prototyping in connection to the metalayer of distributed databases.

8–7 CONCEPT OF DYNAMIC METADATA

The cornerstone of deductive databases is *metadata*, that is, data about data that reflects the constraints. For data to be meaningfully processed, metadata associated with it must be present and accessible. It provides the information required to identify data of interest based on:

- Content,
- Validity,
- Sources,
- Preprocessing, or other selected properties.

The schema of a relation may be considered as metadata. It constitutes information about a collection of data values, but it is generally difficult to alter such schema, for instance, to add a new attribute, or delete an existing one.

For any alteration to be effective, not only must the schema itself in the data dictionary be modified, we should as well reformat every tuple in the relation itself. A better way is to use *dynamic metadata*, changing the structure of the database itself at runtime. This is particularly true with:

- Knowledge engineering applications,
- Scientific calculations,
- Pattern recognition, and
- Ad hoc analytical queries.

Systems programs, too, not only databases, can have *metarules*, that is, rules about rules. These can be helpful in recognizing and resolving rule and data conflicts. It is not a trivial task to match up corresponding records when fundamental differences exist.

Whether centralized or distributed solutions are adopted, user organizations are faced with multiple target platforms, incompatible standards, the need for interactivity with previous commitments in data structures and DBMS, and the goal of hiding complexity from the endusers.

Heterogeneity in databases is not only due to different hardware and software platforms. The structures with which we work may also differ in regard to:

- Data models,
- Query languages,
- Message processing, and
- Transaction models.

This is true all the way from data and rules, which can change dynamically, to metadata and metarules. Information technology is no longer the simple business it used to be 30 years ago—even if many of its people are still thinking in the old terms.

The concepts of *metadata* and *metarules* are fundamental in effectively employing information technology but also in human thinking at large. Many issues in business and industry, as well as in daily life, relate to metadata management. Within any specific instance, metadata must remain associated with the information elements it defines. It is therefore important to distinguish two particular uses:

1. A *low-level* description of the information necessary to provide a data interchange format
2. The *higher level* definition of the characteristics of data, which enable it to be interpreted properly

It would not be wise or even desirable to attempt to impose specific standards across the different domains and areas of wide-ranging implementations. But it is essential to introduce standardization into interchange formats, the methods for describing data and metadata.

A single format does not adequately support all needs and requirements even within a single discipline.

Self-describing formats solve this problem by promoting standardization of data interchange descriptions.

One aspect of this is to promulgate control lexicons of a standardized descriptive terminology appropriate within a given discipline. The data dictionary is the proper vehicle for doing so.

Finally, by applying an object-oriented inheritance mode, the qualities and characteristics of an upper layer are inherited by those below it. This is in conformance with applications practice where microscopic level decisions are typically made under the light of macroscopic ones, as we have seen in Chapter 1.

When the macroscopic solutions are misguided, the microscopic ones too will be misdirected—although they may be quite precise. The macroscopic world presents an integrative view, but to do so it needs concepts and tools. These can be provided by fuzzy logic, heuristics, genetic algorithms, the process of intelligent control of unstable systems, image understanding, and pattern recognition.[*]

---

[*]See also D.N. Chorafas, *Chaos Theory in the Financial Markets*, Probus, Chicago, 1994.

9

Facing the Growing Competition in the Service Industry

9–1 INTRODUCTION

The principles described in Chapter 8 in connection with deductive databases are not theoretical themes but practical issues that find their way into implementation with the aim being to increase competitiveness in the marketplace. A real-life application is the case study with American Airlines presented in this chapter.

Acknowledging that all leading airlines try to catch up in terms of technology, and therefore of services provided to the traveling public, each one of the main carriers has engaged in a race of major improvements for the traveler. This translates into concrete goals:

1. Trying to lessen the time and stress the flyer has to endure before getting on and off the plane
2. Integrating to air reservations other services such as hotel and car rentals
3. Vastly improving current scheduling practices for better performance
4. Depending on a more sophisticated implementation of computers and communications for the next significant service improvements

A recent example among certain European airlines is a system that separates the seasoned and unseasoned travelers. The former is, or will be, offered self-check-in, self-ticketing, telephone check-in, and an all-in-one boarding and baggage ticket.* The aim is to separate those who need assistance from the fast travelers who do not.

Besides this, airlines have ongoing projects to improve the individuality and friendliness of their services. An example is greater flexibility in meal service times, giving passengers a choice of time bands during which their meals can be served, but also avoiding serving the same meal to frequent passengers.

As in all industries, in air travel a small number of customers account for a large part of the profits the airlines make. These are the seasoned business travelers who want both staff warmth and more individual service. The latter can be greatly assisted through a quantum leap in technology as the case studies with American Airlines and United Airlines help in documenting.

The core technology now in the process of adoption rests on flexible and powerful query optimization systems which require both knowledge engineering and object-oriented solutions. The able handling of polyvalent, complex, ad hoc queries has to be performed at runtime in a way that greatly reduces the search space in a network of distributed databases.

American Airlines, for example, has experimental results that show that parallel query execution is doable. One of its projects addresses the optimization of entire queries parallelizing a given sequential plan to achieve minimum duration time with affordable computational resource requirements.

Studies by United Airlines demonstrate that such solutions cannot be effectively supported through mainframes, no matter how many million instructions per second (MIPS) they feature. They require supercomputers able to parallelize and to handle previously unknown parameters—generated by multiple query plans—at real time.

This demanding environment is not limited to the airline industry. Finance today faces the same information technology challenges and the same constraints. This reference is just as valid of merchandizing. Wherever *customer service* is the competitive terrain, the lessons learned by American Airlines and United Airlines are applicable, hence portable to other sectors of the service industry.

9–2 A REWARDING MEETING WITH AMERICAN AIRLINES

Like every other major service organization, American Airlines (AA) finds itself at this moment at the crossroads regarding data management. This is particularly true in connection with its real-time systems—from flight reservations to management decision support.

---

*Automatic check-in is already on trial at both Geneva and Paris airports, with Swissair playing a leading role in this project.

The leadership American Airlines has obtained in information technology dates back to the late 1950s when the SABRE passenger reservation and airline control system was established, in collaboration with IBM. At that time, it opened up great possibilities in customer service improvements and, not surprisingly, other airlines followed suit.

While SABRE has undergone major changes which can be characterized as generations, the management of American Airlines has shifted its emphasis on networking. In 1985, the company retained Booz, Allen and Hamilton (BAH) to identify who will be its No. 1 competitor 10 years later, by 1995. The BAH answer has been: AT&T.

Unlike other companies which disregard the consultant's report, at AA top management got the message and built for its company the largest online network in the world. Today, it features 160,000 attached hosts, workstations, and other terminals.

Investment banks at Wall Street say that presently American Airlines derives more profits from this huge service network than from flying airplanes. This is an issue that was not discussed at a recent meeting with AA executives in Dallas,* as the focal point was technology—which management sees as the tool for obtaining a leading edge.

The reference which has just been made helps explain the importance AA places on the need for able cross-database solutions. Two managing directors, together with their immediate assistants, participated in the meeting at American Airlines headquarters. Both of them expressed precisely the same opinion:

The endusers oblige us to take a new look at their needs—and at our needs as well.

This was stated by executives of one of the foremost companies in computer usage where very few areas have not yet been automated. But management appreciates the time has come to revamp.

A better perspective on the scope of the program which is currently under way can be gained by taking a look at accomplishments that have taken place in the past. Over the years, American Airlines has answered a good deal of user requirements through a number of database solutions:

- *TPF-IMS*—This is an outgrowth of the original SABRE, which was born in 1958

SABRE as a whole has been renovated many times since its inception, although its logo still identifies the reservation system duties through which it addressed client needs. But as a cognizant executive underlined during our meeting, "Though the programs themselves have been largely changed, the

---

*The American Airlines executives and system specialists who participated in this meeting are identified in the Acknowledgments.

system as a whole has retained a great deal of the old databasing structure which now has to be revamped, modernized and integrated."

Obliged to face in a constant manner the growing range of database-intense requirements, over the years American Airlines has added newer means and tools to its solutions. Such additions can be highlighted through three references:

- *DB2*—used, among other areas, for transaction-oriented applications in extension to TPF-IMS
- *TSO-DB2*—particularly implemented for decision support reasons
- *Teradata DBC* (database computer)—installed to enhance the online decision support implementation

There are as well other DBMSs operating online, an example being applications addressing graphics interfaces. They use Sybase and Informix.

"In short, there is a big mix of database solutions characterizing computers and manufacturers, in our information systems environment," said the responsible executive. "To get out of it, American Airlines has established a vision."

The American Airlines vision of the database solution of the 1990s rests on an analogy to power generation: Power can be produced through many types of factories (thermal, nuclear, hydroelectric) and different types of equipment. But as long as a network-wide compatible outlet is there, and the user can employ it, the diversity in the background is transparent to him.

After the guidelines were set, it was time for fine-tuning the mechanics. To implement its strategy, American Airlines relies on three basic building blocks:

- Knowledge engineering,
- Object-oriented solutions, and
- Intelligent networks.

Endusers communicate among themselves and with databases, as well as other resources, through networks. Sophisticated workstations become the entry point to the distributed database system. This is the cornerstone element of the new vision.

9–3 DYNAMIC IMPLEMENTATION OF TECHNOLOGY

"Dynamic, rapid implementation of communications technology and of knowledge engineering boosts competitiveness in today's environments and it is up to all of us to bring the means at our disposal to fruition," said a senior AA manager. "Vendors will support the user organization's standards if the user organization is forceful enough and knows what it wants in different situations."

Along this line of reasoning, the technical experts of American Airlines demonstrated that to be able to face the increasingly sophisticated enduser requirements and the diverse databasing situations these involve, it is necessary to support dynamic schemata. This permits us to manage ad hoc representation by means of both:

- Object-oriented, and
- Relational databases.

"The vendors will still drive the market, but it is up to us to choose and make them adapt their wares to our needs," another American Airlines executive commented. But then he added that *the difficulty comes from within.*

Like in so many other organizations in First World countries, the resistance to adopting a dynamic approach to systems administration is at the middle management level of data processing (DP):

The company's top management fully supports the issue of renewal. The analysts love to use knowledge engineering and object-oriented approaches.

But the middle managers of DP resist both renewal and new tools.

It is precisely because of this resistance that in the past many projects have been proposed but nothing really happened. Now the top management of American Airlines has decided to redefine responsibilities and ask for accountability with specific reference to results. Part and parcel of the "results" criterion is a rapid deployment timetable.

As the vision of the systems solution of the 1990s unfolds, an object-oriented architecture becomes a key player in the redefinition of responsibilities. American Airlines was to mention that this approach:

- Provides an understanding of where *we* are going and why,
- Sets a direction for vendor relationships, and
- Offers a framework for evaluating tools.

Designed by American Airlines, this framework for evaluation and redefinition is shown in Figure 9.1. The company thinks that, among other benefits, it provides an opportunity for reducing future legacy problems.

Management looks at object-based solutions as business drivers, helping to deliver applications faster. Like every other leading organization, American Airlines realizes that it needs to change tools and methods in

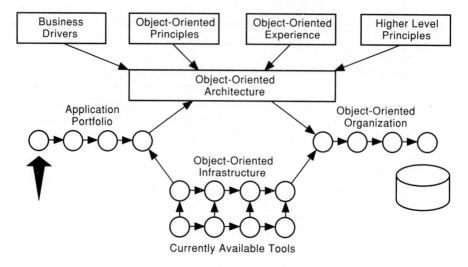

Figure 9.1   Framework for evaluation and definition.

order to reduce application development costs and the associated timetables. The goals are those of:

1. Meeting user requirements in a better, more flexible manner
2. Building computer applications that are more resilient to change
3. Producing higher quality software, all the way from development to maintainability

Delivering applications very close to schedule is one of the goals, but not the only one. Higher quality of software is just as important, and this is true of protecting existing investments as well.

Every major organization today has millions of lines of code that can neither be changed overnight nor written off. By necessity "old programs" will continue to operate, the more centralized ones phased out as the distributed workstations environment unfolds. But even in a dynamic, well-managed information technology organization, this takes time and has to be achieved in an orderly manner.

To reach the business benefits that have been defined and proceed from problems to solutions, American Airlines started in 1990 with pilot projects in *object-oriented applications*. Management is using the new technology in a controlled manner.

First came the training of a selected team of five people, which took place in August 1990.

Then, three prototypes have been produced in less than a year.

Object-oriented programming has been done in Smalltalk 80, primarily on Apple Macintosh—which talks volumes in terms of hardware efficiency when contrasted to formerly used mainframes. At American Airlines, the object-oriented DBMS which has been installed is GemStone. A tested alternative is Versant linking into DB2 and IMS, to permit managing object designs.

As the technology specialists of American Airlines aptly suggested, it is unwise to underestimate the educational effort for the introduction of object-oriented solutions. Management added that an integral part of this effort is the necessary cultural change.

It takes four to six months to train people with DP experience and change their habits. Many companies underestimate the investment that needs to be done for training reasons, yet without it even lavish expenditures in software and hardware will be of no avail.

When we talk of dynamic implementation of technology, what we mean, without necessarily spelling it out, is *reprogramming the human mind*. Unless this is done consistently and in an able way, results will be minimal—because resistance by those who are uninformed and ill-informed will be high.

9—4 THREE PROTOTYPES WITH OBJECT-ORIENTED APPLICATIONS

The first basic reference to be made when a new technological solution is introduced is at the conceptual level. There are numerous advantages to be derived by elaborating a concept, but this has to be done without losing time or sight of timetables. Implementation has to follow in fast succession.

New technology in systems development, such as shells and prototyping, permits interactive work with computers and concurrent software engineering. But analysts, programmers, and management itself have to be both sold and trained on this approach. After the prerequisite of formal training, prototyping is a good way to proceed with hands-on experience.

Prototyping, in fact, has many different meanings. The sense of the word is literally *first of a type*, and it is this concept which is correct. When we prototype we build a real-life working model where some 80 percent of the needed functionality is catered for by 20 percent or less of the code which might otherwise be necessary.

This 80/20 rule is an excellent application of Pareto's law which says that about 80 percent of something represents 20 percent or less of something else.

If 80 percent of the functional requirements are built into the prototype,

Then we rapidly get a quick glance at most of what is needed in a system sense,

While fine-tuning and customizing will be negotiated later.

What is important is that we have a working system on which we can experiment and which we can optimize. Once the prototype is done in a successful manner, other tools put at the disposal of the analysts can help in producing desired results. Let us appreciate, however, that the prototyping approach to software development is not strictly a testing mechanism:

A prototype can be used effectively to evaluate ideas and aspects of system design including conceptual aspects.

No prototype can be done practically unless we have a concept that can be represented in the form of a working model.

Even if it is not a full-size implementation, the prototype permits us to experiment with different representations, inference architectures, certainty factors, and so on. If the prototype is used constructively, then we can benefit considerably by improving the correctness in the final system, hence the quality of a solution.

American Airlines has done a useful assessment of the prototyping approach to information systems development. This has enhanced the company's ability to show that a new approach meets requirements and that the obtained results are satisfactory. By way of example, here are the object-based prototypes AA has constructed:

1. *Management of Regularities in Operations*—For instance, what happens if something goes wrong with a given airline operation? Which specific flight(s) is (are) affected? What sort of problems are there going to be? What happens to resources downline? To customer service?

Such queries have been existing for some time. They did not come up at AA just now. The problems associated with them were faced for many years—and they have been approached through modeling. But the usage of these more restricted models has shown the limitations of the previous approaches.

An example was given with reference to an ongoing 3270-type application. The latter has been judged as inadequate to meet the growing requirements of AA, hence the search for newer, more powerful solutions.

As the analysts have demonstrated, already since the prototyping level, object orientation has proved to be of great assistance. This is particularly true in terms of mapping relationships among:

- Aircraft,
- Gates,
- Facilities, and
- Passengers.

Problems associated with the flight of an airliner from point A to point B have been successfully faced in the past. But as modeling and experimentation have progressed, and experience has been gained, it has become evident that more flexible approaches than those supported through hierarchical and relational databases are necessary to face the growing service requirements.

For instance, even though when the airplane reaches point B the passengers may leave the plane and the crew may change, the craft itself in reality continues from point B to point C and from there to point D. As a result, an irregularity which might have happened in the A to B leg will most likely be propagated in the B to C leg, and culminate in the C to D leg.

The solution to such a propagation problem cannot be addressed in a correct manner through hierarchical data structures.*

Relational approaches have been tested, but they were not found to give real competitive advantages over current models—at least not at the level of sophistication which the company desires.

By contrast, an object-oriented approach provided advantages, satisfying the goals of the project team and opening new perspectives as well as opportunities.

This example from the air transport business, incidentally, is the nearest thing to a *long transaction*—an issue that has an important impact in the banking industry. Like anomalies in the A to B leg which affect the subsequent legs, the modern bank handles long financial transactions with substransactions specific to a tandem of legs.

In the airline business affected events within a given leg are client reservations, cargo commitments, crew schedules, catering—whose interconnections may not be apparent at first sight, but they are there. In banking a tandem of events resulting from a single customer order, hence transaction,

---

*On which the current models run.

may involve commercial paper, credit lines, documentary export, and possibly investments.

The handling of long transactions is complex, therefore challenging. While old approaches will not do, new experience is still at an investigative level. In order to be handled in an able manner, long transactions require a different technology than that we have used so far in short transaction management.

2. *Management Information System (MIS) Type Applications and Their Optimization.*—An example was provided during the AA meeting with object-oriented solutions in connection with problems regarding the planning of food and beverages. Typical management questions are: "What food tablets do you put on which flight? How do you mix particular components to assure that the passengers will not be given the same food moving in and out of a given airport?

In this domain, too, experimental approaches as well as practical implementation examples were modeled some years ago. Typically, these were IMS applications, but as experience and requirements grew they became too inflexible, no longer responding to the problems that had to be handled.

A similar reference was made regarding problems connected to crew management, including checklists and associated items. Heuristics are now being used and they require a much more flexible database structure than hierarchical and relational data models can support, hence the object orientation.

3. *Potential Productivity Increases in Administrative and Other Chores*—An example of an object-oriented project along this line of reference has been airline capacity planning and scheduling. A number of interesting aspects came up, demonstrating that both algorithmic solutions and hierarchical databases are too restrictive.

One specific case is the flight update function. It is directed towards allowing planners and analysts to take a portion of the schedule and induce a partial schedule change, then automatically recalculate changes in flight time and the overall schedule itself. Variations in subschedules are based on functional specifications which themselves must be subjected to experimentation.

Different approaches have been tried. One attempt was to keep on using a procedural solution while switching to an object-based database orientation. But procedural solutions have limitations and the conclusion has been reached that heuristics offer a better basis. Heuristics can best benefit from a full-scale object-oriented approach.

In this as in many projects focusing on intellectual productivity, the goal is to provide interactive business function views. These have to be sophisticated but also flexible and friendly. The user is not interested in technical details. What he or she wants is tangible results.

9–5 NEW GROUND CUT BY COVIA OF UNITED AIRLINES

COVIA started as a fully owned information technology subsidiary of United Airlines. Recently, United sold 50 percent of ownership to USAir, British Airways, KLM, Alitalia, and other carriers. This makes COVIA a wide-based cooperative information technology effort in the airline industry.

The reservations and logistics system underpinning the services COVIA offers is known as *Apollo*. It supports 48 million airfares and handles:

- 12,600 different types of transactions,
- More than 65,000 networked workstations,
- 548,000 miles of network transport, and
- 2,600 data circuits.

Figure 9.2 shows major Apollo components and the special software they are employing. The original system has been mainframe-based, but as a cognizant corporate executive detailed in the course of the First International Conference on Parallel and Distributed Information Systems,[*] the mainframe can no longer handle the systems load—hence the recently done supercomputer benchmarks aimed at establishing value-added capabilities.

Like any other advanced technology outfit, COVIA is greatly concerned at this moment about the refocusing necessary in order to handle the changing business environment in the service industry, particularly so, given the new perspective characterized by complex transaction types which essentially present long transactions handling requirements.

Correctly, COVIA management decided against looking at computer resources in a freeze-frame manner, even though there is an impressive array of them already available. In its current structure, Apollo is served by 1,000 IBM 3380 disk units, with 1.2 terabytes of online storage. There is as well a Unix-based parallel system. Both the central and distributed resources work 24 hours per day, 7 days per week nonstop.

---

[*]Miami, FL, December 5 and 6, 1991.

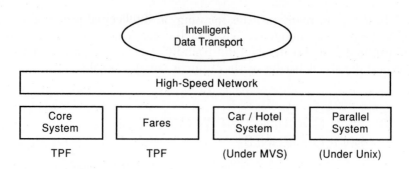

Figure 9.2   Network and computer resources at COVIA.

As far as the current missions are concerned, performance is relatively good, featuring, for the majority of cases, a 2- to 4-second response time. The average TPF transaction is 100,000 instructions; with 40 percent of these transactions characterized by 16 real Input/Output (I/O)[*] as well as 20 virtual I/O.

COVIA management is preoccupied, however, by the significant changes which its operating environment is undergoing. Aptly, it feels the need to respond in an able manner to the new realities:

- The business cycle time is accelerating.
- The complexity of computer-based applications increases.
- The demands posed by globalization create daily challenges.
- There is a rapid evolution in the clients' demands for services.

Although these messages were made by an air carrier and it can be thought that they represent its esoteric needs, the learned reader will appreciate that they fit the financial industry hand-in-glove. Every one of the four points that have been made is equally applicable to banking as well as to the other service sectors of the economy.

COVIA suggested that these four factors of evolution in client service requirements imply a radical change in concept and system structure. At the same time, there is an overriding need for maintaining continuity as well as bettering the current performance levels.

As the context of products and services offered to the market evolves bringing in greater complexity, it becomes necessary to elaborate new transaction types. For instance, one application involves information about

---

[*]Versus an average of 8 to 11 in other service industries.

the properties of a Room Master commitment connected to an airline reservation:

- Location in Miami
- Rooms available on night of arrival
- Priced at, say, less than $100 per night
- Observing a number of client-specific characteristics

Online access to heterogeneous databases and heuristic search is at a premium. COVIA no longer believes that the addition of more mainframes would solve this and similar problems. Therefore, it is benchmarking supercomputers. This situation is not unlike the one other service industries—such as banking—are now facing.

The forementioned client-specific characteristics, for example, may require access to basic proprietary data geographically distributed in incompatible databases, some of which belong to other companies and agencies. A complex transaction cannot be completed unless its subtransactions are executed.

Access to these heterogeneous databases has to be done in a seamless, timely, and efficient manner.

All operations have to be executed online even if some of them may be fairly demanding in computer terms.

For instance, a transaction of the forementioned type may have to check availability and serviceability for each resource to be committed, then cost. Subsequent to this, in order to offer the best service to the client, optimization will need to be done involving the appropriate mathematical model.

At COVIA, models have already been developed for this purpose and they are operating. But they are also very demanding in regard to cycles. As COVIA was to demonstrate at the Conference, very expensive IBM mainframes can handle *only* 20 transactions per second when complex models and database searches are involved—which does not make economic sense. By contrast, modeling on the KSR supercomputer[*]:

- Runs at seven times the mainframe performance,
- But only at one third the mainframe cost.

---

[*]By Kendall Square Research of Waltham, MA, a new computer architecture and a new company.

This means an impressive *ratio of 1 to 20*. Let us not forget that this is precisely the type of application coming up in significant numbers which has to be handled in a flexible, fast, and cost-effective manner for the service company to remain competitive.

9–6 DATABASES AND SUPERCOMPUTERS

The solution to the problems of the 1990s faced by the service industry requires online access to distributed heterogeneous databases which have to be exploited in real time. The databases of United Airlines are distributed and, like other carriers, the company has worked on the problems posed by database integration. In their current distribution, database support lies on:

- IBM mainframes, for commercial operations and airline control
- Univac mainframes for maintenance (installed in California) and for company operations (in Chicago)
- A large number of minicomputers, such as by Hewlett-Packard and other vendors
- A fully distributed workstation environment.

Interfacing has been chosen as an approach to solution, by setting a powerful mini to frontend the mainframe. One of the first cross-database applications was the building of an inventory catalog: homogenizing the business name of objects and creating a seamless access without duplication.

Important investments are being made as well in database management. In one application, for example, 12 man-years were invested from the development of the concept to full-blown implementation. Prerequisite to this implementation have been:

1. Making an architectural plan
2. Cataloging all information elements
3. Establishing reference standards

Item 3 was judged by management to be of critical importance not only to present but also to future implementations. New applications and the information elements that they require will have to conform to standards.

Contrary to practices of the past which looked at databases in a stand-alone fashion, networked databases impose significant prerequisites and imply the use of system-wide criteria. Duplication of information elements has to be avoided through appropriate classification and identification. All new data structures must be streamlined and those already existing must be sorted out according to a flexible classification scheme.

At COVIA, database control became an intelligent node at network level. It generates the proper commands and primitives without duplication. To achieve this goal data dictionary facilities have been extended throughout the network. The aim is to have directory services reach identification detail specific to every callable entity.

Another lesson learned from practice is that internetworking of databases must provide sufficient proficiency for data analysis. This is not written only in connection with existing applications, but also, if not primarily, with a view to the able exploitation of business opportunities through computer applications that did not exist previously.

This is what COVIA calls *the next generation of systems and services*, and it is actively preparing for the challenges it presents as well as the services it offers.

The next generation of systems and services goes well beyond the handling of routine queries of the type we were accustomed to in the past. The answer to simple queries might still be served through centralized corporate data, but simple queries are disappearing from the repertory of dynamic companies, being converted to queries of an analytical type.

As COVIA and a myriad of other organizations have found through practice, the able response to analytical and complex queries depends on algorithms, heuristics, and:

- Online collection of information elements,
- Their storage with interactive retrieval in mind,
- The adding of value to data, and
- The wide distribution of information.

All of these activities have become key factors in the survival and continued success of service organizations. This is the reason why data administration has taken on a critical role, further emphasized by recent developments in database technology, fourth and fifth generation tools, and personal computing.

In order to provide the best of support, developers and users must properly understand each other's objectives, problems, and functions—and they must communicate particularly effectively with senior management. Personnel skills, standards, and procedures necessary for successful implementation must be examined, and the same is true of techniques, disciplines, and other issues to be solved.

9–7 APPLICATIONS DEMANDING SUPERCOMPUTING RESOURCES

As an example of issues demanding high-performance computing resources, United Airlines took the online construction of dynamic schedules which require a significant amount of experimentation and optimization.

> Today, with mainframes, this process takes 50 hours per week and the job is done offline, hence it is not characterized by interactive response.

> But COVIA management has good reasons to be convinced that the application in reference has to be performed online, interactively and with a short response time.

"What we *do not* want to do in programming terms is to develop applications which depend on a number of monolithic processors being there," said the responsible executive. "This will be near-sighted and inhibit flexibility as well as scalability in our operations."

Other service industries have come to precisely the same conclusion. Not only do they orient their plans for the 1990s toward high-performance computing, but they also actively seek the identification of sources of knowledge necessary for understanding the inner working of complex business situations which they confront.

Some of the more imaginative systems efforts undertaken today are oriented toward discovering or devising mechanisms for encoding and applying business knowledge in a practical sense. This leads to the creation of integrative frameworks to control and coordinate the implementation of a variety of knowledge sources—which needs supercomputing to be done properly.

Once sources of knowledge have been identified, whole subdisciplines come into being to study the associated bodies of knowledge, their structure, and methods for their computerization. Some of the major knowledge sources are being unearthed now through the research that leading companies are conducting—and this means even more in high-performance computing requirements.

To face the fast-evolving needs, COVIA has chosen a distributed environment architecture with supercomputers as number-crunchers. As we discussed in Section 9–5, the solution attracting the greater attention in this project is the one tested on the Kendall Square Research (KSR) supercomputer.

As it is to be expected, within the perspective of the new orientation in information technology, particular attention is being placed on the issues that the management of COVIA considers to be of primary importance for a service industry which wishes to remain competitive in the 1990s:

- Complex transaction handling involving many facets of operations
- Analytical ad hoc management queries accessing heterogeneous databases
- High reliability in operations through controlled data redundancy
- Ability to bypass faulty units for continuing nonstop processing
- Quality control leading to online replacement for 24-hour availability

In connection to database software, among the advantages COVIA has found in the KSR solution is a logical view with simple address space and an all-cache (no fixed address) memory approach which migrates where it is needed. All this is supported in hardware, in a scalable fashion.

Hence benefits from the use of a supercomputer go beyond its number-crunching capabilities and significant cost-effectiveness. In a database-oriented sense, such benefits have to do with *recoverability* and therefore with redundancy, leading to online replacement while assuring continuing operation.

These are among the benefits that a parallel architecture can provide in contrast to the old mainframe approaches which have by now worn thin. Significant benefits to be obtained from a parallel system come from the interoperability which it offers with different logical and physical applications levels.

The best results are obtained not only from scalable system constructs but also from the implementation of a transparent parallelism: System configurations should be transparent to the programmer, and there should be an open system management endowed with the appropriate tools. These conditions require advanced management thinking. When they are met, the company can gain a high degree of cost-effectiveness.

10

Setting the Stage for Cross-Database Functionality

$10–1$ INTRODUCTION

As the complexity of computers and communications applications and associated system reliability requirements increase, centralized operations or off-line servicing for a myriad of users become unwise if not outright impossible. Distributed control is the only approach with long-running activities, and there is a need for a deductive database functionality.

Networked applications must be controlled by a set of distributed, knowledge-enriched tasks through a sequence of well-timed interactions. A sound model will:

- Allow local autonomy,
- Provide for flexibility,
- Guarantee a global perspective when necessary, and
- Assure the control of long-running jobs.

The support by knowledge engineering is vital because network-wide database interactions create many technical issues, some of which are not even known at design stage. For instance, how can the shared resources be reliably manipulated as the number and complexity of concurrent cooperative processes grow? Faced with long transactions (see also Chapter 4),

How do we define when a cooperative objective is attained?
How do we determine that a given operation has taken place in a satisfactory manner?

What is the dynamic criterion for controlling interactions among multiple cooperative tasks?

Are we sure these tasks work in synergy toward achieving a common objective?

Other systems queries, too, require deductive capabilities for automatic execution. Not only must responses be automated, but they also have to be handled in real time. Tasks must be informed about changes to the database that occur because of other tasks, as well as changes to other components of the operating environment for whatever reason they happen.

Intelligent database structures must be able to deal smoothly with logically complex notions, such as disjunction, quantification, implication, causality, and possibility. This ability is well beyond some of the models being developed by major vendors which act as if they were handling information containing:

- A fixed, deterministic number of objects and relationships among them
- Immutable relationships and unchangeable patterns

The solutions we are after in response to the requirements of the 1990s have to be flexible and far-sighted. Half-baked approaches, like treating each input as if it were given in isolation, are not acceptable. We have to perceive a problem in its true dimension, though we may not be able to answer at the same time all of the requirements that it poses.

10–2 INCREASING COMPLEXITY OF DISTRIBUTED DATABASES

A great deal of the drive to manage the database resources in a more rational way is due to the fact that current implementation requirements are far more advanced than what available database mechanisms can provide. As Figure 10.1 suggests, the leftmost reference in the time scale, simple centralized database access, involved relatively low complexity and could be served by means of rather naive software. Under this condition, file management was an acceptable practice.

A little further down the time scale, the introduction of DBMS aimed at both improving performance and handling the somewhat increased complexity. It also made feasible a partly distributed database access, which in the 1970s was mainly minicomputer based.

But the explosive growth in terms of user demands for greater sophistication has began with the myriad of networked workstations requiring

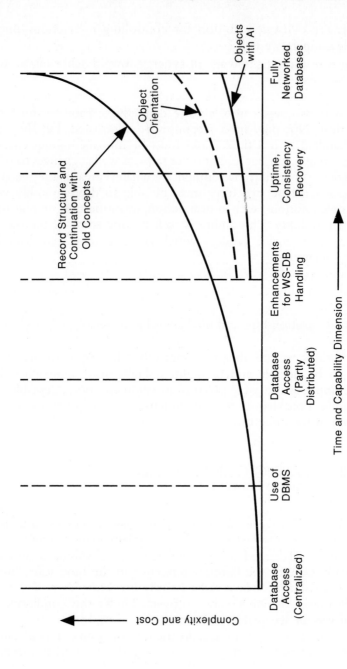

Figure 10.1   Record structure, object orientation and knowledge engineering assistance.

systems with explicit models which operate at runtime and are able to handle complex relationships among information elements, and also between information elements and the types of processes that can alter those relationships.

It comes, therefore, as no surprise that the request for more advanced database management capabilities has come right after this line of reference calling for significant enhancements in terms of modeling, optimization, and management by the participants in the network. The message given by Figure 10.1 is that:

1. As long as we keep with coarse-grain record structures, complexity increases exponentially.

This is the sense of continuing to operate with "old concepts" identified in the figure. The exponential growth in cost and complexity is present no matter what type and how many old-style DBMS are used in the database network.

2. By contrast, there can be a rather significant improvement with the transition to fine-grain object-oriented solutions.

Such improvement impacts on complexity by reducing it, and therefore, up to a point, it swamps costs. Part and parcel of this approach is that in a distributed database sense access to states of instantiation of objects is an inherent part of many applications.

As the preceding chapters have already underlined, application domains that benefit from this object-oriented approach include CAD, CIM, financial engineering, CASE, office automation, and document management at large—as well as practices such as global risk management and company-wide cost control. In these cases, the same object undergoes multiple changes or state transitions, and it is desirable to access or investigate the specific previous states of it.

This process is known as *version management*. Its mechanics require a number of tools and constructs to automate and simplify the construction and organization of different configurations, creating progressively more enhanced versions of classes and objects while leading the curve of complexity and cost.

3. Further benefits can be derived through the use of knowledge engineering concepts and solutions, which enhance the object orientation.

The effect of AI-enriched object-oriented approaches on complexity and cost is shown in Figure 10.1. The reasons should be found in the fact that when objects are distributed among computing facilities at various sites, new and more powerful approaches are needed to tackle the difficult problem of database management.

The reference to exponential increase in cost and complexity is compounded by the fact that databases at various sites are often heterogeneous for a variety of historical and operational reasons. Difficulties show up all the way from architecturing a system that provides effective distributed facilities, to the development of a virtually homogeneous distributed database solution.

10–3 DEALING WITH PREEXISTING INCOMPATIBLE STRUCTURES

Whether we like it or not, we are obliged to deal with preexisting incompatible object structures. This is true not only within the context of distributed databases resources but also with centralized sites. To manage such environment in an able manner, we must:

- Know where objects are stored, as well as what are their formats and data structures.
- Formulate and implement deductive query capabilities over all databases in the network.
- Decompose the user queries into subqueries that can be executed at each database.
- Integrate the query languages of the local DBMS in a way transparent to the enduser.
- Provide the necessary interfaces for the able functioning of global database management operations.

An important implementation issue in developing a reliable system solution involves the strategy of supporting conceptual database evolution: Instant propagation versus deferred propagation is among the choices to be made.

In the former case, changes to the conceptual database structure need to be instantly propagated to the underlying databases, thus a consistent database image is maintained. In the latter case, changes to the conceptual database structure are deferred. However, the representations of objects have to be corrected or filtered as they are used—which is effectively a late binding procedure.

In terms of upkeeping the database context, we should aim to capitalize on the possibilities offered by knowledge engineering. Traditional databases, for example, are considerably more rigid than knowledgebanks. Their structure requires:

- A prior uniform definition for each entity, and
- Explicit storage of all facts.

In turn, this calls for a fair amount of deterministic approaches that are ill-suited in modern environments. Knowledgebanks, on the other hand, represent information elements in a more dynamic fashion.

Facts can change, and the structure and interrelationships among the facts can vary as well, as the knowledgebank is being used. When the IF portion of a rule matches an input pattern, the THEN portion of the inference rule can include initiating an action such as a database update and/or sending a message to another knowledge source. This can be done in addition to making an inference.

Through deductive database capabilities, for very large data files the logical and contextual relationships can often be expressed much more compactly and efficiently than the actual data. The answers to many queries can be determined solely through reference to knowledge-intense relationships with little retrieval of information elements.

One of the important operating references concerns *replicated objects*. Whether partially or fully, objects are replicated in order to:

- Increase database performance and reliability,
- Decrease communications flaws, and
- Better the organizational perspectives.

When the closest copy of an object is accessed, performance increases and communication costs decrease. With replication, if a node fails, another node with the same IE is available.

Chief among the replicated data problems, however, is how to assure that the identical class and its instantiation at all nodes is updated the same way and as quickly as possible. Otherwise, different data values of the same IE may be read at different nodes.

Deciding where to replicate which information elements is a complex problem that can be helped through heuristic approaches. In general, objects should be replicated and distributed so that 90 percent of database accesses are to the local resource site, while the synchronization problems and overhead of updating replicated files are minimized.

Knowledge engineering approaches are as well instrumental in connection with the need to understand database context. This throws considerable doubt on the idea of building, for example, natural language interfaces without the benefit of knowledgebanks. Information in the knowledgebank is often needed for comprehension of a query and for filtering reasons regarding the response.

10–4 FEDERATED DATABASES AND THE NORMALIZATION PROCESS

A normalization process associated with the relational approach tends to fragment real-world entities over several tables, introducing significant reconstruction overheads at runtime when the database is accessed. There are various problems related to the use of primary and foreign keys, a fundamental aspect of the relational approach.[*] But these are not the only ones:

> Our past images of what a distributed database is and is not present significant limitation in creating *integrative architectures*.
>
> The common ground of such limitation is the centralized nature of current databases and particularly the lack of a *global schema*.
>
> Low-level manipulation foregoes the benefits of a higher level approach, as, for instance, exemplified by a *federated database architecture*.

A federated line of reasoning sees to it that each local database continues operating on its own when local problems are addressed. But it is also part of a grand design which assures seamless cross-database operability when global transaction or global queries must be handled.

Along this line of reference, the GTE Laboratories have developed an intelligent database shell known as Intelligent Database Assistant (IDA). Its first practical implementation took place in assuring the interoperability of heterogeneous databases of GTE in Southern California, and it is known as CALIDA. Benchmarks made on this application involved 30 different activities and compared:

1. Response time from a nonnormalized structure with distributed heterogeneous databases as they exist on mainframes, to
2. Response time of a normalized distributed database through the CALIDA metalayer which involves knowledge engineering.

CALIDA views all heterogeneous databases as memory locations. Besides minimizing the number of accesses and interconnections, a feder-

---

[*]The permanently hierarchical approach of IMS and network DBMS (IDS I, IDS II) predates the relational approach and is even less appropriate in a distributed multimedia environment.

ated database architecture is mapped in memory with one address space serving all objects in the distributed environment.

A federated database structure simplifies the job of programming and thus lessens the demand on high-level language interpreters. Objects can be called out from address locations in the same manner as read/write operations. Accesses can be prioritized and processed in the same way.

In contrast to tightly coupled systems, the federated database architecture uses an organizational model based on:

- Peer-to-peer autonomous structures, and
- Sharing control by explicit interfaces.

This limits the effect of heterogeneity, as no database has authority over another. There is *no global schema* in a federation. Rather, each component has direct access to the original IE provided by other components, and it is free to restructure that information into whatever form is most appropriate to its needs.

Control of the shared resources rests with the owner of objects, but the negotiation mechanism assures that changes to the structure of classes and objects proceed in an orderly fashion. The aim is to provide a small set of operations for object definition, manipulation, and retrieval in a distributed environment.

There are other advantages apart from the contribution of normalization done through the metalayer, beyond virtual homogeneity. For instance, reasonable independence from three possible failure types:

1. *Deadly embrace* which takes place when databases in a distributed environment are addressed without global supervision, with some of the object being reached being in lock-up because of waiting for results from other operations including the one now requesting a reply.

2. *Transaction failures* often caused by concurrent transactions conflicting in their access to the shared resource(s). When such conflicts are detected, the DBMS aborts one or more of the conflicting transactions, or there may also be user aborts.

3. *Systems failures* as usually caused by software errors in the operating system, DBMS, or Transaction Processing Manager (TPM), such as a crash in an operating system. When such a crash occurs, the content of the main memory is lost while the secondary disk storage remains intact. Without global normalization and coordination this must be handled case by case.

These three references do not mean that the metalayer of a federated database will do miracles. But normalization does help in the online automatic investigation of a deadly embrace as well as in the recovery from transaction or system failures.

For instance, one simple technique often used with a centralized or a limited distribution topology is to handle any kind of failure through mirroring or replication. If the persistent database is replicated, there will actually be two or more copies of each persistent object.

The underlying assumption, of course, is that there is homogeneity in data structures and formats, which often is far from being the case. By contrast, through knowledge engineering, relationships among objects can be established across workstation boundaries, with objects relocatable within the distributed environment and with mechanisms assuring dependable access control.

An object-naming convention applied with federated databases supports location-transparent object references. This means that objects can be referenced by user-defined names rather than by address—a process supported by CALIDA.

Since the federated database architecture focuses on a higher level than the object-sharing approach, it provides more explicit interobject interfaces. Through knowledge engineering, these are enriched with specific capabilities to support negotiations based on a semantic model. We will return to some basic aspects of federated databases in Section 10-7.

10–5 PROTOTYPING THE METALAYER OF DISTRIBUTED DATABASES

The foregoing discussion provides evidence that AI object-oriented approaches have the potential to improve upon results obtained through relational solutions. The question is whether this will come through system evolution or revolution—the former being more likely than the latter.

Relational databases, of course, are not going to disappear and bridges have to be provided to them by locality and in a networking sense. The able management of a long transition period is most important. Relational approaches will characterize the extensional database (EDB) while an object-oriented knowledge-enriched layer will constitute the intentional database (IDB).

Through this duality, each solution will contribute its strengths and in a way counterbalance the weaknesses of the other. But a balanced design requires experimentation which the appropriate prototype helps to support.

The relative strengths of object-oriented approaches must be properly identified and exploited within a distributed landscape. Through six points of reference, the strengths of an object orientation are outlined in Table 10.1 and compared to the predominant weaknesses of a relational solution.

After the prototype is complete and due experimentation has been done, the results can be listed out for review by the database administrator of each of the local resources as well as the system manager of the distributed network. This usually leads to suggestions of clarification and changes, so that the projected solution meets the requirements of the users. Following modification and approval the model serves three purposes:

1. A formal specification for the projected federated database system
2. A written definition (not just description) of its functionality
3. A basis on which the knowledge engineers would work to provide the primitives

As Figure 10.2 suggests, by working on the prototype we can do semantic, pragmatic, and syntactic checks, controlling for correctness along all three axes of reference. This can be best achieved by means of an expert system and an integrated compiler/interpreter approach.

The compiler will translate the specifications for changes into an intermediate representation, also performing essential checks on it. The

Table 10.1   Relative Merits of Object-Oriented and
Relational Approaches

Object-Oriented	Relational
Able handling of complex objects	Even the best relational DBMS is slow in addressing complex objects
Polyvalent object identification	Not supported through the relational model
Flexible formal modeling	Need to break tabular forms into different files and put them again together; this is a slow operation
Easy extensibility of a distributed environment	Extensibility creates representation problems due to different record structures
Relatively simple aggregation through algorithms and heuristics	Many expensive join operations—although relational solutions are better than hierarchical and network in ad hoc applications
Fine-grain modularization at object level	Coarse-grain modularization at record level

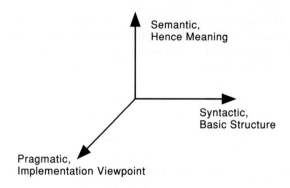

Figure 10.2   A coordinate system helpful in checking for correctness.

interpreter will execute conceptual and consistency controls. This can best be done through a knowledge engineering process of equilibration.

Simple definiens should be presented to help distinguish between two objects that look alike. Such result cannot be easily achieved with relational approaches, which approximate an identification process by using surrogates. At the same time, extensibility requires:

- A predefined set of types
- The ability to treat same types uniformly
- The existence of attractive programming paradigms

The existence of new and old software complicates the mission. New VLSI and ULSI hardware will help in solving some of the current problems; others will remain. The conversion to firmware will interest the lower programmatic interfaces while the top problems will be the investment in legacy systems and the large changeover cost.

These issues point toward a soft conversion with the ability to provide a generic interface for user-defined objects, protocols, and primitives—whether the user is a person, a program, a terminal, a host, or the file server itself.

Simulation and experimentation will see to it that changes of the involved configured elements and of the system as a whole will be performed at prototype level. Results will be checked for consistency according to given configuration conditions.

One of the major tests to be done at prototype stage is database reconfiguration and associated computational aspects. It is advantageous that distributed configuration, computation, and communication issues are expressed into the design language.

- A more elegant integration can be achieved by selecting an object-based model of computation, communication, and structure.
- The structural model should be supported by a configuration language enriched with a set of tools related to database distribution.
- Semantic relations must be the cornerstone to multimedia representation, coupled with basic runtime events.

While the prototype may as well provide a more abstract and global mapping of the distributed environment, it is wise to focus on specific aspects and avoid generalities. This should be done without impairing distribution transparency.

10—6 DEDUCTIVE APPROACHES AND VALUE-ADDED SOLUTIONS

Database management was an early target of the natural language community because many endusers find it rather difficult to interact with conventional interfaces, such as a keyboard. As a result, a number of natural language frontends have been developed that are designed to ease the interaction burden between the user and the database management system.

Unlike progress made in the expert systems domain, however, the natural language community has found that the nature of the challenge is more complex. Good devices must understand the components of language and represent the knowledge necessary for meangingful interaction with the user, observing the latter's profile and natural way of communicating—a requirement which goes well beyond the natural language itself.

This example helps document further that information management problems depend on solutions, and the deductive approaches discussed in the beginning of this chapter are a step in this direction. Rules about user behavior based on an ad hoc query and interrelationships regarding subqueries in the distributed database are issues that can be effectively approached through a *profile analyzer* as well as through statistical observations of past behavior. The output of these processes can greatly help in man–machine communication, including display processes.

Figure 10.3 presents the interactive characteristics built into the system by a project following the approach that has just been described. In this graph, the description of the modules has been simplified so that the figure becomes self-explanatory.

Information modeling concepts are important because a deductive database requires a knowledge representation standard which is powerful enough to be used in applications. But the solution to be reached should be easily comprehended by system users, as well as by developers.

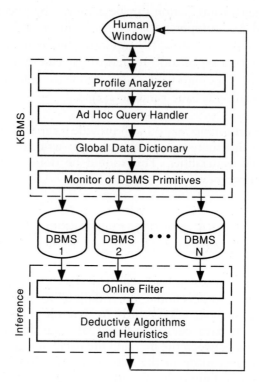

Figure 10.3   KBMS functionality with heterogeneous DBMS.

Properly designed and supported through knowledge engineering, deductive user profiles constitute a value-added solution. This is in line with the concepts presented since the beginning of this chapter and can make good use of fuzzy engineering capabilities, which are discussed in Chapter 3. Fuzzy engineering artifacts can:

- Address themselves to multiple nodes in the database network
- Account for all events whether they are global or only local
- Handle aggregation of changes affecting classes and objects
- Filter database contents and bring required object(s) to the required user node
- Assure system-wide performance through supervisory interpreters (demons)

In essence, this is what we expect from a KBMS structure of the type discussed in Chapter 12.* The bottomline is semantics—hence *meaning*. This is what we are after.

Whether fuzzy engineering or other tools are used, the goal is a flexible and expandable object-oriented knowledge representation scheme. As we will see later, a primary distinction between databases and knowledgebanks is that databases have a predetermined structure, whereas knowledgebanks consist of a set of unstructured facts, their states and instantiated values.

The paths by which facts are related to a knowledgebank are determined "on the fly" as needed to solve a particular problem. This is at the core of object-oriented approaches as well. By contrast, the relationships between data items in relational, network, and hierarchical databases are designed into the database in advance.

To operate in an able manner, a deductive database needs a strong knowledge component, not just Data Manipulation Language (DML) and Data Description Language (DDL) type routines. Another critical distinction between the DBMS approach which we know from the past and the KBMS we have to develop is that:

Databases store all of their information explicitly,

Whereas the bulk of what a knowledgebank contains is inferred from a few basic facts through rules and heuristics.

In a deductive database sense, knowledge representation frames the domain and its objects, providing relations to link objects together and to develop demons to support event-driven programming.

Inheritance helps to pass characteristics from a class to a subclass across relations. Object-oriented programming supports coding methods that assure that objects communicate with one another via messages in the form of global broadcast or narrowcasts.

Within the basic knowledge representation perspective, class and instance frames address themselves to either a generalized type, a more limited category of objects, or a particular member of a class. Attributes storing values such as numbers and character strings are provided, and so are relations reflecting user-defined links between frames in the knowledgebank—as well as messages connected to object-oriented programming methods.

---

*A brief introduction is necessary at this point as KBMS are the kernel of deductive databases.

Using heuristics and algorithms, a deductive database sees to it that, starting at a particular node, frame networks are searched for a specific slot. Slots in frames have both global and local behavior.

Demons are automatically invoked when the associated slot is accessed or modified. Searches can be breadth-first or depth first, correspondingly carried across "*is a*" and "*instance*" relations or across user-defined relations. The latter are searched in the order in a which they occur in a frame.

Inheritance is performance by all functions that access slots and values. The metalayer helps in the definition of constraints as well as in making the semantic meaning more explicit. In a deductive database, the whole context is tuned to support hypothetical reasoning. Subproblem solving metaknowledge permits the:

- Inclusion of background information, and
- Execution of dependency tracking.

Path following looks after the efficient traversal of compound relationships. Declarations and optimizations provide a high-performance environment with dynamic knowledge representation. They also permit creation of objects and relations at runtime.

Within the context of deductive database operations, browsing is used to display the contents of the knowledgebank or of selected databases. There is however an increasing need for tools to help in the convenient and efficient creation and manipulation of documents. There is as well a need for error handling and warning subsystems which permit us to tailor application responses to errors and warnings.

These are no hypothetical statements, but ingredients of a system which has past the prototype level. An example is the Initiative for Managing Knowledge Assets (IMKA) by the Carnegie Group which we have examined in detail in Chapter 5. As will be recalled, this project is done in partnership with DEC, Ford, USWest, and Texas Instruments.

10–7 CONTRIBUTION OF KNOWLEDGE ENGINEERING TO DEDUCTIVE FUNCTIONALITY

One of the value-added issues characterizing a distributed database and its functionality is the way in which the database conducts its own housekeeping. This too requires deductive capabilities since the fact that raw data is heterogeneous can lead to special problems in housekeeping chores.

An example is path finding within a widely distributed object structure. Paths must be supplied for traversing class hierarchies and their instances and therefore developers must be able to:

- Define paths across relations which are both system- and user-established
- Employ path grammar in path definition of stored objects and dynamically at runtime
- Be able to use efficient traversal of compound relationships

Traversal of compound relationships must be kept dynamic, as objects are added to and subtracted from the distributed landscape, and also as their interrelationships change. At the same time, for efficiency reasons, the data dictionary must be at a steadily updated status.

If path finding is deficient, users will discover that the global database system does not provide everything they want for their jobs. As a result, more specialized, parochial databases will be used, and different means of getting the data out of one system and into another will proliferate.

Two approaches examined so far in regard to this import/export problem are the *copy* and the *interface*. In the copy approach the functions of one database are copied into another, provided the appropriate linkages are created between different databases facilitating path finding, conversion handling, and other functions. There are many negative issues associated with this approach.

Interfacing has to be executed both in regard to applications and in respect to databases, leading to the federated solution which we examined in Section 10-4.

Different levels can be envisaged in interfacing applications and databases.

Tightly coupled, fully integrated systems allow users to query the distributed database in executing different operations, whether procedural or heuristic.

The artifact automatically prepares the input to the procedure, locates the appropriate objects, produces the specific commands, and initiates their execution, with the result of the execution saved in the database.

The alternative is *loose coupling*. This is a low integration level where the different DBMS in the network are invoked to produce, for instance, a flat table of IE in a format required by the application.

This leaves a good deal of the ongoing responsibility for creating the appropriate commands and initiating execution up to somebody else, but in itself it is a more flexible approach.

To answer the query, "Who may the somebody else be?" Figure 10.4 suggests a path-finding architecture which, in this specific case, addresses both magnetic disks and optical disks, the latter storing compound electronic documents. An AI-enriched four-layer software support at the user's workstation level will help manage:

- Ad hoc query language requirements
- The rules and heuristics of object search
- The specific path-finding approach which has been chosen, and
- An intelligent filter automating selection activities which otherwise had to be done by the user.

The looseness or tightness of the coupling helps specify the algorithms and heuristics to be used. The overall configuration provides for interfaces to the different DBMS by means of specific drivers.

Knowledge-enriched facilities can allow users to trace attribute value inheritance, browse contexts, navigate (through hypermedia), and display selected objects. Data dictionaries provide essential support to operations intended to manipulate objects conveniently and efficiently.

Programs can create lists by declaring an entity as local variable, global variable, or pointers.

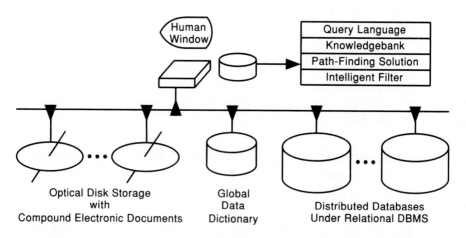

Figure 10.4   Path-finding architecture with distributed multimedia databases.

Once available, all lists can be used by any of the functions that manipulate them.

Such activities are more effectively executed in a knowledge-enriched environment which can permit adding new technology on top of the old one in the context of the application system. This must be done without manually changing existing code, by mapping existing data structures to the basic object model of the application.

At the human window level, a menu system should dislay operations whose choice permits us to access objects at local sites transparently. AI-enriched software makes it feasible to be able to check the validity of a global query and convert the data access part of the original query into internal representations.

A knowledge engineering module decomposes, optimizes, and checks the internal query by using the information stored in the global data dictionary. It also activates the communication network when query processing involves remote site(s).

The path-finding solution links together intermediate results returned from local sites and resolves data incompatibilities. Intelligent filter primitives can see if there is a relationship between the objects being retrieved and the specific query characteristics.

Dynamic knowledge representation provides functions that allow users to modify dynamically class hierarchy and object behavior. Interactive knowledgebank editing adds value on applications, such as knowledge acquisition about a user's preferences, through profile analysis.

Overall, the deductive databases solution produces a high-performance system with distinguished features. Optimizations improve execution time of basic operations. Performance optimizers can be either inherent in the design of the system or a result of user-supplied declarations.

11

Knowledgebanks and Databases

11—1 INTRODUCTION

Within the perspective of a deductive database implementation, Chapter 10 has demonstrated the synergy that exists between object-oriented solutions and knowledge engineering. The latter performs its functions through rules and heuristics stored in the *knowledgebank* which acts as a metalayer on the database.

A knowledge-based system consists of two fundamental parts: the knowledgebank and the inference engine. The inference engine is not the subject of this text. The *knowledgebank* is a repository of *rules* and of information made up of *facts, states,* and *values* about the *domain* to which the system addresses itself. The knowledgebank also includes the appropriate methodologies.

Sometimes the role of a knowledgebank is misunderstood. Therefore, proper appreciation calls for the right definition. A primary distinction between a database and a knowledgebank is that:

The way they are practiced today, *databases* have a predetermined structure, while *knowledgebanks* consist of a set of rules and unstructured, even isolated facts—which may be objects.

Knowledgebanks abide by the *class concept* describing a set of object instances with similar structure and behavior. As with all object-oriented systems, each class has a name and a set of attributes, which may be instance variables or properties. These hold state values of the object as well as a set of operations to which an object is subject.

The path by which facts are related in a knowledgebank is determined ad hoc, as necessary to solve a particular problem. This is the sense of a *heuristic* search versus a structured approach—whether probabilitistic or deterministic.

Path finding within an environment of object-oriented distributed databases is discussed in Chapter 12, as well as the approaches adopted for its execution (copy, interfaces). It will be recalled that such approaches are knowledge based, legitimating the need to look at the concept of knowledgebanks and the services they offer prior to examining the role played by intentional and extensional databases—which is done in Chapter 14.

Comparing knowledgebanks to databases is practically synonymous to discussing *intentional* versus *extensional* solutions to database management. The intentional lead to the notions of *expert databases* and *idea databases*. However, prior to approaching this subject it is correct to establish the concept of knowledge-based operation with object database goals. Typically, such solution:

- Is equipped with knowledge stored in rules and heuristics
- Can be applied flexibly in unanticipated paths within the distributed database environment
- Is able to cope with ambiguity in terms of user queries
- Can proceed with and the object identification and the search criteria they imply

The role of knowledgebanks is more pronounced in problems that are not readily solved by conventional database approaches. Such problems typically involve issues based on complex interaction of many factors hence they can best be handled through semantics and knowledge processing.

11-2 CONCEPT OF KBMS VERSUS DBMS

No database can be managed without the proper methodology. A good example on this statement is the use of a DBMS. Some methodologies have been available in connection with distributed database systems but they have not yet been formalized. Formalization requires rules and this is done through the knowledgebank.

A methodology for database management should be application-independent, but it should also take full advantage of the underlying database model. The process of formalization ranges:

From the establishment of proper formalisms in a distributed database sense

To the provision of the appropriate software modules for their management, and

To the implementation and policing action necessary to assure the rules are observed.

A key question in establishing such methodology is whether all information—text and data, graphics and images, edited voice (for input, transport, output), design specifications as well as the rules governing the methodology itself—can be normalized in a valid manner. Databases are not known to behave in that manner, but knowledgebanks do so.

Normalization and formalization are achieved through a layered architecture which works along the lines shown in Figure 11.1. The concept involves a physical layer and four logical layers each divided into two sublayers.

1. The upper logical layers are those of the knowledgebank.
2. The lower layers correspond to the distributed database which may hold diverse data structures and incompatible DBMS.

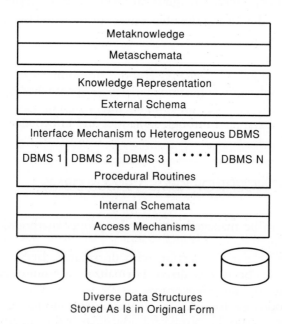

Figure 11.1   A layered structure from metaknowledge to database access.

In a way, assimilating the relationship among classes in an object-oriented sense, the metaschema can be seen as *generalization*. It observes the principle of inheritance and works in a way similar to that of the superclass and its subclasses.

In the general case, the structure of a knowledgebank includes domain information (facts, states, values), rules and heuristics, methodologies, a shell and other linguistic artifacts, as well as a beginning of learning ability. This is the general definition which, however, will be better focused in the present section to correspond to the implementation of a knowledgebank in a deductive distributed database mission.

Metaschemata, knowledge representation, and external schemata are handled by the knowledgebank management system. The contrast to the job to be performed to that provided by the DBMS became apparent before the KBMS came around as a formal discipline; one of the first manifestations of this approach has been *logic over data* (LOD) (see also Section 11-3).

Among the better known issues connected to LOD are *logical clustering* and *caching*. This approach is an elementary notion of a knowledgebank, primarily done for fast data switching; we will talk more about it in the next section.

A knowledgebank may handle the rules it stores through multiple cycling.
Interpretation would then require its own rules and inference engine to govern the flow of control.

Since knowledgebanks use the kind of knowledge that a human does, they bring to the tasks being executed all the benefits of intelligent action, not just of computer-based programmable processes. This requires a polyvalent approach and is a key reason why *cognitive psychology, complex database management*, and *machine intelligence* can be seen as different perspectives on the same aggregate of notions. The sort of contribution a knowledgebank can make is exemplified by considering the difference of *knowledge versus belief*. Knowledge is generated by:

- Instruction,
- Experience, and
- Discovery.

Knowledge is always accompanied by a true account of the grounds on which it rests, based on laws which at any given time are taken as *evident truths*. Therefore, it is unshakable by persuasion, which is not true of belief.

Quite often, data-type queries are subjective and their making is based on beliefs. In an object-oriented database, there is, for instance, an essential difference between attribute-defined subclasses and user control.

Membership of some types of classes can be directly and explicitly controlled by users.

Membership of other types of classes may be determined by information in the database.

In principle, it is possible to emulate the effect of a user-controllable class by an attribute-defined class. This is done through the introduction of a member attribute of the parent class whose sole purpose is to specify whether or not an entity is in the class. Class membership could then be *predicated* on the value of this attribute.

This is practically what the knowledgebank is doing by way of capturing the semantics of the application environment. Such approach exploits the fact that there are cases in which the method of determining membership is beyond the scope of the database schema—but can be defined by a knowledge-based predicate.

This example helps document that there is a synergy effect between knowledgebanks and databases, as well as a significant difference between them, which is also exemplified by distinguishing between:

- *Knowledge*-type queries, and
- *Data*-type queries.

By and large the database implies quantitative references, and when we access it we more or less know what we want. By contrast, when we are using a knowledge-assisted approach, we only have an *idea* of what we *might* want in qualitative and quantitative terms. Through the rules embedded in the knowledgebank, the online system uses its expertise to provide us with answers.

As these references help document, there are similarities and differences between knowledgebanks and databases—and therefore also between KBMS and DBMS. Both similarities and differences are of substance; they have to do with:

- Objectives,
- Contents, and
- Behavior.

The knowledgebank operates through the rules and heuristics which it contains. For instance, a financial knowledgebank includes rules linking received data to market performance hypotheses, combining pertinent factors to exploit information elements in the database and presenting a decision-oriented output.

By contrast, the global database includes pricing history, past volatility references, and the results of different diagnostics as well as of tests on current hypotheses. There may as well be limits and prices as they come from information providers.

The paths by which facts are related in a knowledgebank are determined ad hoc, as necessary to solve a particular problem. This is the sense of a *heuristic* search versus a *structured* approach—whether probabilistic or deterministic.

The heuristic search has an instantiated structure that may be hierarchical, but, as we said on other occasions, is ephemeral. This is precisely what an object orientation needs; the semantic instantiation as well as the supervision is provided by the knowledgebank.

11–3 CAPITALIZING ON LOGIC OVER DATA

The statement was made in Section 11-2, that logic over data was the first, primitive approach towards a knowledgebank. Most particularly, LOD focused on metadata, utilizing Pareto's law that 20 percent of something represents 80 percent of something else. For instance,

> 80 percent of all accesses to the database have to do with the 20 percent of the information elements stored in it.

There is another rule as well which defines the probability of the next record (or class of objects) to be called up given the record (or class of objects) currently handled. LOD moves that group of information elements of high recall probability to the cache, in what amounts to selection logic applied to data on storage. Only selected IE need be brought to the cache memory for further processing.

The selection representation chosen impacts on the speed of memory access and therefore the overall processing results, hence the interests on representations and mechanisms able to handle the marking of appropriate objects beforehand—in a feedforward way. This is an action of the knowledgebank, although at first sight it might not be recognized as such.

The implementation of Pareto's law and feedforward capabilities can be combined into a powerful mechanism with significant aftermaths. The clustering of objects around a network and within a physical disk can have a great impact on performance.

A single object can be contained in any number of different logical clusters.

Logical clusters provide a way of grouping transfers of objects independently of physical storage.

In a distributed application it is also useful to be able to control the physical location of objects in the database.

Rules and heuristics can help in this direction. They can assure as well that the working data set of an application is kept small enough so that it fits within real memory and does not get paged out to disk by the operating system. In other terms, it is essential to control the caching of IE between auxiliary and central memory.

Information elements have to be brought into memory around application usage *patterns*, but bringing in too many objects may degrade performance. Hence, caching control is provided through logical clustering of objects defining classes that can be moved between database and central memory:

- As a single unit, and
- Through a single operation.

For instance, the programmer defines a logical cluster around the runtime usage patterns of the application, grouping objects that exhibit locality of reference into a single logical cluster. The size and content of a logical cluster can be changed at runtime according to:

- Evolving usage patterns,
- Dynamically adjusted object volumes, and
- Specific hardware characteristics.

A logical cluster may contain objects of a single type or objects of several different types. Such clusters are independent of the physical locations of objects on physical databases so that in a distributed application a single logical cluster could contain objects that are distributed around the network.

11–4 SMART AND INTELLIGENT ENGINES

Wider relations in forward data management can be accommodated by using more complex rules, essentially moving from a *smart* to an *intelligent* engine, hence a knowledgebank. This transition is necessary in order to confront complexity in database management, and can be observed all the way from strategic to tactical issues.

The incorporation of logic over data mechanisms has led to the creation of the *database engine*, providing a facility to handle system functions automatically for the optimization of functions. The latter can, however, be network-wide database accesses but also areas such as recovery and concurrency control.

An example of early knowledgebank-type implementation is high-level data retrieval and manipulation rules able to shield the enduser from:

- Data formats,
- Access methods, and
- Storage management.

These have been largely linguistic constructs with appropriate primitives, reflecting the fact that since predefined physical access paths are not used, databases must be searched in breadth and in depth to satisfy a query.

Searching is slow on conventional computers, and that is why in the late 1970s with the first relational releases the user was allowed to specify optionally a prior access path. The specification of storage structures, access paths, and data structures was a characteristic of DBTG (Codasyl's Database Task Group) approaches (owner/member network). This solution was, however, characterized by inflexibility since:

> Access paths not predefined at database load time cannot be used through this approach, while the storage structures, generally constructed of pointers to linked lists, tended to be quite complex.

In other terms, as perceived at the time, the advantage of a relational solution was that it shielded the user from the complexity of storage structures, data structures, and access paths. But this advantage was largely lost with compromises within the database management perspective which tried to do too much in one setting. Hence the wisdom to distinguish between KBMS and DBMS.

According to this layered definition, the KBMS establishes the constraint mechanism that is shown in Figure 11.2. Other expert systems may as well be added for an overall control of networked databases and for presentation purposes at enduser side.

This approach is applicable both with object-oriented databases and with relational record-based models, provided that they abide by the rules and functions of managing database requirements in an intelligent manner. A basic criterion of any valid solution is that it must:

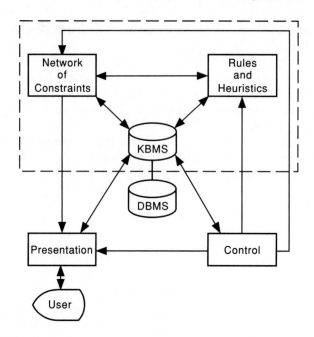

Figure 11.2   Component parts of a constraint mechanism.

- Be streamlined in its operations
- Be easy to understand
- Lend itself to real-life implementation

Supported operators should produce powerful relations as they manipulate the database elements. While this is done, supervisory rules must assure that the system itself never gets out of control, while demons specify the extent to which, say, a transaction is isolated from the effects of other transactions.

The Microelectronics and Computer Development Corporation (MCC) originally hoped to answer these requirements by developing a single database engine that could satisfy the needs of computing programs. As the project progressed, it became evident that two different types of database structures had to be developed:

1. The first type, accounting for a large share of the program's effort, is a *logic database.*

In this type, data is entered and retrieved through logic (Prolog-like) assertions, hence through a knowledgebank.

2. The second type is an *object-oriented database* which constitutes the underlying distributed layer.

This, too, makes use of symbolic processing to give the programmer maximum control. The goal is that of logic programming optimized for database operations.

One of the specific objectives of the logic database is to implement a new language that MCC experts developed: logic data language (LDL). This is an upgraded version of Prolog. The next objective is to combine the two database engines onto one integrated operation. The raw database problems have to be solved first, MCC suggested, because databases are "lower in the food chain."

Those elements that are lower in the food chain can be dumb or simply smart. The original intention of logic over data was to provide a smart approach. But as the population of these information elements vastly increases, and they take on polymorphism and multimedia characteristics, a new higher-up layer is necessary to manage them. This is the function of intelligent databases—hence of KBMS.

11–5 EXPLOITING DOMAIN AND METHOD

A *domain* is a set of values. In the general case, a class of operators does not need to be specified but when we defined *objects* we said that an object includes both information elements and operations; this is alike to a *microdomain* where operators are included. The domain may be:

- General purpose, or
- Specific to an issue or entity.

Rules associated with a domain look after an interactive assimilation of new knowledge. They may also manage the domain information or guide a process of *memory-based reasoning* in the context of episodic information.

Under certain circumstances it is useful to label a class as containing *concrete objects* or *events*, hence episodes. Such distinctions, however, are not directly supported by the typical DBMS, although those that are object-oriented do address the meaning and contents of the class. For instance, they can be used to:

- Describe the specific nature of the entities that constitute a class, and
- Indicate their significance and role in the application environment.

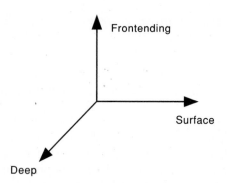

Figure 11.3   Types of orientation with knowledge-based systems.

Since the class has a collection of attributes that describe the members of that class, or the class as a whole, these attributes are often classified according to applicability. This brings under perspective the issue of the *method*, which can be:

- Model driven (top down) or
- Data driven (bottom up).

A method may also be classified as being deterministic (subject to noise) or stochastic (noise resistant).

Different methods may be chosen, depending on where and how we apply the concept of a knowledgebank. Typically, an expert system may be employed along any of the three axes of reference in Figure 11.3: Frontending existing applications to improve upon their man–machine interfaces, for deep modeling reasons, and for surface-type implementation in the exploitation of large distributed databases.[*]

The concepts of the domain and the method are interleaved in the context of an *idea database*, which may consist of object-oriented distributed databases of a deductive nature. This has been explained in Chapter 8.

An idea database takes its name from the search methodology that is employed: We are looking after distributed objects that fit a certain *concept* or *idea* of ours, and that may be crisp or fuzzy. Identification does not need to be a complex expression, but it does require intelligence.

Within a given domain and subject to a chosen method, an idea database can be served even by simple rules of the form:

---

[*]See also the discussion on knowledgebank organization in Section 11-6.

IF   a text mentions a conceptual unit anchored in <Argument>
THEN   start in-depth processing of that class
ELSE   skip otherwise irrelevant reference

But it may as well be that an idea database search calls for a method that is quite sophisticated, based on experience from previous similar projects and utilizing an extensive set of object selection criteria.

An idea database closely resembles man-made document and data searches. For instance, using the appropriate criteria, cognizant personnel goes through an extensive application domain evaluation and selection process, identifying diverse candidate objects as major possibilities and investigating them in great detail.

As briefly discussed in Section 11-2, looking at the knowledgebank in a structural sense, we can say that it generally consists of three main components:

1. Facts, states, values—facts being seen as superclasses, states as classes, values as their instantiation
2. Inference rules for determining new facts, states, values—and for execution reasons such as answering queries
3. A methodology to link together the inference rules, typically following a process of induction or deduction

The domain may be *loans*, the *facts* specifying that we are after loans, for instance, to private individuals. *States* are loans in specific classes: new housing, house repairs, appliances, automobiles, and so on. The *values* for each class are given, say, by a score system which permits us to evaluate loan risk. The latter is an inference application.

Within the so-defined domain, the loan scores will be stored in the database as episodes, but using an evaluation methodology the loans officer will look at them as a *pattern*. The search for the scores in the database calls for the use of a surface expert system, but their representation as a pattern needs deep knowledge.

The expert system with deep knowledge has its intelligence, hence its problem-solving structure, compiled into it. The domain model addresses itself to data search within the range of the problem that it handles. As such it contains no data and/or rules alien to the domain.

As this example helps demonstrate, the domain is characterized not only by facts, states, and values, but also through the use of expert knowledge, judgment, and experience which are mapped into the software. An object orientation provides significant assistance to the management of such complex, polyvalent aggregates whose instantiation and dynamic handling cannot be effectively approached through traditional methods.

The same example helps document the role played by knowledge engineering. Classical databases and conventional programming (algorithmic) approaches are not satisfactory. Knowledge-enriched solutions to domain and method offer significant advantages over conventional techniques, such as:

- The ease of updating and maintaining a distributed database
- The process of obtaining patterns out of the objects which it contains
- The ability to instantiate, compute and explain results.

In many cases, there are recognized experts who can solve a given problem, but if an area is too new or too quickly changing, there may be no real experts. Besides expertise is not and will not be available on a reliable and continuing basis over wide-ranging very dynamic situations, hence the need to capture and map such expertise, which is practically what we do by domain and method.

11–6 KNOWLEDGEBANK ORGANIZATION AND OPERATION IN A DISTRIBUTED ENVIRONMENT

We said that the difference between a knowledgebank and database can be explained as that between information contained in a program (the knowledgebank) and information accessible in a storage device (the database). The objects stored in the database have attributes.

There may be a degree of commonality among some of the attributes of these objects.

These commonalities should not be eliminated, to encourage consideration of the different aspects of domain selection.

The commonalities, however, should be controlled, and this is done through the knowledgebank.

Very few of the desired attributes are absolute, and it is unlikely that any domain will meet all of them completely. Furthermore, in each different situation the weighting of the factors will be different, and additional factors may apply.

The reasons just enumerated help document that we have to provide a fairly extensive list of aspects to be considered in domain selection; this too is done by the knowledgebank. We have to keep in mind as well that the solution domain and the problem domain both consist of the same entities, and while there is no need to map problem domain concepts into data structures, we should never lose sight of execution knowledge requirements.

A knowledgebank organization task is separate but indivisible from that of the database as a whole, in the sense that the former is done to help the latter. The many component parts of an *intelligent database* system are shown in Figure 11.4, ranging:

- From multimedia and hypermedia to a fully distributed environment,
- From semantic modeling to an object-oriented implementation,
- From deductive capabilities to user interfaces and analytical queries,
- From intentional databases (IDB) to extensional databases (EDB), and
- From knowledgebank management systems to database management systems.

Overall, the organization task dominates and it primarily requires symbolic reasoning. Most often, it also calls for the use of heuristics, particularly when there is need to consider a large number of possibilities and database searches based on incomplete or uncertain information.

Such problems are difficult to attack by conventional approaches, but may be amenable to expert system methodologies, provided the task is defined very clearly. However, it is neither necessary nor desirable that the task definition be fixed for all time. The knowledgebank evolves as the situation changes, therefore its rules must be dynamically adjusted.

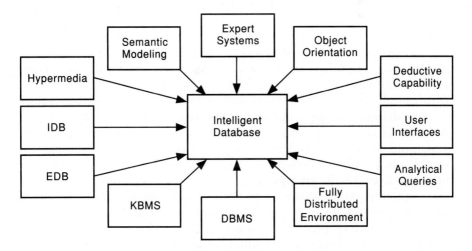

Figure 11.4   Component parts and functional description of an intelligent database system.

AM, the first expert system with self-learning characteristics, provides a good example of the role of a KBMS in *knowledgebank organization*. To organize the knowledgebank, AM uses elementary ideas in finite set theory. Heuristics is employed:

- For generating new mathematical concepts by combining elementary ideas, and
- For discarding "bad ideas," that is, ideas whose usefulness proved to be null or substandard.

The knowledgebank of R1 has been structured around the properties of some 400 Vax components which, in a way, can be considered as objects in the database. There are rules for determining when to move to the next subtask based on system state. There are also rules for carrying out partial configurations. A KBMS has been necessary for knowledgebank organization and administration.

The knowledgebank of EL employs rules that represent general electrical principles, make conjectures, and decide what to forget when contradictions occur. SYN, an MIT expert system which uses propagation ideas of EL, contains in its knowledgebank electrical laws. KAS takes a different approach. Its rules focus on:

- Inference networks for expressing *judgmental* knowledge,
- Semantic networks for mapping the *meaning* of the propositions employed in the rules, and
- Taxonomical networks for representing basic *knowledge* among the terms of the domain.

These three key references can be found among the pillars of object-oriented solutions, particularly those enriched with AI capabilities. There are knowledge mechanisms employed by all advanced type artifacts for representing and using objects, as well as for mapping consistency rules.

In all these examples, the taxonomical reference is important because it helps represent the instantiated hierarchical tree of search into databases, which can nicely be considered as object orientation. Taxonomy helps in sorting out problem domain concepts and is an element of fundamental importance in the design process.

Taxonomy is as well the key process in the instantiation of a hierarchical structure, the way object-oriented databases operate. Figure 11.5 exemplifies this reference by presenting a schematic decision tree for classification which can be used very successfully for searches in a distributed database context.

This taxonomical tree is ephemeral. A sunset clause deletes it once the searched-after categories have been identified, selected, and ported for further processing. While the term category is used to avoid confusion with an object class, the example is applicable in an object-based implementation sense.

The knowledgebank exploiting the object-oriented distributed database is a general-purpose thinking machine. Its rules may, for instance, say what the engine shall think in a specific situation instantiated through a query. Searches can be made:

- Breadth first
- Depth first
- Priority first

Breadth-first (or surface-first) approaches permit us to concentrate on data-based reasoning, considering in the process other paths of causality. A *depth*-first approach focuses on design steps and design operators.

A *priority*-first approach is usually depth-oriented, but centers on rules and information extracted from a plan and kept as a trigger for goal detection. This requires the facilities of an inference engine and brings issues related to knowledgebank management into perspective.

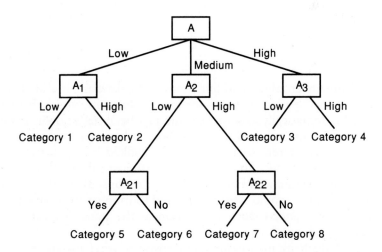

Figure 11.5   Schematic decision tree for classification.

$11-7$ DEMONS AND KNOWLEDGEBANK MANAGEMENT

It has been stated that a knowledgebank contains *facts* and *rules*. Facts have states and values. Rules are long-lived. Facts (or assertions) are medium-life information. Values are short-lived. They can change rapidly during the course of user interaction.

As longer-term information, rules direct an object-oriented and knowledge-based construct on processes which require an intelligence quotient. For instance,

- How to generate hypotheses from what is presently known
- Where to locate the objects necessary to respond to a query and its subqueries
- In which way to proceed in order to create new facts from incoming information elements

How does this approach differ from conventional database methodologies? The answer is that because of its *intentional* characteristics, a knowledgebank is creative, while the information elements in a database are normally passive.

Processes initiated by the knowledgebank require supervision. The most popular way of running as well as controlling a distributed information system is through *demons*. There are three possible types of demons:

1. If added
2. If needed
3. If removed

Demons are enabled by adding them to the database. If-added demons would typically be used to make forward deductions, which have to be performed automatically as soon as some fact becomes known. If-needed demons are also used to perform backward deductions.

By contrast, if-removed demons are invoked by the actuation of a built-in function *remove*. They are the opposite of the if-added but work in very much the same way. For maintaining the consistency of the database, if-removed demons would typically be used to mop up the explicit deductions made by if-added demons, as soon as the item that caused those deductions is removed.

Knowledgebank management also involves other aspects. As we have seen in the preceding section, the results of an able exploitation of object-oriented databases will quite often be a set of patterns. Patterns play a very important role in database exploitation and object solutions are no exception to this process.

Rules invoked by pattern-matching may have features of an environment that comes alive through *analogical reasoning*.

Patterns may be added to, modified, or deleted by the user—a person, a program, a terminal, a host, or an intelligent database.

A database of this special type benefits from the services of the knowledgebank.

The importance of analytical reasoning in the handling of complex object-oriented databases sees to it that when it comes to knowledgebank management we aim not only to improve the ways in which we get answers to problems, but also to improve or increase the system's knowledge. Subsequently, we harvest such knowledge for productive use. Harvesting is done through:

- Instantiations of classes in the global database, and
- Initiation of searches to locate and collect the appropriate objects.

Crucial to the successful execution of this process is the selection and implementation of a method of choosing which objects are applicable to the current problem. As an example, the diagram in Figure 11.5 should be seen in connection with that of Figure 11.3 which distinguished between surface (shallow) and deep-knowledge engines. The shallow processes, it was said, are an intelligent approach to the exploitation of large databases. Its goal is learned search in a globally distributed database environment using domain knowledge.

The deep-knowledge machine is an inference mechanism, and expert knowledge plays an important role in its development. Many current applications of diagnostic systems, for instance, are built using the rule-based approach. There may be, for example, a rule to include each possible fault in the system, organized so that one or more intermediate hypotheses are computed and then combined to provide a final analysis.

Surface approaches account for much of what a physician does, a process of matching the current case to the relevant indices in memory.

This is essentially a process of associating patterns of symptoms to diagnostic categories, and offers an example on how a standard rule-base is built.

A deep-knowledge approach is exemplified by entering a feature space mapping through the pattern matcher to produce an experience-based solution.

Not always appreciated is the fact that both methods use *similarity-based learning* and *classification*.

Organization-wise, surface knowledge systems are typical of database exploitation through pattern-decision pairs. They support a simple control structure to navigate through the object-oriented database.

Sometimes, surface-level similarities are all that we need in our database investigation. If the underlying causal relationships are very complex, incomplete, or unavailable, surface-level reasoning can be a very effective approach. Its shallowness is exactly what makes it possible to build an effective approach to database search.

By contrast, deep knowledge helps in solving problems of significantly greater complexity than surface, although this distinction is often imprecise. Some surface systems support the hypothesis of similarity-based induction whose goal is to make decisions by looking for patterns in data.

Deep knowledge may be obtained from specification documents of a manual type: "How to program," "How to write syntax." A heuristic form is difficult to describe in a manual.

In the financial business, for instance, success depends on the precise exploitation of the domain and needs deep knowledge—as in the case of buying and selling securities. A similar example can be taken from engineering design. Generally, deep knowledge is very difficult to develop.

Whether structural, causal, or functional, deep models can provide powerful central organizing mechanisms for diagnostic systems. However, not all tasks need to be expressed in terms of a deep model, and this may not be cost-efficient either.

One of the central problems of model-based solutions is that of efficiency.

Deep reasoning is slower because of a more sophisticated control structure.

In the general case, the use of the term *deep knowledge* to describe those systems that use representations more rigorous than heuristic rules (a shallow representation) reflects the new awareness that rules alone are often insufficient as a representation for expert knowledge.

Some practitioners employ the term *second-generation* expert systems to denote those that combine heuristic reasoning through rules with deep reasoning based on a causal model of the problem domain. The use of causal models:

- Avoids the need to construct large rule sets, and
- Makes explanation facilities much more effective.

When we talk of deep models, however, it would be unwise to place excessive reliance on any approach that did not have a strong theoretical underpinning. For this reason, it would be premature to suggest that at the current state of the art deep models are applicable with object-oriented databases, whereas surface-type models can definitely be used.

12

Toward Knowledgebank
Management Systems
(KBMS)

12–1 INTRODUCTION

During the 1990s, the integration of artificial intelligence and database management systems will quite likely play a significant role in shaping the policies followed with databases and databasing. Hybrid AI/DB solutions are crucial not only for next generation computing but also for the continued development of DBMS technology.

In a paper, "The Interpreted-Compiled Range of AI/DB Systems,"* Anthony B. O'Hare and Amit P. Sheth describe various approaches to AI/DB integration in terms of the degree of compilation that is performed by the artificial intelligence component. This component is a rule-based system permitting a user, terminal, or application to construct and manipulate a knowledgebank and to pose queries entailing firing of relevant rules.

In the context of such an integrative AI/DB approach, the term *compilation* refers to the translation of some of the relevant rules into DBMS queries or, alternatively, a Data Access Program (DAP) necessary for addressing the database.

With the *interpreted* approach, DAP is little more than a simple retrieval operation (relational algebra select-type) corresponding to a single database predicate.

*Published by Unisys Corp., New York, 1989; project financed by ARPA under contract N00039-88-C-0100.

This will make the approach just a little better than naive SQL. In the Unisys/ARPA research, the results of DAP are used by the AI component in further inferencing. This may involve the generation of additional DAPs before the processing of the AI query is complete.

With the *compiled* approach, DAP acts as a complete program for computing all solutions connected to the AI query.

As O'Hare and Sheth emphasize, compiling and interpreting are the two basic ways of handling query processing. These are, as well, the two basic alternatives with any programming scheme.

The particular aspect connected to database usage is that, with the compiled approach, access of the database is delayed until all the processing required for query evaluation is reduced by the deductive component to a set of accesses. The deductive component accesses the database as it encounters instances of relations in the process of responding to a given query.

In reality, however, the compiled approach is an end point on a range that extends from little or no compilation to full compilation. The fact that several options exist makes the design of a knowledgebank management system (KBMS) even more challenging.

12–2 BRIEF HISTORY OF KNOWLEDGEBANK MANAGEMENT SYSTEMS

The first knowledgebank management system on record was built in 1986 by ICOT, the Institute for New Generation Computer Technology in Tokyo. The concepts that went into its design are important inasmuch as they both characterize the functionality of a KBMS and define what exactly enters into the fine-tuning of an intentional database, which is elaborated in Chapter 13.

The best way to look into the functionality of a KBMS is to start with the internal schema such as is looked at and manipulated by a classical DBMS. Traditional database management systems store a relation as a file in which:

- A tuple is treated as a record, and
- An attribute is treated as a field.

Indexing and hashing techniques are applied to rapidly obtain tuples satisfying specific criteria. Such methods, however, are helpful when the user knows how to employ the relation in reference, which is not always the case.

Contrary to a classical DBMS which has to scan the entire relation if an indexed or hashed attribute cannot be used as an access path for a given query, a KBMS employs intelligent access characteristics. This conforms to the goal of a knowledge-enriched structure storing facts for inference machines.

Knowledgebank management systems do not address only information elements in databases, only processes, or only communications channels for message switching and other purposes. As Figure 12.1 suggests, they address all three at the same time, in regulating the prevailing dataflow in networked distributed computer resources.

It is precisely this plurality which presents opportunities with the implementation of the intentional and extensional database concept. In ICOT's case, to explore these opportunities a database server Delta was designed, adopting an attribute-wise schema as the way to efficiently process queries and other kinds of requests. Instead of storing all the attributes of a tuple together, a relation is split into a collection of attributes memorizing all occurrences of each attribute.

- A tuple identifier is attached to each attribute.
- A two-level indexing method is used for clustering.

The fact that most relations have only a few attributes was capitalized upon, though the attributes used as conditions are unpredictable. The ICOT researchers have established two merits of an attribute-wise schema:

- Attributes are treated uniformly, and
- Operations for attributes unnecessary for a given request are avoided.

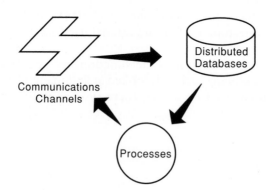

Figure 12.1   Regulating the prevailing dataflow in networked, distributed computer resources.

The method is good but not foolproof. A transformation is necessary between the tuple-type format and attribute format and this can become complex as the number of internal commands among the units tends to grow. Also, tuple identifiers occupy additional storage space, thus increasing overhead.

In the duality KBMS-DBMS which has been adopted, the lower layer is a Relational Database Engine (RDBE) projected as a specialized processor to perform operations on the distributed information elements. Whenever the RDBE acts, IE are transferred to it or from it. An alternative is to place the RDBE as logic over data between main memory and secondary storage—as we have seen in Chapter 11.

The LOD solution reduces transfer time and improves system throughput. However, this alternative was not chosen by the ICOT project because of difficulty in modifying the disk controller—which may not be a constraint in other cases.

The RDBE offers various kinds of commands using its hardware modules, specific sort and merge capabilities, and a general-purpose microprocessor. The sorter and merger is dedicated hardware designed to perform intertuple commands requiring comparison between records.

For ease of implementation, the comparison is limited between a contiguous field of one tuple and a contiguous field of another, typically an attribute or the entire tuple. Performed through this scheme are:

- Comparison between an attribute value of each tuple and a list of constant values, and
- Comparison between two attribute values of one and the same tuple.

By contrast, all other commands are executed through the microprocessor itself or a combinatorial way involving the comparison mechanism and the microprocessor. This decision was made according to the frequency expectation of the commands and their processing time. The functional flexibility of the RDBE was instrumental in the choice of the described solution.

Since that the operations performed by the sorter and merger are limited to intertuple comparison concerning one field (typically one attribute) for each relation, other activities must be performed by the microprocessor. These are:

- Selection under complex conditions
- Arithmetic operations
- Aggregate operations

To improve system performance, RDBE has a compiler which generates the native machine instructions into the main memory. Instructions generated by the merger are executed on the tuples and stored in main memory.

By virtue of the fact that the use of the microprocessor can overlap with sort-and-merge operations, a combined approach can be performed in one shot. This is important in queries, particularly those involving a join operation with a conjunctive condition.

12–3 RECONSIDERING THE RELATIONAL DBMS FUNCTIONALITY

Since Delta primarily addresses itself to the extensional database level, this solution is akin to conversion into hardware of a great deal of relational DBMS functionality. This makes the engine in reference *a true* database server, as contrasted to other approaches which essentially use a general-purpose computer (mainframe, maxi, or mini) for database management purposes.[*]

Although Delta adopts the attribute-wise internal schema, working records exist that have several attributes and RDBE must process them. The basic idea is that a join operation is performed efficiently by:

- Sorting tuples of each relation according to their values, and
- Comparing tuples from these relations in a manner resembling a two-way merge operation.

Such an approach is appealing since it can be applied not only to an equal join function, but also to nonequal join operations and other functions that involve two relations. This gives the extensional (relational) database engine the following advantages:

The combination of sort and merge improves performance, as is the case in pipeline processing.

The RDBE can process efficiently null values and duplicate values.

Projection operations can be performed during another operation.

The use of parity check and sorting check mechanisms improves reliability.

IE processing by the RDBE's microprocessor enhances overall functional flexibility.

---

[*]For other examples, see also D.N. Chorafas and H. Steinmann, *Supercomputers*, McGraw-Hill, New York, 1990, Chapter 14, "Dedicated Database Computers (Teradata 1012)."

Data transfer is performed in the handshake mode between the modules involved in one of the operations in reference. Each module is designed to achieve a processing rate as high as the transfer rate.

Built-in features assure greater reliability. A parity check mechanism and the sorting checker detect hardware errors with very little increase in processing time. When an error occurs, the microprocessor resets the modules and controls the adapters, retrying the data transfer.

During the power-up sequence, the microprocessor performs RDBE operations on test data. Test IE in main memory are provided to the IN module and the result is stored in main memory via the OUT adapter, while being checked by the microprocessor.

As a specialized database engine, Delta has solved many of the problems general-purpose computers face. But it has also demonstrated that even the conversion into hardware of database management system primitives leaves other issues wanting. Hence the two-layered IDB-EDB architecture which has been chosen by ICOT and which is discussed in Chapter 13.

Regarding the functions of a KBMS, the ICOT findings are that operations concerning knowledge should be added to system functions. This particularly concerns:

- Inference, and
- Pattern matching.

Such strategy is necessary in order to realize both an intelligent database management system and to open the possibility of knowledge manipulation. The ICOT research revealed the following six problems in connection with a conventional DBMS:

1. In a query system with a natural language interface, a traditional DBMS cannot make an incomplete query accurate enough because of lacking common sense and knowledge about the contents of the database.

2. The presently available commodity DBMS can process a query only when the database has the immediate answer.

3. In a conventional retrieval system using keywords as a search condition, the keywords must be originally registered by the users.

4. The more a database grows in size, the more important its integrity check becomes.

5. In a traditional database system, the user must choose a suitable file organization for each relation in order to achieve greater performance.

6. Parochial file organizations lead to heterogeneity and furthermore need considerable skill to develop a path.

Classical choices become inadequate in a growing range of situations and this, as we know, has a negative impact in overall database performance.

Due to its special design, Delta has significantly greater functionality than a conventional DBMS. It can handle knowledge of a tabular form, which in Prolog corresponds to facts with constants as arguments. It can also approach query processing as a breadth-first evaluation of an intentional goal.

These characteristics add considerable power to the performance of a distributed database. However, if the choice of an intelligence-enriched approach is the first key step, there really is nothing universal about the *right way* to choose a method. As in any design process, this is a skill which must be acquired through knowledge and experimentation.

12–4   OBJECT VERSUS RELATIONAL DBMS

There are many critics of relational DBMS and the relational approach at large. Henry G. Baker suggests that:

> Relational databases performed a task that did not need doing; e.g., these databases were orders of magnitude slower than the "flat files" they replaced, and they could not begin to handle the requirements of real-time transaction systems. In mathematical parlance, they made trivial problems obviously trivial, but did nothing to solve the really hard data processing problems.[*]

Making a comparison of relational versus object solutions, other relational critics suggest that: "The road is not flat, yet a relational approach obliges to look at and use flat files."[†] In Chapter 10, Table 10.1 provides a long list of advantages object-oriented approaches have over relational approaches.

By contrast, systems specialists inclined toward relational approaches suggest that one of the attractions of the relational model is its simplicity, which largely rests on an algorithmic basis. Manifestations of relational representations, as well as operations on them, have often reflected the underlying theory.

Other systems specialists who would rather keep with relational solutions cite as an advantage that relational ones provide referential integrity, which object approaches find it difficult to match. There is no easy answer to this issue, though research is going on.

But listening to this argument, critics of the relational approach would immediately point out that work carried on during the last 4 or 5 years

---

[*]ACM Forum, Communications of the ACM, April 1992, Vol. 35, No. 4.

[†]From a discussion during the Symposium on Parallel and Distributed Systems, Miami, FL, December 5/6, 1991.

documents that relational solutions are not compatible with the evolving information technology requirements, for example, such domains as:

- Concurrent engineering
- Long transactions, and
- Complex queries.

Relational approaches respond well only when transactions and queries are short and simple. Also, the information elements being handled must be rather simple, which is less and less the case. Relational models also lead to semantic type problems. Hence the need for object orientation in order to:

- Represent nonhomogeneous data,
- Map data characteristics more effectively, and
- Increase the efficiency of database operations.

Indeed, as database implementation work gets more sophisticated relational DBMS reach their limits. Another constraint is that many relational approaches assume that user access patterns are *static*, which is less and less true.

Furthermore, one of the major constraints with relational DBMS is that the user as well as the systems specialist has to think of all the contingencies before developing the application. In a complex environment, this invariably fails. But relational databases have a more sound mathematical basis, even if this comes at the expense of a restrictive, low-level abstraction, forcing the program around it, and a lack of semantic meaning.

Object databases are built upon the advances in data independence pioneered by the relational model. But unlike the relational model, and its structured query language (SQL), object databases integrate a semantically rich object programming language which enhances database capabilities:

- From conceptual modeling,
- Through implementation,
- All the way to maintenance.

Companies that have tried object solutions say that this approach assures an improved architecture, increased flexibility, and reusability of system components, as well as improved manageability of systems that can be readily evolved and enriched with knowledge engineering artifacts.

12–5 MANAGING A DISTRIBUTED ARTIFICIAL INTELLIGENCE ENVIRONMENT

Whether relational or object principles dominate, the making of a KBMS requires a great deal more in terms of technology than what the DBMS have implied so far. Useful examples can be found in past research, particularly projects which have exploited distributed artificial intelligence perspectives.

Research in the implementation of distributed artificial intelligence began in earnest at around 1980. Several early projects have been based on prototypes, such as the Hearsay speech construct, but subsequently new approaches have been proposed with database orientation and multiagent systems, for instance:

• Actors of Agha
• Air traffic control models of Steeb
• Agora of Bisiani
• Contract-Net of Davies and Smith
• DVMT of Durfee
• Mace of Gasser

In a way, several of these references can be seen as descendants of Hearsay, as most are based on its blackboard architecture which has been used to advantage in real-life implementations.

A blackboard is a message display and message passing paradigm whose function is explained in Figure 12.2. A blackboard architecture is essentially a communications environment which:

• Permits distinct modules to display and exchange messages, and
• Provides a cooperative solution between processes and information elements necessary for solving complex tasks.

The Hearsay-II blackboard organization stands as a model for all current implementations. However, there are times when it is not possible to generate a single abstraction hierarchy, the way the original blackboard architecture demanded. This was the case with two systems: OPM by Hayes-Roth and Crysalis by Terry (1983).

OPM is nearer to a database type implementation because it was designed to model the behavior of human subjects planning a sequence of errands in a hypothetical town. The subjects were given:

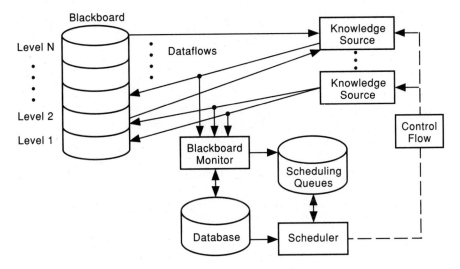

Figure 12.2   Dataflows and control flow in a blackboard architecture.

- A list of errands to run, and
- A time within which they should complete them.

The time allocated was insufficient for all errands to be run. An opportunistic method was established for planning: Subjects would select errands on the basis of the physical proximity and not necessarily in a top-down fashion.

As a result, additional structural divisions of the blackboard were introduced into OPM, called planes or panels. These are workspaces that help to solve problems in different subject domains or which concern different topics. OPM contained five planes:

1. Plan
2. Plan–abstraction
3. Knowledgebase
4. Executive
5. Metaplan

Embedded in each plane were entries which dealt with qualitatively different kinds of knowledge, while the executive plane was charged with controlling the overall system functioning, rather than only planning, and the metalevel focused on problem-solving strategies.

This is indeed an approach applicable to distributed databases which need general-purpose knowledge-enriched facilities to retrieve and update information elements in servers. Even if supported through AI, an intelli-

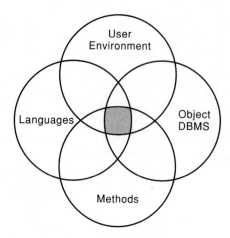

Figure 12.3   The four domains Hewlett-Packard sees as pillars of object orientation.

gent database does not automatically produce global solutions from computation but provides schemata that help in data retrieval and manipulation.

The contribution a blackboard model can provide in a distributed database environment is exemplified by the fact that the better projects in this domain adopt a strategy which includes:

- An environment model,
- Participation schemata, and
- Communications facilities.

The environment model specifies metainformation and command types as well as their capabilities. Metainformation is used to carry out the first level decomposition of database tasks, which are then assigned to agent classes.

The environment model is important inasmuch as it permits us to take the proverbial long hard look at all players entering into the distributed landscape. As shown in Figure 12.3, Hewlett-Packard, the American computer vendor with most experience in object orientation, sees four domains entering into this perspective.[*]

A participation model is largely an instantiation of the environment model. It specifies information on individual acquaintances and necessarily involves the schemata proper to the local databases. Such information helps the preliminary allocation of subtasks.

---

[*]See also D.N. Chorafas and H. Steinmann, *Object-Oriented Databases*, Prentice-Hall, Englewood Cliffs, NJ, 1993.

However, information held in instantiated environment and participation models could be partial and could become out-of-date. Hence the need for a facility to help update these models dynamically by providing flexible communications mechanisms. This is the role of the blackboard.

Still one of the major challenges in a distributed environment is that of overcoming impedance due to incompatible information elements and rule conflicts. Data incompatibility in distributed databases has been studied to a reasonable extent but rule conflicts have not. With a blackboard approach, one agent can pass to another the knowledge regarding:

- Facts, and
- Rules.

Hence we need to assure the compatibilities of both facts and rules, as well as to check rule conflicts. This is one of the main tasks knowledgebank management systems are required to perform. Several projects have pointed in this direction, but there are also other crucial issues to account for as we will see in the next sections.

12-6 USING FUZZY ASSOCIATIVE MEMORY: A PRACTICAL EXAMPLE

The Laboratory for International Fuzzy Engineering (LIFE) of Yokohama, Japan, has developed an associative memory approach called Fuzzy Associative Memory Organizing Units System (FAMOUS), and has shown its usefulness with applications to control systems. This implementation is close to the concept of a knowledgebank management system. As it should be appreciated, there exists no unique way to approach KBMS design challenges.

Fuzzy IF-THEN rules as well as fuzzy inference[*] have been used in connection to FAMOUS. Also developed is a Learning Vector Quantization (LVQ) to automatically create membership functions of these fuzzy rules.

FAMOUS with LVQ has been applied to two different examples to show its service in computer simulation.

LVQ is useful for mapping input vectors to fuzzy concepts shown in IF-part of fuzzy rules.

Two fuzzy control applications have been performed: One is an adaptive control system for a parameter variance process, the other a robot

---

[*]See also the introductory discussion to fuzzy engineering in Chapter 3.

interface. Among them, they have three features that resemble KBMS functionality:

1. Membership functions created by LVQ in IF-part of fuzzy rules
2. Fuzzy inference by means of the associative memory system
3. Fuzzy knowledge representation using fuzzy rules as well as relationships interpreted from fuzzy rules.

All three features are just as important in the management of large databases involving vagueness and uncertainty. In the practical applications to which this system was put, they underly decisions that are typically made under fuzzy conditions.

While these two implementation examples address themselves to industrial applications, the meeting held with LIFE in Yokohama also pointed out that the approach is just as valid in a broader, intelligent database landscape. In the financial world, for example, risk management and cost control are two areas requiring access to large, distributed heterogeneous databases where FAMOUS can be of service.

Whether it is a financial, transportation, or manufacturing environment, the theory of fuzzy control can be effectively used in conjunction with many real-life systems. Its impact is assured by fuzzy IF-THEN rules, set by means of membership functions.

In the implementations done by LIFE, LQV is employed to create membership functions of fuzzy rules and fuzzy data. LVQ output is inference input, and the fuzziness of the function may increase or decrease. Correspondingly, FAMOUS is useful for controlling fuzziness by means of association and has three features:

1. Fuzzy knowledge representing causal relationships
2. Hierarchical knowledge realized by means of associative memories
3. Fuzzy inference implemented by means of association

As shown in Figure 12.4, LIFE has used FAMOUS to realize approximate reasoning through fuzzy rules. The fuzzy processing consists of three elements: IF-part, IF-THEN-rule-component, and THEN-part. The fuzzy rules represent expert knowledge describing the relationships between the reference models and output functions.

One of the practical applications of FAMOUS has been in connection with a sewage pump station whose plant is characterized by a strong system of nonlinear behavior. In most of these plants, rainfall is measured at the pump stations. Therefore, to operate them, experts presently predict the inflow of rainwater based on:

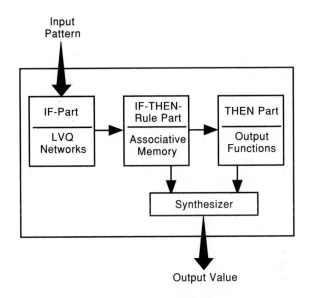

Figure 12.4   Applying fuzzy rules with an associative memory system (famous).

- Their past experience reflected through statistics, and
- Observations such as the state of rainfall, water level, and its change.

LIFE has demonstrated that some interesting similarities exist between this guesswork and information retrieval in databases. In either case, the experts' knowledge is represented with a fuzzy cognitive model; such a model would make inferences on how the future situation would change if the present conditions continue.

In the pump example, the input data are normalized values, and the data intervals involve a single step. Through the use of FAMOUS, the rate of change and the degree of change of the water level were successfully predicted. The same is true about the change of pump discharge and the status accompanying it. The forward and backward relationships of events—that is, cause and effect—were accurately expressed.

The input pattern was fed into a LVQ network for evaluation. By means of unsupervised learning, LVQ can classify the input space, which consists of input patterns. Functionality is supported by means of three-layered neural networks.

In the LVQ structure, the first neural net layer handles the input; the second layer receives an input vector from the first and creates membership functions of fuzzy rules by unsupervised learning. The third evaluates the truth value of each rule.

Each neuron of the second layer has an activation function that is inversely proportional to the distance between the synapse weight vector and the input vector.

Membership functions are trained by the LVQ, through a fast algorithm which realizes a continuous mapping according to the distance between two vectors.

Using bi-directional associative memories, the LIFE researchers connected the mapped reference models to output functions of fuzzy rules. According to LIFE, this approach has been instrumental in integrating the advantages of fuzzy logic and neural networks techniques, achieving an intelligent fuzzy control which is self-organizing as well as capable of inference and learning.

12–7 NATURAL LANGUAGE AND FUZZY COGNITIVE MODELS

Natural language (NL) has been an early target of database management systems in appreciation of the fact that it is difficult to interact with most conventional computers. Hence vendors have developed a number of natural language frontends designed to ease the interaction burden between the user and the information management system.

Among the alternatives available today are dedicated as well as universal natural language artifacts that can be coupled with a variety of DBMS. However, these efforts have not given truly NL results. By nature, the natural language challenge is more complex than that of other artifacts. Good solutions:

Must understand the components of language, and

Represent the knowledge necessary for meaningful interaction with a user.

Language arose and persisted because it serves as "efficient means of communication, especially for abstract concepts," say Antonio and Hanna Damasio[*] "It helps to categorize the world and to reduce the complexity of conceptual structures to a manageable scale."

Lexical knowledge concerns individual words, the parts of speech they belong to, and their meanings. *Syntactic* knowledge has to do with the grouping of words into meaningful phrases, distinguishing between similar sentences. From the little we know, in the human brain:

---

[*]"Brain and Language," *Scientific American*, September 1992.

A large set of neural structures serves to represent concepts.
A smaller set forms words and sentences.

The contribution of semantic knowledge is both to integrate and to distinguish meaning. Ever since the Tower of Babel, our use of language has given rise to diversity of expression rather than conformity, leading to the regular creation of new languages and new dialects—as well as different meaning within these dialects.

Diversity in meaning leads quite frequently to misunderstanding and resolution requires powerful *paradigms*, that is, examples full of meaning of the type object-oriented approaches aim to support. Apart from *semantics*, an important issue with object orientation in general, and most particularly KBMS and languages based on objects, is the concept of *class structure*.

Just as helpful in a linguistic sense is the concept of inheritance between classes. The idea of multiple inheritance and polymorphism also develops as our use of language becomes more sophisticated. Polymorphism occurs in our use of metaphors, implying different classes that superficially seem in no way related.

This brings machine language issues nearer to human language, although object languages and natural languages are by no means the same. Several issues exist that can complicate a natural language system development process, including ambiguity due to incompatible database structures, as well as domain-independent and domain-specific natural language processing.

A *domain-independent* approach has very little or no knowledge about a particular subject matter, while a *domain-specific* approach has a lot, but is more restrictive in terms of utilization. But there are tools that help to overcome the constraint connected to domain-independent solutions.

As we have seen in Section 12-6, such tools can be provided through fuzzy engineering and neural networks. Topics having a relation to this and similar projects include high-speed learning, knowledge self-refinement, deductive inference, modeling using fuzzy causal relationships, and sophisticated fuzzy neural networks media.

This is written in full understanding that one of the most important and feasible areas of the application of natural language processing is accessing information elements in distributed heterogeneous databases. Billions of dollars have been spent in collecting, encoding, entering, and reentering data into computers. Yet, today information is generally not readily available to the people who need it, while approaches enriched with fuzzy sets and object orientation could help in solving this problem.

That is why it has been so important to learn and appreciate the basic features of fuzzy information processing structures such as FAMOUS, its theory of learning, knowledge representation, and high-speed inference with association—by using parallel processing.

A great deal of research still remains to be done. One of the important issues is the evolution of a parallel fuzzy information processing architecture. Another is modeling theory; a third, image processing; a fourth, pattern recognition.

13

Intentional and Extensional Databases

13–1 INTRODUCTION

Intelligent database solutions represent the convergence of research in knowledge engineering and database management. They endow object-oriented database systems with planning and reasoning capabilities. They also make it possible to set effective specifications, to do prototyping, to perform tests, and to debug complex database applications.

Chapters 11 and 12 outlined the basic functionality necessary for supporting distributed object-oriented database server facilities. The message has been that we need intelligence-enriched database management tools and a development environment based on the semantic model. The keyword in the databases of the 1990s is *meaning*.

As we will see in Section 13-2, the contribution of knowledge engineering, which in this chapter we define by means of the intelligent database, focuses on the *schemata* level and involves *metadata* and *constraints*. The more intelligence we bring into the software commanding this level, the better the performance we can obtain in a system-wide sense.

The able implementation of database management within global object-based environments, starts with the early recognition of the importance of conceptual schemata separating the meaning-based specification of a database from its physical implementation detail, and providing a complete generic set of manipulative operations. The importance of semantics, as well as the specific notions of objects and abstractions cannot be stressed too often.

The modeling of behavior and the meaning of derived data are the business of the intentional layer. These must be integrated into conceptual database models, accommodating multiple points of view on data semantics. This is known as semantic relativism.

- The deductive rules,[*] will be embedded in the *intentional database* (IDB) while
- The *extensional database* (EDB) will handle the bare facts, or more precisely, their values.

This two-layered structure requires very good organization because, without it, it will not function properly. Given the proper organizational perspectives, we will never lose sight of the fact that the object-oriented database models and systems that we are examining all in contrast to the record-oriented approaches.

13–2 INTENTIONAL SERVICES THROUGH KNOWLEDGE MANAGEMENT

Seen under an implementation perspective, the object-based design becomes a natural approach. Objects and classes are both the subjects and the tools of operational modeling.

As discussed in the Introduction, the contribution of knowledge engineering in the context of an intelligent database, focuses on two schemata:

1. The external schema is *metadata*, as seen by the enduser.
2. The internal schema is a list of *constraints* impacting database behavior.

The tools designed around the concept of the external schema must support the enduser's conceptual functions, as well as efficient interfaces and natural language question/answer facilities. Conceptual functions are ill-served through the semantically limited "Select...From...Where" query languages.

In order to contribute to the evolution of large object-oriented databases, the linguistic interfaces at the database management level must go beyond indexing-type manipulation. This calls for integrating AI and DBMS functionality into new and more powerful software and hardware environments.

The significant finding of the ICOT research that we have discussed in Chapter 12 is that even a highly improved relational DBMS functionality

---

[*]See also Chapter 8 on Distributed Deductive Databases.

does not respond to the requirements posed by a distributed database structure. Hence we must conclude that a solution should be found that is capable of handling more generalized knowledge than Delta. This is the function of the Knowledgebank Management System (KBMS).

The Japanese researchers' experience with Delta led them to the following fundamental ideas on this issue.

1. *Conventional Databases Can only Process Knowledge as Data*—In other words, it is impossible for the database to recognize the contents of knowledge or to execute specific operations regarding knowledge, such as matching and inference. However, these operations are vital to an object-oriented distributed database system.

2. *The Knowledge Needed to Handle a Distributed Database Is Represented as Facts and Rules*—It is well known that many facts can exist with the same predicate name. It was also found that the number of rules with the same predicate name is almost always fewer than 10. Nevertheless, the Delta architecture, which was designed to handle facts only, proved insufficient to address this issue, which requires a specialized processor able to perform a breadth-first evaluation.

3. *A KBMS Should Treat Several Kinds of Knowledge Representations*—ICOT information scientists put semantic nets, frames, objects, relations and Horn clauses (for Prolog-like programs) in this category. The KBMS should treat knowledge representations directly for efficiency and ease of understanding.

It has also been established that specialized mechanisms will be required for each knowledge representation and for the necessary conversion to take place among them. In this sense, Delta-like engines should be regarded as a special component for tabular knowledge (relational representation).

4. *Unless Efficient Linguistic Solutions Are Found, a KBMS Would Take up a Considerable Portion of the Main Memory*—While the development of semiconductor technology has helped in reducing the cost of memory, the bottleneck between the processor and the memory remains. Accordingly, ICOT led its research toward an intelligent memory system that stores knowledge and is able to manipulate it. This constitutes the intentional database layer, with Delta running the (lower) extensional database level.

Table 13.1 gives a snapshot of what a knowledgebank and a database contain within the perspective of this discussion. Figure 13.1 outlines the system architecture of this setting.

The workstation, which is at the upper part of the local area network (LAN), acts as an inference engine.

Table 13.1   Contents of a Knowledgebank and of a Database

Intentional Layer, Knowledgebank Management	Extensional Layer, Relational Database
1. Facts and states	Information elements—hence values—subject to:
2. Relations between objects	1. Input
3. Decision rules and heuristics	2. Update
4. Methodology	3. Retrieval
5. Consistency control	preferably expressed in an object-oriented form.
6. Propagation actions	
7. Dynamic extensibility	

This type of solution has several advantages, one of them being that it can be used effectively with hybrid-type AI/DP applications.

The upper layer of the intentional database (IDB 1) resides in the workstation.

The lower layer of IDB (IDB 2) is in the distributed database servers.

The extensional database is run by a DBMS. Existing DBMS are *passive*. They respond only when invoked by a user (person, program, or another machine). Therefore, they cannot provide effective access to diverse object types. The result is that without the services provided by a KBMS:

Applications suffer unacceptable retrieval errors and delays, particularly in a distributed database context.

Information is not always compiled, as it should be, from a variety of sources to meet inference requirements.

An object orientation is not promoted efficiently for reasons we have seen in preceding chapters.

Processing primarily regards only limited kinds of knowledge; however, we need capable supports for object types, relationships, and constraints.

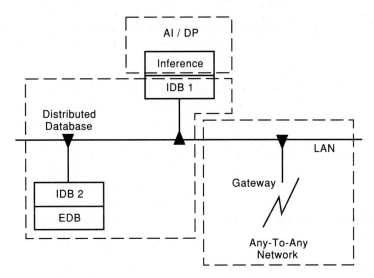

Figure 13.1   System architecture with intensional and extensional databases.

Without the assistance of a KBMS, a network's overall object-oriented operation becomes deficient in a number of areas; for example, identification of sources of knowledge necessary for understanding or generating complex operations. The latter requires discovering or devising mechanisms for applying such knowledge in a fully automated way.

A similar statement can be made regarding the creation of an integrative framework to control and coordinate object-oriented applications. Once sources of knowledge have been identified, whole subdisciplines come into being, permitting us to study the database objects themselves, their meaning, attributes, structure, and methods.

To do this ably, the knowledgebank management system must provide a great deal of functionality, which can be described at five levels of reference, top to bottom.

1. User queries and user program(s); the highest level

2. Knowledgebank management proper at the workstation level (IDB 1)

3. Communications interface through an object-oriented language or horn clause(s)

4. Knowledgebank management program (IDB 2) at the database server level—a breadth-first evaluator

5. A relational DBMS able to exploit the objects stored at the extensional database

Levels 1 and 2 are in the inference machine. IDB 1 includes a subset of the global data dictionary and may also require lexical knowledge and/or clauses on how to handle compound electronic documents. The latter will reside in the EDB.

No doubt, this requires a sophisticated approach. ICOT's *Kaiser* is a distributed KBMS, resting on myriad workstations (IDB 1 level) and the many database servers attached to the network (IDB 2 level). The aggregation of these parts constitutes what is known as the *distributed deductive database,* which we mentioned in Chapter 8.

To recapitulate, the contribution of KBMS is particularly important because the relational model has semantic limitations. KBMSs provide a solution to semantic modeling; they give meaning to database management; and through metadata, they interpret the user's meaning to the DBMS.

13—3 INTENTIONS, EXTENSIONS, AND CONSTRAINTS

A *logic database* defines the meaning of objects and semantic relationships between objects. The rules in the knowledgebank perform object-level operations, such as generating a new object of *atomic* flavor in the database. For instance, *object-id* is a user-defined identifier for a new object, and *object-key* its system-generated identifier.

These rules take upon themselves the function of removing a given object from the database, creating a relationship among objects, as well as its inverse relationship, or removing a specified relationship from the repertory. In contrast, set-level operations define a specified, closed atomic set object by enumerating its members (if any), or adding members to a given class.

This may seem similar to some of the work being performed by an object-oriented DBMS. This should hardly be suprising because the KBMS has been developed largely through a DBMS evolution toward the handling of semantic models enriched by knowledge engineering.

Figure 13.2 is a graphic presentation of the transition from DBMS to KBMS. The following should, however, be noted.

Not all the KBMS functions we are discussing are being handled through an object-oriented DBMS.

The most widely used DBMS today, and the best established ones, are not object oriented.

There is significant merit in adopting the two-layered architecture of KBMS-DBMS, even if an object-oriented DBMS was doing most of what is required in a knowledge-engineering sense.

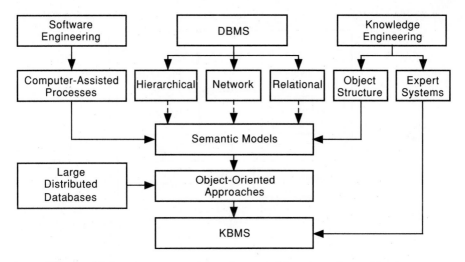

Figure 13.2   Transition and integration of functions: from DBMS to KBMS.

One example wherein the functions of KBMS and object-oriented DBMS meet is the so-called object-flavor operations, which can be achieved through rules invoking methods associated with types. An evolutionary type of retrieval addresses itself to relationships satisfying input parameters that can match all objects in the database, in terms of domain, mapping, and range.

Encoded knowledge is necessary for such high-level object manipulation as Create-type. This generates a new type of object with all attributes inherited from the specified class. Delete-type and Add-attribute are other examples. Such knowledge is expressed by:

- Rules (intentions),
- Facts (extensions), and
- Constraints.

Constraints are extended before and after the action taken in the database, and they are a vital part of any KBMS.

Figure 13.3 further explains this concept of intentions, extensions, and constraints by presenting a block diagram of the main components of a KBMS according to the ICOT version. As it will be appreciated, these are distinct from those we have known for years in connection with a DBMS.

A reference to the transition that has taken place in databases and their management, including that from DBMS to KBMS, helps explain the

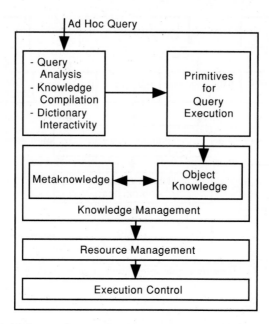

Figure 13.3   Vital parts of a knowledgebank management system.

distinction between extensional and intentional concepts from a different viewpoint. It also serves to identify more clearly the transition taking place in information science. Such a comparison is presented in Table 13.2.

At the bottomline, the aim of *logic databases*, and therefore of knowledgebanks, is the efficient handling of:

1. *Intentional Rules*—These are necessary not only in the class–object frame of reference but also to ensure global database access and in order to establish a more intelligent resource administration.

Such a mission cannot be fulfilled simply through relational database management structures, which have a different goal to achieve. However, as we have already seen, intentional constructs are linked to relational databases through:

2. *Extensional Features Handling the Objects Themselves, and Their Instantiation*—Hence, knowledgebanks and databases do not conflict with one another, overlapping or canceling each other's functionality. Rather, they are complementary.

The extensional database has only an instance of the objects in the global structure and acts at a lower level than the intentional database. The

Table 13.2   Extensional Versus Intentional Concepts and Transition
in Information Science

From	To
1. Relational database	1. Knowledgebank
2. Data	2. Multimedia
3. Query search	3. Query analysis
4. Response compilation	4. Knowledge compilation
5. Presentation of results	5. Explanation of results
6. Record handling	6. Object handling
7. Procedural generator	7. Rule and heuristic generator
8. Database management	8. Knowledge management
9. Descriptive language	9. Natural language

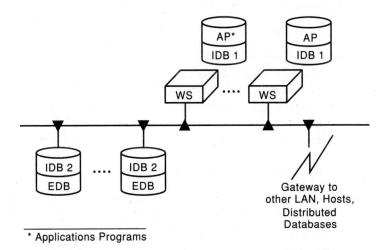

* Applications Programs

Figure 13.4   A networked approach with IDB and EDB.

EDB cannot rule on IDB; however, the inverse is true because the IDB includes *conceptual* facts (rules).

Logic engines must use both IDB and EDB. Logic programming should include *intentional* and *extensional* knowledge (Prolog does so). This context can be extended in a networking sense, as is shown in Figure 13.4.

Within this distributed object-oriented environment, member attributes will describe aspects of each member of a class by logically connecting the member to one or more related entities in the same or another class. A class attribute helps to define a property of a class taken as a whole.

A *base class* is defined independently of all other classes in the database, and it can be thought of as modeling a primitive entity in the application environment.

Base classes are mutually disjointed in that every entity is a member of exactly one base class, although at some level of abstraction, all entities are members of a superclass.

The KBMS should promote interclass connections because each nonbase class has associated with it one interclass connection. This must be reflected in the schema definition.

If the class is a base class, it has an associated list of groups of member attributes, and these too must be managed. Each of these groups serves as a logical key to uniquely identify the members of a class. Typically, there is a one-to-one correspondence between the values of each identifying attribute or attribute group and the entities in a class.

Another crucial DBMS function, which forms part of the constraints, is that of equilibration. A base class is specified as either containing duplicates or not containing duplicates. Stating that duplicates are not allowed, amounts to requiring the members of the class to have some difference in their attribute values, with all of the member attributes of a class taken together constituting a unique identifier.

13—4 SUPPORTING A HOMOGENEOUS SCHEMA THROUGH IDB AND EDB

A user-visible *homogeneous schema* is the database intention. Relevant *individual values* constitute the database extension. IDB takes care of the external schema by concentrating on how users view and process information. This is done at the knowledge-intense level (IDB 1). At the level that is nearer to database implementation (IDB 2), emphasis is placed on internal schema handling, but in an AI-enriched manner.

Exemplified through the work done in Japan by ICOT on new generation computer technology, this concept of *intentional databases* merges the best of our experience in relational solutions with that of knowledgebanks. Intentions are rules; hence, the intentional database is a surface expert system associated with defined applications domains, but focusing on object-oriented database management.

As shown through the layered structure of Figure 13.5, applications and IDB 1 together form the inference engine. The ICOT product for IDB 1 management is a KBMS known as Kappa (Knowledge APPlication-oriented Advanced database and knowledgebase management system). A crucial part of the work added in an object-oriented environment is the instantiation of an *inheritance hierarchy*. (This particular reference does not necessarily mean that KAPPA *is* an object-oriented DBMS; rather, it tells what an object-oriented DBMS should do.)

> This will be a real hierarchy only when single inheritance is allowed. If multiple inheritance is supported, the structure becomes much more complex.

Schema homogeneity should, however, be upheld at all times. This fits well object-type functionality where every subclass inherits, by default, the attributes and methods of its parent class.

Using the intentional clauses of the KBMS, a subclass may add and delete attributes, as well as add or override messages and methods within its own definition. Inheritance increases the modularity of the system, and also helps to simplify associated development and maintenance.

It can be appreciated that in this specific implementation, the midlayer consists of guarded horn clauses (GHC) as an interface. A Prolog development, GHC provides the linguistic primitives interconnection to the database engine Delta of which we spoke in Chapter 12.

Such an approach makes it possible to connect processes running on an inference machine through many-to-many relationships. As stated, IDB 2 is an intentional database running the extensional database. In the case of ICOT, its knowledgebank management system is known as *Kaiser*.

The methodology outlined above makes it feasible to construct layered conceptual models in order to simplify, idealize, conceive of, and understand

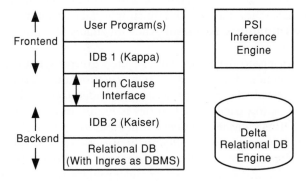

Figure 13.5   A layered solution including IDB 1, IDB 2, and EDB.

complex database situations. It also permits us to gain insight and to exercise foresight before taking action.

Developing knowledgebanks on top of databases ensures that new experiences are integrated with know-how that has been acquired over the last couple of decades. New experiences must not be alien to the store of knowledge already available. Rather, they should expand it, enhance it, and manage it.

Metaknowledge and *object knowledge* ensure knowledge management. This is what IDB 2 is doing as the knowledge management layer of the database server, through control predicates. The relational database system in the EDB integrates with the logical programming language, but at the IDB level, knowledge and IE are treated in the same manner.

There are no unique rules to follow along the line of our discussion, but it is valuable to know what has been achieved so far in avant-garde projects. As the ICOT experience documents, a knowledgebank should encompass the following.

They should be built on top of a database in a fully layered but functional manner.

Relationships between information elements should be encoded and mapped into the predicates.

High-level mechanisms must be provided for inferences and consistency checks.

Knowledge engineering should be used for queries, diagnostics, and help facilities.

This will create the infrastructure of an agile, user-friendly, and self-contained environment that can deal effectively with *semantic expressiveness*.

The semantic expressiveness of the hierarchical and network models is limited; that of relational models is even more so. None provides mechanisms sufficient to allow a database schema to describe the meaning of a database because they employ overly simple data structures to model an application environment. As a result, they inevitably lose information about the database.

Object-oriented databases have a much greater semantic expressiveness by consequence of the fact that their structures are not record oriented. As we have stressed, the appropriateness and adequacy of the record construct for expressing database semantics is highly limited, and permanent hierarchical DBMS models are very inflexible.

However, to be exploited effectively object-oriented approaches must have formal fundations as well as a systematic methodology for handling abstraction and conceptualization of the problem space. This is what is provided by the knowledge-based intentional database solution.

It is also essential that the database model to be developed and maintained ensures class expressions and a rich set of features. These are necessary to allow the direct modeling of the application environment's semantics. They should support the view and meaning of a database, permitting alternative ways of looking at the same information.

13–5 INTENTIONAL DATABASES AND QUERY OPTIMIZERS

Query optimizers use proprietary strategies to enhance the overall response capabilities and to better the *response time*. This is done through semantic modeling as the query optimizer attempts to:

- Reduce the number of input/output or disk page accesses, and
- Cut down the computational overhead for executing the query.

Through knowledgebank implementation, query optimization is completely hidden from the endusers. This is one of the characteristics of intelligent databases.

Chapter 12 treated the issue of queries in the sense of a distributed deductive database. Having spoken of KBMS, we must now approach this subject from the viewpoint of conceptual modeling supported by means of primitives of the knowledgebank management system.

To begin with, in order to construct a conceptual model for knowledgebanks and databases, we must handle knowledge types; for example, the rules and regulations of an organization whose activities are mapped into its databases.

We must also stress that the primary requirement for databases and knowledgebanks is not a computer, but the rules defining the organizational structure about which we process large volumes of data, text, images, graphics, voice, and knowledge. Then comes the representation procedures.

In order to accommodate multiple views of the same multimedia information elements and to enable the evolution of new perspectives in query handling, a database model must support schemata that are:

- Flexible, but with meaning (semantics),
- Potentially logically redundant, and
- System-wise integrated.

Flexibility is essential to allow for multiple, nearly equal, or unequal views of objects. In a logically redundant database schema, the values of some components can be algorithmically or heuristically derived from others. Incorporating such derived information into a schema can simplify the user's manipulation of the database.

The use of derived IE eases the development of new applications because information elements required by these applications can often be readily adjoined to the schema. Experimentation can help in this direction by simulating events and messages expected in a variety of operations.

For instance, a simulator assists in experimenting on whether the system returns the kind of responses defined in the logic model. It also provides a means to test the functionality and sufficiency of the model prior to actual implementation. These responses are generated from the:

- Function, event, and action descriptions in the logic model;
- Configuration definitions giving the type of query or application program;
- The type of communication system in operation; and
- The type of distributed database organization available, or the one we want to project.

The logic model of an *idea database* (idea processor) is free form. Free form means that information is viewed in a semiorganized manner rather than being regimented through the structure known from record managers. Object-to-object links can be enhanced substantially if metadata concepts characterize this implementation.

Idea databases have much to do with messaging and communications. Among the weaknesses of current approaches in terms of query handling, including the better known query languages, are:

- A rather rigid database addressing
- The manipulation of primarily passive IE, and
- Noninterpretation of presentation contents.

Query optimization should be object oriented because such approaches are particularly tuned to handle new requirements also providing greater adaptability in building more complex response structures. The response often involves actions that form the basic frame of reference, and actions cause events.

The action of asking a query generates an interpretative sequence and database search.

The action of sending a message causes the event message to be sent.

The action of storing (or retrieving) an object leads to the event object being stored (or retrieved).

A report generation action causes a presentation event.

For optimization purposes, such events should be defined through logic modeling that leads to the recognition of an action that triggers the initiation of a new function. That secondary function carries out actions of its own, generating new events, some of which lead to functions and tertiary actions. A chain of:

- Events,
- Functions,
- Actions, and
- New events

tends to continue until conditions are reached where none of the actions triggers any new functions, and the chain is complete. Until this happens, there is plenty of scope in the optimization of queries—involving actions, communication paths, and databases accesses associated with boundary functions that are known or unknown. A careful study would address all these categories.

13—6 ADVENT AND USAGE OF EXPERT DATABASES

When we approach a human expert for assistance in solving a problem or completing a task, the first thing we do is state our goal. The expert would then ask questions, mentally sifting through facts and rules, using our answers to ask more questions, and eventually he or she would target the best means to reach a given goal.

A different way of looking at this mental process is to say that, in effect, the expert brings a base of knowledge to bear in resolving the problems encountered, or to be encountered, in reaching a stated goal. This is precisely what the KBMS is doing in determining goals and constraints, or in containing a particular subject matter.

The formalization of such an operation by means of an artifact is feasible because the knowledgebank exhibits three important characteristics.

It already contains the facts and rules with which it must work. If it does not contain a given fact, it infers it, or alternatively it looks to well-defined external sources.

It knows what to ask, as well as what not to ask. Because most of the answers are already in the knowledgebank, user consultation is kept to a minimum.

It determines the interfaces between query (or any other application) and objects sought online through the DBMS.

The inference process is determined largely by how we choose to codify knowledge in goals and rules, and partly by how we structure the knowledgebank. To understand the inference process fully, we must be familiar with the components that make up a knowledgebank.

One of the most important issues in man–machine communication is the consultation design. What information must be produced on the basis of the query being made? What is the best way to present that feedback? The queries the user makes are ad hoc, but the mechanism that will respond to them has to be made a priori; therefore, it needs to be polyvalent.

The knowledge engineer determines how effective the consultation will be by carefully considering content, structure, timing, and placement of each available dialog option within the knowledgebank. The final consultation design should make dialog between user and system as easy as dialog between the client and a human expert.

Indeed, the artifact is both simplifying and making more sophisticated the external schema and its semantics. This can be achieved because knowledgebanks contain rules, domain values, and methodologies. The rules focus on expertise for problem solution. The inference engine is the interpreter of the knowledgebank.

Metarules guide the interpretation of rules but also impose constraints. We said that metadata is data about data, and we also stressed the fact that the concept of *meta* is very important in object-oriented databases as it relates to contents, intention, extension, and usage of expertise. The latter is mapped into the:

- Knowledgebank,
- Metarules, and
- Metadata.

As we stressed in previous chapters, with classical computers, efficiency is 98 percent a function of database design and only 2 percent a function of the means by which the query is generated. Idea databases change this frame of reference by nearly inverting the percentages.

These benefits are quite significant, but they are not the only ones to be derived from expert databases. Another contribution is *text animation*, which is most important in multimedia solutions. Animation represents information contained in large chunks of text organized in the form of a knowledgebank, its rules being used to drive a computer-based consultation.

For instance, Microelectronics and Computer Development Corporation (MCC) actively works on a program animation to endow analysts and programmers with the ability to overfly their software construct on a 3-D video presentation

This way they can examine the functionality of query node.

They can experiment on the evolutionary steps needed to enhance such functionality.

They can preoperate a programming system before it is released.

The outcome of a database query handled through the dual structure of KBMS–DBMS may be presented as *hard-data* or *soft-data*. As stated in Part One, soft-data is derived data often useful to accommodate multiple viewpoints on information and for maintaining frequently referenced multimedia objects.

Hard-data is explicitly stored facts and their values; hence raw data that have not yet been subjected to derivation rules. A hard-data update is done by means of the more classical DBMS. The handling of derived data is more complex, involving update propagation.

An expert system embedded in the KBMS will keep statistical evidence of soft-data usage with a view to *optimization*. Optimization procedures should consider:

- Repetitiveness of equal-type queries requesting a given object or objects,
- Computational requirement for a derived version versus update propagation, and
- The fact that update propagation is not always unique, and the associated transaction can be ambiguous.

The derived data update problem is similar to the view update problem in relational database terminology. Given the inherent difficulty of this process, most relational DBMS permit view update in very limited cases, for instance, only if such procedures are explicitly specified by designers or users.

Much of the problem of supporting derived data update in semantic databases is largely open. However, using knowledge engineering and capitalizing on the facts that:

- Conceptual schemata specified with semantic database models are richer than
- The corresponding record-oriented relational schemata,

it is possible to perform update propagation in a more substantive way than has been possible so far.

Update rules generally are gathered from the constructions of classes or attributes and from the restrictions applicable to them. The former is structural information, whereas the latter constitutes the constraints whose importance has been often brought under perspective.

In an object-oriented sense, structural information includes class definitions, subclass derivations, and attribute descriptions. Constraints are specified in the class or attribute definition sense, and among other issues, involve cardinality limitation of attributes. Also classes and restrictions, such as an attribute value, cannot be null or cannot be changed.

The manipulation of update rules and constraints is made more effective through parameters that are set by the knowledgebank on the basis of certain inputs. Goals define rules and facts, as well as the sources of knowledge. Intelligence-enriched definitions determine the type of classes to be handled in a given situation. All these together make up the expert database.

13–7 BENEFITS FROM THE INTENTIONAL DATABASE APPROACH

When a human expert is presented with a problem, he usually breaks it down into subproblems, resolving them one-by-one until the total problem is solved. The intentional database works the same way. In the knowledgebank, a complex query or transaction is broken down into a series of subproblems that:

- Can be represented as specific goals, and
- Each benefits from a knowledge approach.

A goal may be thought of as access to an object or objects within the distributed database environment, or as a type of conclusion that we want the knowledgebank to reach during a consultation. It is specified in the intentional database by a goal statement.

Each database-related goal is made up of one or more rules or facts that conclude a value for that goal. Even a single goal may have several possible values concluded for it, reflecting the way it is defined in the statement.

All rules in the intentional database that conclude a particular goal are logically grouped under that common statement. The order in which those rules are listed is important to the inference process. This order is instantiated. Its execution is likely to be hierarchically structured, but the existence of such structure is ephemeral.

The rules in the intentional database permit us to perform tests and to manipulate database accesses. This process offers an extensive set of expressions, with two kinds of premise clauses: simple and complex.

A *complex* premise typically consists of two or more simple premise statements joined by logical operators.

An AND operator, for example, can connect two simple premise statements, dictating that both must be true in order for the conclusion reached by the rule to be valid.

An OR operator also connects two simple premises. It dictates that only one of the premise statements needs to be true in order for the conclusion to be valid.

This form of a Boolian expression is the simplest that can be implemented in handling database objects. We also spoke of memory-based reasoning, which is the most sophisticated approach (among several alternatives). At the bottomline, however, a complex premise is determined to be true or false by the combination of all the simple premises.

Although each premise is tested individually, the logical operators that connect the simple premise statements dictate a processing pattern. This pattern creates the methodology followed in searching the object-oriented database, with *semantic* approaches being the more powerful alternative we have available today.

In the intentional database are included description and structuring formalism that are intended to allow a schema to capture more of the *meaning* of a database than is possible with other types of database models. However, it is wise to analyze many database applications to provide a pallet of features for the modeling of database application environments. This helps in:

1. Determining the structures that occur and recur in connection to this pallete of features,
2. Developing scenarios to address the problems of pattern recognition of objects in the database, and
3. Assessing the shortcomings of the finer programmatic interfaces being tested.

The process in reference is iterative. Features are added, removed, or modified during various stages of experimentation prior to reaching a valid mechanism for describing the meaning of the database.

A valid approach typically addresses semantics because of the level of user interfaces to the distributed database. Human windows can be constructed as frontends to existing database management systems helped by powerful query languages. Such intentional database approach uses predicates and does much more than retrieve information stored in computer memory.

It *interprets* the user's external schema; be it for a query, for processing, or for communications reasons.

It searches into its *data dictionary* (as well as the dictionary and its directory) to find the location of the database(s) whose objects satisfy this external schema.

It *converts* this external schema into an internal schema (or schemata), which can be understood by the database management system that runs the specific database.

Essentially only the third step is done by older query languages, such as DM 4 and SQL. In these, the all important first step is absent, and the second step is very limited.

The artifacts of an intentional database provide for the explicit specification of a large portion of the meaning of each component of the distributed environment. This contrasts to many contemporary database models that make a compromise between:

1. The desire to provide a user-oriented database organization, and
2. The need to support low overhead database storage, retrieval, and manipulation facilities.

In contrast, the intentional database solution emphasizes both the importance of understandable modeling constructs and that of appreciating user-oriented interfaces.

In the course of his or her interactivity with the distributed database, the enduser employs the knowledgebank embedded into the system almost without knowing it. His or her interest is not in rules and heuristics or the philosophy of computer-generated space, but it rests in the able and rapid implementation of his or her intentions in terms of man–machine communication.

In conclusion, intentional databases are AI artifacts. The system analyst who thinks only in terms of an extensional database ignores their powerful qualities, which have significant bearing on the lower layers of a storage space where the retrieval problem lies.

The less sophisticated computer professional works close to the physical space, separated by only one logical layer, that of the DBMS. In contrast to this, the sophisticated computer professional (as well as the enduser) starts at the top layer, supported through metaknowledge.

This layered structure in object-oriented database management is a good example of the *meta* concept. The DBMS is metadata to the information elements; the external schema is metadata to the internal schema, and the idea database is metadata to the external schema.

The bottom layer consists of the pattern of chips, wires, printed circuit boards, and physical disks that form the memory.

The top layer is that of problem dynamics that enter the particular solution we are elaborating.

The space between the top and the bottom layers—hence, the logical space—is not simply computer memory freed of its physical limitations. It is much more than that. It is computer memory reduced to its essence—the intentional and extensional capabilities it represents.

14

Computer Graphics and the Enduser

14–1 INTRODUCTION

Multimedia involves concepts from video production, audio recording, animation, and other fields novel to computer experts, system analysts, and programmers. In the past, multimedia operations implied special hardware and software, which led to the need for appropriate study in order to implement such operations. However, the wider spread of multimedia technology changed this.

As we know it today, the concept of the graphic user interface (GUI) was developed by Xerox Research and was commercialized at an affordable price by Apple, in 1984, with *Macintosh*. Rapidly, it came to be regarded as a dominant issue in operating environments for personal computers, with its major features being:

- Device independence,
- Look and feel composition, and
- Seamless data interchange capabilities.

However, there is a stratification of GUI products that seems to follow the dividing lines of operating systems, with Microsoft's *Windows* increasingly becoming a de facto standard, at least in the MS-DOS environment. We talk more about the alternative GUI possibilities in Section 14-2.

The review of commercial GUI offerings is important because of the primitives and software routines they support. In a multimedia landscape, basic software components play a great role producing and transforming information elements. Beyond the primitives:

Advanced software concepts and programming products are an integral part of multimedia.

New software approaches are necessary to handle such fairly complex user interfaces as in *virtual reality* applications (see Chapter 15).

Multimedia programming and its associated concepts require a general model for describing and developing applications. In contrast to past practices with incompatible solutions, a unifying conceptual mode can guide the designer's hand toward homogeneity.

As user organizations gain experience with multimedia, they come to appreciate the benefits to be gained from both simple and complex conceptual models of an increasing functionality. Even the simpler systems should be general enough to capture sound, video, music, and animated sequences, as well as text, graphics, and data.

The best GUI approaches are those that are open and extensible, so that further enhancements are possible, and more experienced programmers are not constrained. I use "approaches," not "approach," because there are different alternatives, as we shall see in Section 14-4. However, prior to that we briefly examine the business perspectives of the multimedia market, then the evolution of computer graphics.

14–2 BUSINESS PERSPECTIVE OF INTERACTIVE MULTIMEDIA

To a very significant extent, competitiveness in the 1990s will be defined through the availability and usage of interactive multimedia, as reflected in the current interest in the emerging markets growing out of the fervor over network systems integration, interactivity, and multimedia computing. Strategic planning on networked solutions involves the integration of:

- Cable television,
- Telephone lines,
- Personel computers, and
- Two-way television.

Under development are simultaneously operating TV and computer solutions that allow, for instance, home computer owners to use their machines for learning, entertainment, and shopping, among other things. This merging of formerly distinct disciplines into a single system will eventually lead to two-way television.

The thrust towards this type of development can be seen in a number of recent merger, acquisition, and investment activities. It takes place not only among computers, communications, and software, but also within the telecommunications industry itself: from the multibillion dollar investment that Pacific Telesis is making in fiber optic cable to be brought into offices and homes, to the sale of Tele-Communications and Liberty Media to Bell Atlantic.

John C. Malone, whose $11.8 billion Bell Atlantic deal gives him a 1.5 percent stake in the new company, says he had been looking for ways to get TCI into the telephone and interactive media businesses and the merger is really far broader in scope than a simple joint venture.[*] It takes a large variety of skills, from computers to cable and software, to develop the solutions that the market demands for the end of this century.

- Merging cable TV and telephone business expertise will allow us to explore new technologies, such as *interactive media*.
- Microsoft has also been in talks with Tele-Communications, Time Warner, and other companies about possible alliances in interactive media solutions.

For telecommunication, computer, and software companies alike, the goal is to define and capture some of the evolving markets. That is why Microsoft has stepped up its efforts at developing the so-called *content*, that is, educational and information programs featuring sound and high-grade graphics that will run on multimedia personal computers.

In terms of business perspectives and practical income-earning implementation, practically every company entering this market has the goal of bringing multimedia into the growing world of client-server computing, where

- Powerful servers run large databases, and
- Dish-up information and programs to workstations across networks.

Hence the race is on to create software needed to store different varieties of information elements (e.g., electronic mail, financial transactions, magazines, video) that will be interactively retrieved through remote access and will flow through the *Information Superhighway.*

The lucrative market that lies ahead has induced network operators, cable companies, software firms, and others to position themselves for what they believe will be the world's largest market for interactive video services. In Europe, for example, both the voice monopoly and the video monopoly have ended—and with that, the door is open for the leading multimedia companies of the world to come in. There are, however, two problems:

---

[*]*Business Week*, October 25, 1993.

1. *The market* of which we speak is not yet so well defined and its boundaries are fuzzy.

Lots of investments will have to be made on foresight and faith. Yet, without these investments the market potential will not develop and the business opportunity will remain difficult to judge.

2. *Multimedia* is a word used by different people to mean different things, one of the reasons being its evolution over the years.

Originally, in the late 1970s, the concept behind multimedia was the integration of voice, data, text, and graphics. Then live video was added to the list. While this definition is still in the background, in the foreground has come the "who's who" in technology. A comprehensive list could include:

- Interactive graphics
- Moving image
- Audio annotation
- Compound electronic documents, and
- Virtual reality.

Megastreams and gigastreams in carrier capacity, video compact disks, and knowledge engineering are enabling technologies with multimedia. *Virtual reality* will eventually integrate the other disciplines in this list into one major environment with powerful tools to be used for the customization of deliverables. We will return to this issue in Chapter 15.

14–3 BRIEF LOOK INTO EVOLUTION OF COMPUTER GRAPHICS

Physical and logical representation capabilities add up to *visualization* requirements—the turning of tables and numbers into images. Computer graphics is about 3 decades old; however, only recently has it become an integral part of computing: from visualizing information formerly presented in tables, to seeing three-dimensional objects in photorealism.

Most of the impetus in computer graphics has occurred in the last 10 years with workstations, and it is foreseen that by the end of this decade many applications will be developed for graphics. Even consumer devices will routinely have a three-dimensional realistic graphics capability.

The computer graphics history started in the early 1960s at MIT. Working on his doctoral program, Dr. Ivan Sutherland wrote a series of interactive graphics programs on the TX-2 (transistor experiment 2) computer, which had a vector-drawing monitor connected to it. Dr. Sutherland's work relied on the computer to do the graphics calculations, while he focused on the development of a wide variety of concepts, including:

- Object-oriented approaches,
- Constraint-based visual computing, and
- Real-time interactive programming.

Sketchpad, Sutherland's solution, however, was a 2-D system. Three dimensions required too much computer power for the then available machines.

After his MIT research, Sutherland joined the Harvard faculty and helped one of his doctoral students, Danny Cohen, to develop a 3-D flight simulator. This led to the making of wireframe virtual images, which then became the high tech of computer-aided design (CAD), until full-blown 3-D models were worked out.

Joining forces with Dave Evans at the University of Utah, Dr. Sutherland helped to plant the seeds of 3-D computer graphics from which several development trees sprang. Among the better known are:

1. The widely used standard of real-time graphics, and
2. Ultra-high-quality rendering, or photorealistic graphics.

Image quality and time considerations divide these two classes. Real-time graphics depend on very fast turnaround, interactivity, and speed of rendering. In contrast, ultra-high-quality graphics focus on the realism of a computer-generated picture; the time required to compute it is of secondary importance.

Under these two different but complementary lines of reasoning, 3-D computer graphics entered the scientific and industrial world. The first real-life implementations have been in engineering, emphasizing conceptual models of potential man-made product configurations.

Three-dimensional CAD makes the design process smoother, and in the opinion of cognizant designers, it takes only one-half to one-third of the time required by an equally skilled 2-D CAD user to produce the same results.

However, 3-D CAD is more than a process that has production speed only going for it. Nontechnical people, including managers and professionals in such fields as finance and trading, find solid images easier to understand and use.

In fact, as of late, graphic solutions from engineering disciplines became embedded into other professional fields. Nikko Securities, for example, employs concurrent engineering design for financial products. This has an impact on the way financial products are designed, as well as how they are delivered.

Lessons can be learned from manufacturing, where companies mastering concurrent engineering avoid being stuck with products that existing assembly lines are ill-suited to produce. One advantage of computer graphics is the ease they bring to experimentations.

Since engineering firms have discovered how to profit from computer graphics, banks and other service industries are finding out that animated graphics are useful for more than an impressive display alone. By simulating a product's appeal or the market's behavior, both opportunities and problems can be spotted and corrected.

Three-dimensional presentation through visualization offers a dynamic viewing and plotting environment.

Multimedia modeling is putting uninmagined power into designers' hands.

Users can model reality more closely than has ever before been possible.

Such modeling has prerequisites. We examine them in Section 14-6 when we discuss graphics metafiles and object solutions, as well as in Section 14-7 through the discussion on integrative graphics projects and frameworks.

Standards are needed in order to ensure that results are portable and they are reasonably homogeneous. As we shall see in Section 14-3, in this domain approaches to graphic user interfaces provide good solutions, which, however, are not normalized.

14–4 GRAPHIC USER INTERFACE

A graphic user interface is the user-visible part of the system; the application frontend. GUIs typically consist of windows, scroll bars, pull-down and pop-up menus; that is, logical devices displayed on the screen and generally driven via mouse.

The term *graphic* is not precise because etimologically it implies a more sophisticated graphic content, such as 3-D graphs, engineering drawings, or animation facilities. But GUI has caught the user's imagination and has become a habit.

There are a number of toolkits available for the generation of friendly GUI interfaces.

GUI presents significant advantages over earlier man–machine communication methods, such as the character user interface (CUI).

A graphic approach has been found to be a major contributor in cutting training costs.

The more advanced GUI tools provide the developer and the enduser with the ability to create graphic objects with encapsulated and inherited behavior. It also permits the user to "cut and paste" together (link) effectively pages or parts thereof containing multimedia objects.

The growing range of GUI facilities permits the complete creation of an application state hierarchy through development tools, without the extra labor third generation languages demand. As we shall see in subsequent sections, GUI has distinct advantages over character user interface tools.

To understand the philosophy of GUI, we must appreciate that a basic element in programming is the assumption that the user must always be in control of the development process. This notion, also known as *feel*, is central to GUI behavior.

Hence, a GUI application must be structured to accept and deal with asynchronous user inputs at any time. Such inputs are known as *events*. This calls for a very different style of programming than that demanded by the more classical computer applications. The latter generally assume that the machine is in control. Therefore, conventional programming follows a rigid sequence of input, processing, and output.

Even if the term is not very precise, graphic user interfaces do present much of their information content to users in graphic form. But the interpretation of GUI can be somewhat elastic.

Graphics need not necessarily mean only pictures or icons (familiar objects).

Even a word processor with multiple text faces, sizes, styles, and a ruler line (for indicating tab stops and margins) is sometimes taken as a graphic application.

One of the basic characteristics of GUI is that it handles flexible *windows* that present information in overlapping rectangular areas of the screen. Users can manipulate these windows, changing their size and position.

Through GUI, endusers can select objects to work on by means of pictorial representations, the icons; and through the mouse. Commands typically are chosen from menus rather than being typed, or input from

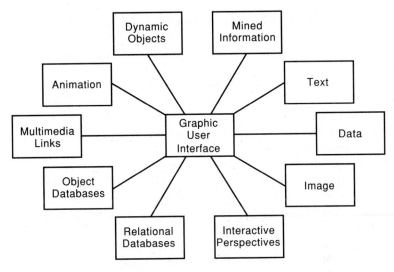

Figure 14.1   An application development environment can be both extended and enhanced through GUI.

function keys. But Windows also contain other graphic entities, permitting the user to provide input to the application program.

As suggested in Figure 14.1, an impressive application development environment can be served through GUI, but some constraints must be considered. One of the most important is that graphic user interfaces found in many commodity offerings are diverse and incompatible. Let us examine these, starting with the earlier artifacts.

Although GUI predates the announcement of Macintosh by Apple Computers in 1984, it is Macintosh that made graphic user interfaces an affordable solution. As a result, it has captured a big chunk of the market for the electronic publishing media, apart of its acceptance as user-friendly business computer.

The Macintosh GUI software is embedded in the read-only memory (ROM) chip, providing a good degree of standardization in that environment. Software developed by Apple, the User Interface Toolbox, ensures the means of constructing application programs that conform with Apple's defined graphic user interface standards.

Another comprehensive and mature GUI is offered by Microsoft *Windows*; therefore, NT* also. Windows has become popular as a bridge for MS-DOS users wishing to enter the GUI world, although the number of its users is somewhat smaller than that of Macintosh.

---

*Microsoft's New Technology operating system.

The *Presentation Manager* (PM) of OS/2 can be considered to be an offshoot of Windows. It has been jointly developed by Microsoft and IBM but as do some other GUIs, it lacks rich application software, and the number of its users is quite small.

Presentation Manager embodies the main principles of IBM's approach to the design of such user interfaces as the Common User Access component of the System Application Architecture (SAA). Contrary to the design concept of MS-Windows, Presentation Manager is an internal part of the operating system.

In the mid-1980s, Project Athena at MIT, brought forward *X-Windows*. Some people do not consider it a GUI; however, others tend to include it in the GUI family because it offers windowing and graphics. *DECWindows*, by Digital Equipment, is built on an X-Windows infrastructure, adding scrolling, dialog boxes, and text fields.

Among the so-called GUI standards, we can distinguish *Motif*, by the Open Software Foundation (OSF). Motif runs under Unix and does present similarities to DECWindows, from which it has been derived.

In contrast, substantially different from DECWindows and Motif, in both in the user interface and the programmatic interfaces, is Open Look. Open Look features have also been derived from X-Windows, a development of Sun Microsystems and AT&T.

Among the major players in the GUI field it is appropriate to include NeXTstep. From its inception until it was phased out, the NeXT Computer Company addressed itself to the high end of graphic user interfaces. It featured first-class techniques, but as with the Presentation Manager, it suffered from lack of applications software.

NeXTstep, Open Look, and partially DecWindows address the Unix world. DECWindows also operates under VMS. X-Windows, in contrast, is only an enabling technology—a foundation on which to build GUIs, rather than a GUI itself.

14–5 PROGRAMMATIC INTERFACES AND COMMUNICATIONS PROTOCOLS

The majority of GUI design tools are integrated with other software modules within a systems environment, leading to seamless reusage without reinvention of objects already dealt with. Experience has shown that the general requirements may be expressed in a similar way for most cases, although particular applications place more emphasis upon certain types of interfaces.

This experience can, however, be generalized only partly because at the same time, as Section 14-2 suggests, there is a growing range of heterogeneous GUI tools. The more evident issue among them is the Application Program Interface (API). This is the library of routines that perform functions such as:

- Creating windows,
- Displaying graphics, and so on.

Unfortunately for the users, practically each GUI approach has its unique set of API routines, differing in parameters, calling sequence, functionality, and even in name.[*]

As we have seen, there are different graphic user interfaces in the Unix world: X-Windows, Motif, Open Look, and NeXTstep have been mentioned. Unix is a favored platform because most applications for a GUI environment are resource intensive.

Diversity in GUI APIs is just as pronounced among non-UNIX systems. Yet, these too would need to tie into any comprehensive Open Systems computing architecture. In Section 14-3 we mentioned Windows 3.0 (DOS), Windows NT, Macintosh, Presentation Manager (OS/2), DEC Windows, and we can also add Character Mode, Block Mode, and so on.

Such diversity is bound to grow rather than shrink as the next generation of GUI tools will aim to meet many new requirements. Therefore, there is a need to provide an integrative tool set with specialist modules dedicated to the particular functions that are portable among different GUI platforms.

New tools and protocols are needed to assist further in decreasing the development times for applications.

Norms are necessary to broaden the user base of application development to people who do not want to be locked into proprietary architectures.

There is a reason why emphasis is on more versatile—as well as more simple—normalized and user-friendly programming interfaces. According to most forecasts, the majority of tools people will be using in the future will be GUI oriented. This is not only true of programming but also of communicating, as for instance, in electronic mail.

Even today, graphic user interfaces have become the expectation of every workstation user. Consequently, the application developers are moving rapidly toward incorporating GUI tools.

---

[*]For a while, the productization work done by the SQL Access Group on ISO's RDA attempted to normalize the API. But such norms never really got implemented and by now a de facto standard is developing with Microsoft's ODBC.

Endusers are looking for easy, friendly—but also expandable—application interfaces.

Management wants to have increased productivity; thus, a more cost-effective implementation, with early delivery.

Both of these goals require methodologies and tools for fast prototyping and software development, in the way that previous chapters have explained. Competitiveness can no longer be maintained with limited functionality of and/or lack of new development tools. Indeed, protocols can create a bottleneck also, as seen through the use of 3270 on graphics workstations.

A different way of making this statement is that the emergence of the *graphics workstation* must influence the whole system design, not only the applications. Furthermore, we must account for its significant impact on endusers who pose new demands on software and hardware vendors.

Programming must be minimized, requiring less analysis and coding expertise to achieve the desired solution.

The methodology to be selected should enable he shortest development timetable imposed upon endusers and developers alike.

Today, endusers demand a level of software integration beyond what old concepts and obsolete protocols can provide. Therefore, they exhibit a degree of intolerance with 3270 because it inhibits the functionality of GUI tools and limits their capabilities. Nothing short of a totally user-friendly, streamlined, and complete application development environment can be acceptable.

There are more than presentation reasons connected to the emphasis being placed on protocols. Leading-edge organizations have been identifying applications that can fill the ever greater bandwidth that becomes available at affordable prices. But there is a systems problem having to do with today's model of the relationship between:

- Networks,
- Databases, and
- Computer processing services

Past relationships do not necessarily work for tomorrow because by year 2000, the roles of computer and communications will be reversed, with communications being the master.

Two issues are relevant to this reference. First, nearly all the experience we have accumulated in protocols and communications has come during the time when computers had the upper hand, and at the same time were faster than the communications links. By the year 2000, however, the opposite will be true. Communications will work faster than computers, even if the latter have teraops capacity.

Second, fiber optic communications is significantly cheaper than copper-based solutions. This has numerous consequences for which to account, as costs are turning into prices, and prices fall dramatically.

The systems concepts, the communications protocols, and the graphics presentation tools must all be thoroughly reexamined for the new generation of communications–intensive services. Today's models are wrong because they are based on obsolete assumptions. But how soon will vendors and user organizations grasp the opportunities offered by the new technology?

14–6 MODELS OF EVENTS AND OPPORTUNITIES IN VISUALIZATION

A number of subjects come under this title: Visualization approaches, screen technologies, graphics modes, character-mapped displays (alphamosaic), bit-mapped displays (alphageometric), keyboard, mouse, joy stick, tracker ball, infrared controller, bit pads (graphic tablets), and image digitizing systems. Also included are issues connected to monochrome versus color, resolution, and compatibility.

A GUI example is given in Figure 14.2. On the display screen, the graphic user interface presents a menu structure and iconic representations. It also maps a workplace into a window, and can have many windows

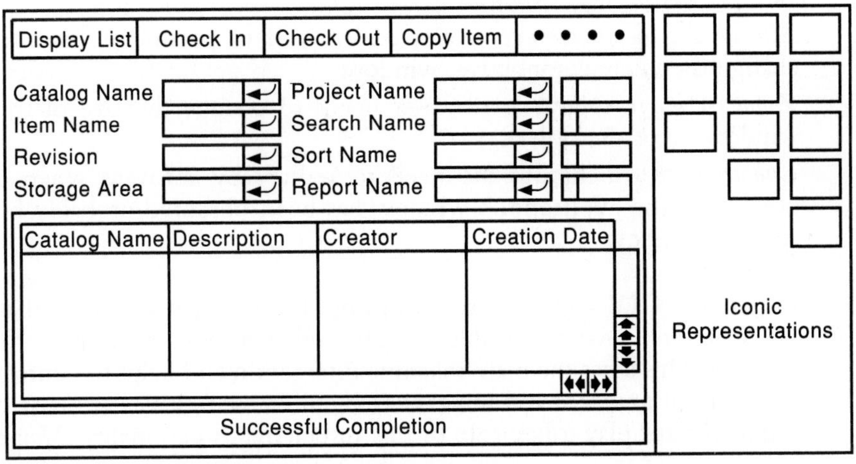

Figure 14.2   Example of a graphic user interface.

displayed at the same time. The user can manipulate with a pointing device objects that are represented as icons.

Effectively handled through GUI, icons and graphics significantly improve the ease and quality of the man–machine interface. *Visualization* is the eyepiece of the computer, able to present through a human window:

- From simple graphic forms
- To the behavior of complex dynamic systems.

The interest in sophisticated visualization is fed by enduser demand. It is also promoted by the fact that by the mid-1990s microprocessor-based workstations might reach a peak of 500 Mflops, providing 25,000 flops per dollar, or 10 times the projected cost effectiveness of a supercomputer.

Also, with the advent of high-definition television (HDTV), low-cost, very high video can be distributed directly to the desktop. As a by-product, users would have video conferencing and telepresence (see in Chapter 15).

Many companies fail, however, to appreciate that multimedia and visualization are for interactive environments, not for batch. To exploit the advantages visualization presents, the whole concept of programming must change—and change well beyond the protocols whose case was stressed in Section 14-4.

Another issue in need of thorough revamping is the concept of user input, as well as the system events being supported. The following event types need normalization and streamlining:

Initialize and *finalize* events delivered to an entity just after it is created and just before it is swept away.

Activate and *deactivate* events created by GUI to permit the user to change the current, or active, window.

Zoom or *resize* events, as the user needs to change the size of the window or of the object.

Update events, including the need to redraw by software when a portion of the application's window has been obscured probably by another window.

In general, GUI approaches use an object–action paradigm, so that the user is presented with available objects, and then acts on them as he or she wishes. This eases the man–machine interaction and helps to control the processing of graphics and images.

Input devices play a key role in this interactive functionality. *Mouse events* may indicate that the enduser has moved the mouse into, out of, or within an entity. *Menu events* are generated when the user selects a command from a pop-up, pull-down, or other menu. Events are produced as well when the user presses or releases a key on the *keyboard* or *keypad*, or moves a *scrollbar* and with it the application's contents of the window.

The execution of such events rests on primitives and, as we noted in Section 14-2, GUIs differ in their primitives and in the way they handle them. With Macintosh, for example, the application must contain an event loop. This loop calls a Macintosh library routine to see if there are any events pending. If yes, the routine returns the event, and the application processes it.

In contrast, Motif has a callback event model. With it, the application must register an event-handling function for each entity that it creates. When the GUI has an event for the entity, it calls the application's event routine. Other commodity GUI software present different functionalities.

The message remembered here is that there is much more in functionality terms underlying the main mouse actions—clicking, pressing, dragging—and this depends on supported primitives. Each time the user needs to perform an event such as:

- Answering the questions of a dialog box, or
- Selecting the source of a link,

there must be available software capable of simplifying this task by offering interactive features. These typically are mnemonic and take the form of graphic objects such as controls or icons, but they don't work the same way with all offerings.

What the different commodity GUIs have in common is a rather extensive use of mouse and graphic interactions by the enduser. That is good because it contributes to the clarity and attractiveness of the system, but it is not homogeneous among different offerings.

14–7 GRAPHICS METAFILES AND OBJECT SOLUTIONS

Metafiles for storing, retrieving, and communicating information elements, database-to-database, are important parts of modern graphics systems. Graphics metafiles are not only valuable for device-independent storage and retrieval of pictures within CAD, but also offer an interface to other computer systems, allowing efficient use of graphics devices.

A graphics metafile can be described as a mechanism for the transfer, storage, and retrieval of graphics information in a manner that is both device- and application-independent. Its minimal capability must include all functions necessary to describe pictures independently of one another. Such graphics expressions must be able to:

- Store on different media,
- Transport between graphics systems, and
- Display on a variety of graphics devices.

The metafile should not require nonsequential access to graphics primitives to display the picture. Its native set of functions should not preclude the addition of application-dependent data or picture-structure information. The specification of functionality should be separated from that of coding formats.

The foregoing paragraphs contain aspects important for incorporating graphics metafiles into a CAD database. With such guidelines, based on the knowledge of existing metafiles, the ANSI X3H33 task group has undertaken an effort to develop a general graphics metafile proposal, with the goal to achieve an international standard.

The use and exchange of records, files, fields, and object-oriented information should be feasible without interrupting the daily use of the system. If both the file descriptions and the procedures are well-defined, then it becomes possible to answer useful questions in terms of metafile functionality.

Metafiles are typically resident in a language file, which is itself part of the applications database. Their contents are represented by information elements generated as the result of functions being invoked. Such functions typically are grouped in upward compatible levels, featuring increasing capabilities.

Not everything can be found exclusively in the domain of metafile import/export. A thoroughly studied database implementation must also respond to a number of other issues of growing importance, such as:

- Security,
- Consistency,
- Integrity,
- Semantics of the database (conceptual modeling), and
- Concurrency in database handling (interactions, deadlocks, synchronization).

Among the foremost design characteristics the metafile concept should consider are: the information content; the size of the projected database; its internal organization and structure; access capabilities; data protection; and policies to be followed, such as device independence.

The principle is that databases must be managed in an efficienct manner through appropriate software. However, today's database management systems are not designed to cope with metafile information.

Interactive design and graphics requirements differ from data handled by commercial systems. An object being designed can be described from several viewpoints.

- Functional description
- Circuit diagram
- Layout, and so on

Although representing the same object, some descriptions are derived from others in the course of design activity. Hence, consistency between the different descriptions must be maintained. This is a basic notion underlining engineering databases.

While the now classical hierarchical, Codasyl, inverted files, and relational DBMS cannot effectively handle graphics metafile information, the basic requirements may be answered by object DBMS. These allow us to take advantage of object features combined with a rigorous database management to develop an application with the following characteristics:

- Multimedia storage and manipulation,
- Different data formats and locations to be integrated,
- Complex and varied data structures,
- Constantly changing environmental conditions, and
- Multiuser access to information resources.

Metafile solutions facilitate rapid prototyping, design, and testing. They also help provide to basic query, administration, and editing capabilities.

The use of graphics metafiles is particularly important in a client–server architecture, in terms of enabling us to utilize the available networked databases efficiently. As shown in Figure 14.3, client workstations can use an object approach with associated programmatic interfaces to integrate multimedia information, such as:

- Product description,
- Design specification,
- Materials billing, and so on.

A metafile approach can be instrumental, with external functions allowing the user to access multimedia information stored outside his or

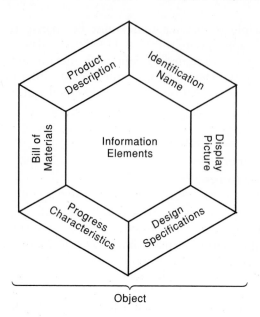

Object

Figure 14.3   Example of a user-defined type of product design.

her database, regardless of format or location. In Figure 14.3 Display Picture can be an external function that executes codes outside the local database to display the stored picture.

Solutions make use of the fact that objects are a combination of multimedia information and stored functions that operate on the information elements. The whole of Figure 14.3 is an example of an object. Functions operate on multimedia information in the database and also define the behavior of these information elements.

14–8 INTEGRATING GRAPHICS PROJECTS AND FRAMEWORKS

As multimedia applications progress, they involve fairly complex effects, for example the synchronization of audio and video signals, the juxtaposition of two video signals, and the creation of compound electronic documents. One of the solutions proposed is shown in Figure 14.4, which consists of a two–level architecture with:

- A system–oriented layer, and
- A user–oriented layer.

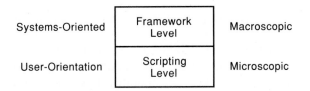

Figure 14.4   Framework and scripting levels help create an architectured approach to GUI.

The former is known as *framework level*.* It is macroscopic, concerned with hardware and basic software, as well as with their control and synchronization in a networked sense. The latter is called the *scripting level*. It is microscopic, concerned with enduser presentation and its specification, in a manner similar to the one we examined in Chapter 1.

The role of the *framework* is to provide a technique for aggregating *multimedia objects*. This approach is known as *temporal composition*, and it exists because of the necessity of modeling situations where:

- A number of media components are simultaneously presented, and
- Each contains audible as well as visual nformation.

The multimedia object not only integrates a collection of component parts but also includes specifications of their *temporal* and *configurational* relationships.

Temporal relationships indicate the synchronization and temporal sequencing of the components. Configurational relationships address the connections between their input and output ports.

Each multimedia object can be viewed as a collection of ports.
A port has a media data type, and it is used either for input or for output.

Given the varying nature of components, multimedia objects must be flexible and must support a variety of synchronization techniques, this is done through synchronization mode attributes. Typically, a media object is an active object that produces and/or consumes media values of specified types at their associated information rates:

- *State*, that is instance variables, and
- *Behavior*, or methods.

---

*The CAD Framework Initiative (CFI), an international effort formed in 1989, closely follows this concept.

Each active object is associated with a process that may be running even if no messages have been sent to the object. Media objects can be sources, sinks, or filters. A *source* produces media values, a *sink* consumes values, and a *filter* screens; hence, it both consumes and produces.

A different way of looking at a framework is as a collection of abstract classes that define interfaces and the implementation of a generic method. Such artifacts are designed to work together with the aim to solve a particular class of problems.

Given their polyvalence, frameworks can take some time to stabilize, being subjected to much experimentation and redesign. However, once it has been well defined and enriched with a components set conforming to it, use of the framework to construct many applications without further infrastructural programming should be possible.

In the case of the CAD Framework Initiative, for example, this concept is used to overcome the fact that different sources of computer-aided design programs have:

• Heterogeneous interfaces;
• Incompatible data structures; and
• Unrelated ways to store and access information elements.

This means that the tools do not naturally talk to one another, with the result that user organizations spend fortunes piecing together the integrated environment they need.

Within a given application perspective, multimedia objects can be *composed*, but this requires that they are well understood both individually and in partnership. Obviously, an advanced composition calls for knowledge-enriched programming that leads to the notion of scripting.

As with all programming concepts, a scripting model defines the permissible ways for objects to be composed. Scripting can help to smooth over certain incompatibilities between objects, allowing their composition within a multimedia programming environment to proceed successfully.

As with any software, scripts are constraints on the types of components allowable, as well as on their composition and configuration. Such constraints are part of the specification of scrip classes, and they are enacted through a scripting language.

A scripting model contains multimedia hierarchies, connection types (e.g., message passing, buffering) and *port* descriptions. The latter identify:

• Whether the port is for input or ourput,
• The media data type of the port,
• Connection types that can be attached to the port, and
• Whether the port accepts multiple connections.

Another important component of the script are object interfaces. Part of the interface of a multimedia object is used only within the framework level, whereas other parts are available for scripting purposes.

A visual scripting tool can be a graphic editor able to present software components interactively, thus permitting a user to connect them together to construct applications. The standard interfaces typically are embedded in a scripting model, with every component being shown together, with its input and output ports.

Input/output ports, their parameters and services, may be presented visually in a variety of ways. Direct manipulation permits us to construct running applications without the need for edit/compile or edit/interpret. A self-documented approach both shows and explains component interfaces. Higher-level components can be built-up as scripts and encapsulated.

15

Physical, Logical, and Graphic User Interfaces

15–1 INTRODUCTION

Chapter 14 presented multimedia manipulation and search strategies, with attention to their theoretical foundations and an examination of their practical applications. Increasingly, search problems call for the building of intelligent information gathering and filtering systems to serve graphic presentation better.

Some research projects along this line focus on methods, models, and algorithms for analyzing and clustering knowledge-based information elements. They use attributive and behavioral information, as well as clustering methods to produce groups of different entities.

A logical regrouping of objects in the distributed database into ephemeral hierarchies has several advantages. Among them, multimedia objects in each cluster are closely related because of common functions, dependencies in behavior, and/or common attributes.

By means of documented and factual grouping, searches for and accesses of objects within clusters are localized by capitalizing on the interdependencies of common objects within the clusters. Such interdependencies can be:

- Functional; or
- Behavioral.

Independent clusters of knowledge information can be handled through separate processors to improve overall performance. Parallel processing permits subtransactions and subqueries to be mapped into relevant clusters and to be evaluated by different processors and/or processes.

This approach also can be instrumental in regard to the development of advanced user interfaces. New software and hardware tools have opened up interesting capabilities for user-interface design.

Sophisticated techniques can use the latest software technology to change the way the user interacts with the computer.

This permits the enduser to recognize actively the benefits of agile interfaces and to look for methodologies to exploit the new tools.

As we shall see in this chapter, the more effective man–machine interface environments currently emerging place particular emphasis on graphics. Implementation characteristics can be improved significantly by solutions of graphic presentation issues, provided that the user interface design is characterized by consistency and normalization.

15–2 PROCESSING BANDWIDTH IN AN OBJECT ENVIRONMENT

The clocked nature of real-time voice, image, text, and data connections requires that an application is capable of scheduling itself. To do so, it must consume ample resources beyond object orientation and local intelligence, which brings into focus the issue of processing bandwidth.

Giga-instructions per second (GIPS) will be necessary, not only for processing per se, but also to meet deadline requirements for servicing ongoing connections. Ongoing connections are affected by the implementation of an object-oriented methodology, as contrasted to a record- and procedure-driven approach.

We pay in computer processing cycles for the agility and flexibility of the object-oriented methodology, hence the need for processing bandwidth. At the same time, the processing strategy or strategies we employ, as well as the different concurrency control mechanisms, must be established in a way to ensure customization and adaptation.

Processing bandwidth should be counted at the levels of both central and distributed resources—the latter concerning departmental computers and personal workstations. Its aftermaths can impact *database bandwidth**[*] and channel capacity.

Precisely because the requirements for processing bandwidth are quite significant and growing, it makes no sense to attach 30 or 40 million instructions per second (MIPS) workstations to 50 MIPS mainframes.

---

[*]For database bandwidth see Sections 16–4 and 16–5 in Chapter 16.

However, this is what most companies are still doing in a curious violation of basic system design principles.

To get the best advantage of available physical solutions, today's powerful workstations should be networked to high-performance computers that work at 10,000 MIPS or greater capacity. This will provide the user organization with:

- The ability to exploit processing bandwidth that is available at low cost, and
- Make feasible very effective approaches to the handling of multimedia information, as well as of object paradigms.

The cost of processing bandwidth can shrink by more than one order of magnitude to nearly two orders of magnitude when we move from mainframes to supercomuters, making high-performance computation by far the best strategy.

An IBM 3090/600 with a vector processor costs about $8 million and delivers a meager 120 MIPS. A Mas-Par supercomputer with 1,000 processing nodes costs only $125,000 but delivers 1,600 MIPS. The difference in cost:effectiveness is a cool 1:80—but how many user organizations take advantage of it?*

In a way, the term, *processing bandwidth,* is a misnomer because only part of the available computer power is really used for processing applications. A big chunk of the very expensive processing power featured by mainframes is necessary for operating systems, DBMS, transaction-processing monitors (TPMs) and the utilities serving them.

As we can see from the issues in the preceding paragraphs, the document-processing discipline the information systems community has been seeking for years comes at a price—and this price increases when we fail to take advantage of opportunities presented by new physical computer characteristics

On the one hand, we are looking for methods to simplify and improve the labor-intensive and error-prone ways of document handling and to enhance our applications development capabilities.

On the other hand, the major steps taking place in computer technology are often left unassessed, with priority given to the beaten path of mainframes and other obsolete hardware.

---

*Interestingly enough, the market takes notice. A New York bank bought a 3090/150 for $2.5 million and, because it did not use it, a year later put it on the block. The best offer it got was $150,000—or 6 percent of the purchase price.

However, there is a real and urgent need to take advantage of physical solutions because implementation of the appropriate methodology in handling multimedia and object-oriented solutions poses not only organizational prerequisites but also major bandwidth requirements.

A similar statement is true in regard to serving agile human interfaces. The work of a user who interacts with multiple applications can be simplified significantly if the appropriate bandwidth is available. At the same time, power needs can be optimized if the interface primitives are consistent.

Applications consistency in the user–interface domain also depends on semantics, syntactics, and pragmatics at the grammatical end, not only on physical consistency.

Semantic consistency refers to the meaning of the elements that make up the interface.

Physical consistency concerns the hardware and how it is used.

Because the more sophisticated user typically has access to several applications, consistency in all the aforementioned aspects is important both within and across applications. Semantic consistency, for example, permits the user to develop strategies that are independent of application boundaries.

The problem is that, by and large, the outlined approach runs contrary to current practices where the majority of users employ interfaces with little or no consistency. As a result, endusers are not as pleased and productive as they could be, while at the same time, they are consuming a high-processing bandwidth that otherwise would not have been necessary.

Failure to ensure the appropriate consistency standards can cost the organization dearly. Therefore, it is not enough to provide more and more processing bandwidth. Something also must be done in bringing a new culture in applications development.

15–3 HOW CAN WE BENEFIT FROM OBJECTS IN MULTIMEDIA ENVIRONMENTS?

To answer this query we must return to the fundamentals. Whether in a data or in a text and image implementation, the *object-oriented* view is that:

Programs are collections of interacting software components.

This approach differs greatly from the classical DP opinion that:

Programs are sequences of actions that are cast into code step-by-step.

By taking a generic approach to the dynamic recombination of software modules, the object-based solution provides a more elegant and more direct way of modeling document-handling activities than procedural programming can ever do. Within the object orientation, the units of program structure are callable entities rather than statements or expressions. Thus they are much more flexible to

- Develop,
- Reuse,
- Incorporate,
- Eliminate, or
- Alter

abstract data types and associated rules. As a result, an object-based solution offers significant advantages, not only in terms of multimedia implementation, but also in our ability to capture the behavior and knowledge of a given system.

Object-based facilities can be enhanced greatly through knowledge engineering, which permits us to capture *document level* interactions, rather than having to deal with much smaller units representing a lower granularity. This is important as multimedia approaches become necessary for a pragmatic modeling network, which involves

- Communicating workstations,
- Distributed databases, and
- Distributed computational environments

that are able to cooperate on substantially common tasks. Figure 15.1 exemplifies this reference to *common tasks* by presenting the steps called for in a computer-aided design situation: from logical design to the use of common modules and interfaces, the definition of specifications and tolerances, and the concurrent chores.

Past practice often ensures that each component function has its own development database. However, concurrent engineering requires not only that these databases communicate among themselves but also that they integrate with other development databases that belong to clients and suppliers—in short, to business partners.

This integrative approach to a computer-aided design methodology also can be applied to business functions. When this is done, a number of questions are raised that we must address.

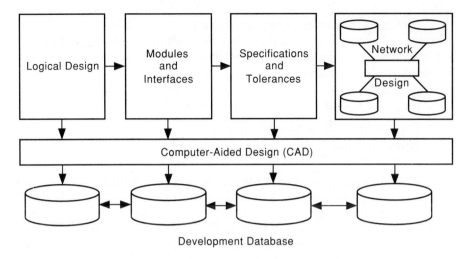

Figure 15.1   Taking an integrative approach to common tasks.

What should each area of activity encapsulate: information elements, knowledge, concepts, concurrency, and specifications?

How should the workstations communicate with each other, with the distributed database, and with users?

What document conversion facilities are needed for the different modules, so that they can understand one another?

How should the multimedia, object-oriented libraries supporting such activities be organized?

Viable answers to these queries become more pressing as computer technology exhibits increasingly greater internal diversity, featuring heterogeneity of storage as well as higher levels of communications and control requirements.

Communications, databasing, processing, and visualization necessarily lead to the management of heterogeneous components. Solutions to interdependency have become as important as the construction of more limited functional systems were in the past.

In order to respond capably to this challenge, we need a breakthrough in *modeling power*, capable of augmenting the human intellect and increasing the expressiveness of software modules, particularly in regard to multimedia operations. In turn, this brings under consideration a contribution that can be provided through:

- *Semantics*-oriented solutions; and
- The use of *metalevel* concepts.

Metainformation elements are dynamic, and can be modified in a manner analogous to that used to alter fact objects. Within a multimedia environment, object uniformity will have to be addressed by semantic database models including:

- Object identity,
- Explicit semantic primitives, and
- Behavioral issues.

This approach is necessary for accommodating different application-specific methods designed for handling multimedia objects in the database. Interobject relationships must be defined to describe associations among multimedia objects that can be modeled as attributes of objects: logical mappings from one object to another, as well as by association of objects.

Multimedia object classification typically will group together objects that have some commonalities. Relationships among object classifications will specify interclass associations of the type we examined with simpler objects: subtype/supertype, adding to this approach both specialization and generalization capabilities.

15–4 PHYSICAL AND LOGICAL PRESENTATION CAPABILITIES

There is a basic distinction between a *record-based* database structure and one that is *object oriented*. The latter benefits from a semantics database description and structuring formalisms that constitute a flexible, proactive database model.[*]

Database models of this type are best fit for multimedia solutions because they are designed to capture more of the meaning of an application environment than is possible with record-based approaches. Their power lies in:

1. Description of databases in terms of entities that exist in the real life application environment
2. Proper classifications and groupings of those entities, executed in a dynamic manner
3. Well-defined structural interconnections among them, some of which are instantiated and perish after rendering the required service

---

[*]See also D.N. Chorafas and H. Steinmann, *Object-Oriented Databases*, Prentice-Hall, Englewood Cliffs, NJ, 1993.

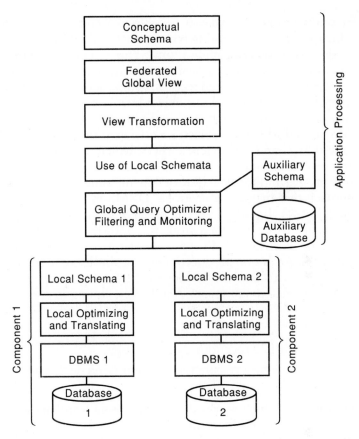

Figure 15.2 Example of a federated database architecture that might be extended to multimedia.

When generic solutions if this sort are refined, eventually they constitute the workhorses of multimedia processing schemes. To visualize the way in which they will work we examine a data-oriented cross-database approach in a heterogeneous (but relational) environment.[*] This is shown in Figure 15.2.

The engineering of this approach has required a collection of high-level modeling primitives capable of mapping the semantics of the application environment. Extending this model, we can see that such an approach permits the multimedia information elements to be viewed in object-oriented ways.

---

[*]The DAPLEX project by General Motors and Relational Technologies involving DB2 and Ingres DBMS.

The outlined strategy makes it possible to accommodate directly the variety of mappings and processing requirements, which are typically present in multimedia database applications. This is not easy with current software because most of today's database management programs have been created to organize lists of printed records: names, addresses, bank accounts, and product inventories, not along object lines.

Some people may say that this does not really matter. We can twist the DBMS around to handle objects or messages; or alternatively, we can squeeze the objects under a current DBMS, whichever is easier. However, what if our records consist of color photographs, video footage, and sound?

To do an elegant job, we require a new multimedia database management approach that may use a relational DBMS in the background (as a lower layer), but we also need to reach a level of sophistication well beyond the functionality to be obtained from this DBMS. In other words, we move toward the KBMS/DBMS approach that we examined in Part Two.

Media Manager[*] is one product addressing this issue, starting with the necessary approach to database homogeneity. It does so by developing a filtering program able to convert to ASCII files, aiming to ensure a transition:

- From different heterogenous data structures,
- To a homogeneous presentation through lower-level code.

The software, which works through scripting, can handle animated information elements, and it permits the use of select criteria. One of the programs in the utilities library does the scanning.

The solution advanced by this approach is to start with a relational DBMS for extracting from heterogenous databases, assuring, however, that the output is Media Manager compatible. The following brief description of functional characteristics helps to explain how this approach works.

The Media Manager's underlying premise is to provide a multimedia database with the capability to append text, image, and audio files that can be:

- Recalled,
- Played,
- Viewed, or
- Heard by the user.

---

[*]By the Harvard Software Co. (HSC) of Santa Monica, CA. This example does not require a large processing bandwidth; however, the sophisticated virtual world setting presented in Section 15–7 requires great amounts of computer power.

To facilitate this process, the Media Manager presents a linear program environment, offering the user all the command functions supported by the program from a single screen. In some activities, such as Load Data, Search, and Print, a submenu is presented prompting further definition of the command.

Because there are no mode changes affecting the selected main screen and the operations on it, a user-friendly approach is possible. The PC-based Media Manager employs a graphic interface that lets the user understand and access operations quickly, providing him or her with the ability to:

1. Retrieve records including graphics, audio, text information, and
2. Display imaging and audio in a context-sensitive search environment.

Specific files can be found through multiple search-and-retrieve functions. This approach is not very different from the one we examine in Chapter 16 in connection to hypermedia.

Search includes the ability to locate information elements in *text, graphic,* or *audio* form.

Still images, video, and audio can be appended to text files from existing databases, or newly generated ones can be constructed with the Database Creator—a utility routine.

A showtime presentation feature allows the user to generate presentations directly from database queries. A multiresolution window makes it possible to look quickly through images and decide which one(s) should be used.

One interesting feature of this utility is that it allows the enduser to view images in multiple resolutions without having to load different drivers or reconfigure the software. Once the user establishes what kind of video card he or she has, the rest is done automatically.

The software utilizes expanded memory to provide *a virtual page.* When the video mode is changed, the expanded memory is used as a buffer for the image. Once the user creates a database and the appended image and sound files, he or she is ready to do a presentation. He or she can either:

1. Go through the database selecting particular records for presentation, assigning a slide number to the record, or
2. Set up search criteria, perform the search, and then present the records found through this search.

Applications of the Media Manager software include videographics and photorealistic still imaging. The multimedia solution that has been developed allows for not only text and images, but also sound effects and live voice to become part of database files.

However, caution should be exercised because this software will not act as a universal database interpreter, which might, for example, make it feasible to query the different heterogenous databases that exist in the present environment. The example of the Media Manager has not been presented as a complete all-encompassing solution, but rather as a workable application, even if it has limited implementation because of database heterogeneity.

More rigorous approaches are needed for a large multifunctional implementation, accounting for an environment that is both distributed and object oriented. However, it is comforting to know that results can be produced based on the essential first steps that have already been taken.

15—5 ADVENT OF KNOWLEDGE ROBOTS (KNOWBOTS)

Physical and logical representation capabilities, the way we have known them so far, have their constraints. This is particularly true when we deal with complex applications requiring approaches that must operate in a networked environment and in the context of large database structures.

To help solve problems connected to the automation of network exchanges and database mining operations, particularly in a wide-area context, a research project at the University of Michigan investigated the use of *knowledge robots*, or *knowbots*. These are intelligent programs that act as *agents* by going around the network and executing specific missions.

Operating through a simple search mechanism in a large database, the user must go carefully, piece-by-piece through the stored information elements that interest him or her.

In such environment, searching can be simple, but voluminous.

Searches should be made not only in one node but, most likely, in many network nodes.

Under these conditions manual operations are not feasible, and classical programming provides no results.

However, if *meaning* rather than *name* is sought, and the search is executed in parallel, then the procedure is effective, although filtering can be very complex.

In connection to large databases, both searching and filtering by semantic means are necessary to keep track of the information explosion and still obtain meaningful references. This must be done while the information elements not only are online but are steadily changing as well.

Searching for and filtering specific multimedia information may require massive amounts of work that simply cannot be done serially. Moreover, as stated earlier, neither can classical programming be of help. It is necessary to use artificial intelligent artifacts that operate in parallel, along the lines of a distributed deductive databases. Knowbots would do:

- Effective network-wide *node searchers*;
- *Database mining*, in a local or global sense;
- *Sorting and merging* of multimedia distributed information elements;
- *Filtering* of massive amounts of information, such as market data feeds; and
- *Analyzing* of contents and interactively on reporting the outcome.

As advanced by Vinton Cerf and Robert Kahn,[*] the idea of knowbots is that of having knowledge artifacts capable of visiting the nodes of a network in search for specific information or action upon it. The knowbot

- Communicates through messages with its master,
- Performs tasks such as rooting through databases, and
- Negotiates transfer terms for information elements.

Knowbots can work for people, for software, or for other knowbots, being programs that essentially cause actions to occur on another system component. They typically act through *teleportation*, moving themselves over the system.

This concept of intelligent artifacts fits within a Digital Library System (DLS) that offers a generalized approach capable, among other services, of providing users with a Personal Library System (PLS). A PLS is responsible for launching knowbots out to networked servers, to get the information the user needs.

The approach advanced by the research at the University of Michigan promotes a variety of utility servers supplementing the database servers; for example,

- An accounting server,

---

[*]Both have contributed to the Arpanet and to the Internet projects. Vinton Cerf has also been a major contributor to the Open Document Architecture (ODA) of the International Standards Organizations (ISO).

- A statistics server,
- An input/output server, and
- A registration server.

Apart from the generalized network-oriented DLS functions, know-bots can be applications-dependent intelligent constructs capable of providing links through a distributed environment. The PLS contents can be dynamic and may include personal documents, copies of frequently consulted references, and/or a cache of recently accessed multimedia information.

Knowledge artifacts are being promoted as capable of communicating using network protocols. They can move between heterogeneous environments, docking into a port of another system that provides a knowbot-operating landscape able to give each artifact the resources it needs.

When a knowbot moves to a different system, it may bring work documents along with it.

These documents might contain results, search criteria, format templates, and so forth.

Knowbot information may also be multimedia messages and/or other intelligent constructs.

In the sense described in the foregoing examples, the best way to think of knowbots is as *active objects*. Some, but not necessarily all, have a courier service. At times, the courier may be passive, equivalent to a read-me file, or it may help to perform a function the object supports.

The real challenge in proceeding in this way does not lie in software, because we know how to develop knowledge-engineering artifacts. The challenge lies in the proper study of operational characteristics that should, in principle, be broad in scope but focused for each user, in a PLS sense.

The proper study of the development and implementation of knowbots would have to exploit the semantic content of multimedia knowledge, as well as of information sources, in two senses:

1. The more generalized Digital Library System
2. The better focused Personal Library System

This dual approach can help in the exploitation of complex graphics-based applications, as well as in the personalization of network services. Knowledge engineering is vital because even extended relational solutions cannot answer sprawling semantic requirements. The best approach is object oriented, with artificial intelligence support.

15–6 USING KNOWBOTS IN CONNECTION WITH AN INTELLIGENT NETWORK

Studies done by Citibank help to prove that an intelligent network can be instrumental in database integration. It is possible to make a heterogeneous system work by taking vertical applications with different customer identifications and/or semantics, and normalize them.

This approach makes sense, and the priority given to this concept in terms of implementation is well placed. Customer service must be the topmost priority. In one specific project, Citibank projected the institution of a new customer code fairly similar to SWIFT numbers, but with associated standards for classification. Enriched with knowledge engineering, these will permit development and interactive exploitation of *customer reference trees*.

The normalization of keys for cross–database search of customer accounts is part of the work currently done on restructuring customer identification. The challenge was described as being:

- Partly organizational, and
- Partly technical.

Of the two, the organizational problem is by far the more difficult to solve. The goal is to take the customer ID, with its synonyms and homonyms, put it into the online directory services, and then develop standard names, process and information elements to best assist in customer account management and relationship banking.

Although restructuring information elements in a global database sense may seem to be the preferable alternative, senior Citibank technologists suggest that there are good reasons to believe that a large organization may not be in a position to:

- Fully restructure its databases, and
- Standardize information elements running into terabytes.

Therefore, it may be wiser to work along the line of *knowledge robots*, building rules and relationships about customer identification and classification, and leaving to artificial intelligence artifacts the mission of performing the integrative job by customer account.

The basis of this is the development and implementation of a dynamic *knowledge tree* equipped with appropriate artifacts that permit their user to:

1. Flash out knowledge embedded in account information;
2. Identify the semantics of customer relationships;

3. Elaborate the syntax of a distributed database; and

4. Proceed with dynamic indexing capabilities in a network-wide sense.

The underlying idea comes from the research project on intelligent networks by the University of Michigan—the *knowbots* we reviewed in the preceding section. Put into practical implementation, the concept is that of encoding a knowledge network letting the artifacts find out information within database resources residing in the nodes.

Such a concept can be of significant assistance to database mining, which is high on the agenda of most leading financial institutions and other organizations. "We would like to discover knowledge relationships in our databases," stated Colin Crook, Chairman of Citibank's Corporate Technology Committee. Solutions relative to the construction of knowbots involve:

- Machine learning,
- Inductive logic,
- Fuzzy engineering,
- Neural nets, and
- Generic algorithms.

The design of such artifacts can range from simple to very complex. The exploitation of the most sophisticated database-mining models requires massively parallel computers for rapid response time and deep search.

For example, one of the applications foremost in the agenda of banks is automation of *individual customer relations* activities and *mapping of their patterns*. Each customer has a unique pattern; however, this is lost in the mass of information, snowed under by large volumes of data, and unavailable through simple searches. In contrast, high technology makes it possible to:

1. Critically analyze through knowledge constructs a customer relationship, its strengths and weaknesses;

2. Know in a factual and documented manner how to work best with the customer for mutual advantage; and

3. Almost to replicate the times of the small local bank, when the banker knew the customers personally.

This is akin to database-oriented marketing studies but applied to profiles with ad hoc evaluations criteria, such as trends, cross-selling, credit risk, account integration, and customer profitability.

An intelligent database approach, Citibank suggests, can use decision trees to analyze whether a given customer relationship is in the proper area of criteria established by management; for example, in terms of:

- Risk
- Fees
- Volume of business

Fuzzy engineering can help to analyze the synergy of different factors further, rather than to examine only one value at a time. It is also possible to use clustering, experimental design, and statistical decision trees in connection with regression tree analysis, rather than a simple straight regression procedure, which gives limited results.

Furthermore, recent work has helped to demonstrate that the exploitation of an intelligent network concept permits the user organization to introduce a set of value-added services, such as:

- Greater security
- Seamless database access
- Intelligent dictionary/directory

In regard to directory services, Citibank coordinates its activities with Bellcore's project ORCA, exploring ways and means a large corporation can utilize to its advantage the existing directory infrastructure, which has been established and is maintained by a telephone company.

15–7 CONCEPTS AND APPLICATIONS IN VIRTUAL REALITY

Virtual reality (VR) is the next generation in man–machine communication, currently being evaluated in terms of prototypes in different implementation areas as well as in real-life applications. These areas include power engineering, construction work, motor vehicles, aerospace, weapons systems, medicine, and finance. The process involves real-time execution, with a conversational mode addressing data capture, computation, and visualization necessary to present a multimedia continuity for the human perception.

From the point of view of a real-life practical implementation, the goal of virtual reality is to induce a real-world sensation. This impacts both on the application developer and on the user. The process:

- Involves visual, audio, tactile, and other senses for input/output;
- Employs realistic backgrounds and animation;

- Meticulously reproduces in a realistic manner immediate surroundings; and
- Often employs parallel processing to meet real-time demands.

Application examples include deployment of weapons systems, aircraft cockpit simulation, and automobile driving simulation. Other examples are molecular structures, fluid flows, and vehicular body contour design.

Portfolio management involving equities, debt, real estate, and other assets denominated in different currencies and traded in different markets, offers a good ground for practical VR implementation. Financial flows can be represented by market activity and the resulting patterns can be seen in a man–machine conversational mode.

In fact, during 1993, my research in America, England, Continental Europe, and Japan identified a significant number of imaginative and practical virtual reality applications. These constitute a whole book and therefore cannot be described comprehensively in a few lines—but they do convey the message that VR has practical applications well beyond the entertainment business.

Virtual reality involves *rendering*—that is, direct display of physical phenomena whose characteristics may, or may not, have an obvious visual representation. Therefore, it is not absolutely necessary that animation be used. Virtual reality applications can be:

- Immersive, or
- Nonimmersive.

Immersion allows a direct, dynamic, and intuitive manipulation of objects, through gestures and human body movement. It generates a direct and intuitive feedback, regarded as a significant step in advanced man–machine communication. But it also requires special gear such as head-mounted display and data glove, which have not yet been perfected and can be cumbersome in certain environments.

Nonimmersive solutions are almost as realistic, but do not need the aforementioned equipment. In fact, they can be seen as a reasonable extension of 3-D color graphics which have by now established themselves well enough in business and industry—after the long developmental process discussed in Chapter 14.

Whether immersive or nonimmersive, one of the characteristics of virtual reality representation is that what the user sees can be composed of an infinite number of spectra, frequencies, and textures.

- Typically in everyday work human senses perceive some of these and simply ignore others.

- By bettering the sensitivity threshold, computer-generated VR allows its users to represent things with greater accuracy or even create entirely new worlds.

By the end of this decade, advanced software that lets a user interact with the computer-generated virtual environment will most likely form the heart of any system. The concept is simple: The reality engine takes a stored set of objects and landscapes and manipulates them, such manipulation being interactive and user directed within a virtual world.

15–8 VIRTUAL WORLD AND TELEPRESENCE

A *virtual world* has its origin in two related fields—*simulation* and *instrument monitoring*. The key element is a man–machine interface that can be implemented through such different devices as DataGloves, EyePhone, DataSuits, and so forth.

Virtual worlds typically are immersive and shared digital environments. Ongoing research investigates problems that occur in such a wide variety of applications as walkthroughs in buildings or other settings.

Through virtual world technology, the feeling of actually being in the setting can be enhanced.

Design may not only be watched but also felt by feedback, as in the case of ergonomic issues and in layout studies.

An article in *Business Week* (September 28, 1992) on the work done by the advanced research laboratories of Hitachi predicted that before the end of this decade, *virtual reality* technology will be widely used. This will allow users on a network to meet and interact in computer-simulated environments.

Within a virtual reality setting, cooperative work can be performed by means of concurrent engineering. Groups of people can participate in the same virtual world without being in the same physical location. The implementation of this concept leads to *telepresence* in shared virtual world environments.

Telepresence is a virtual reality term that refers to the remote participation in an activity, from a meeting to the manipulation of single machines or more complex systems. Fujita, a major Japanese construction company, built a system that permits an operator to direct earth-moving equipment remotely.

- The operator views the work site on a computer screen, then employs controls that signal the robot to do a specific job.
- With VR, the image is so painstakingly exact that the human makes no mistakes in directing the operation.

Telepresence in shared virtual worlds can be seen as a sophisticated extension of teleconferencing, which has proved useful in bringing together people in different geographical locations. In its fundamentals, telepresence is based on shared virtual worlds by means of applying techniques to assemble participants from different sites to the same virtual environment.

Participants to a telepresence meeting can experience a feeling of interacting with each other within the virtual environment. The concept gives the user a sense of being there. For example, every participant in a telepresence session may be represented within the virtual world by a 3-D model allowing a stronger experience.

As opposed to teleconferencing, this could permit better visual interaction between participants.

Even simple mappings can cause a realistic impression, whereas video effects equipment can handle signals and complex objects in real time.

Within a given virtual world, telepresence can be established by a medium through which people can physically experience virtual places, which typically are remote. However, telepresence has a subjective quality: sensory factors are crucial, and there is also an issue of device sophistication (hardware and/or software) that affects the outcome.

Technical issues of device quality have an impact on the user's ability to compensate for the lack of physical presence and to make abstractions from the information passed on through various sensors. This issue is valid all the way from display devices to consistency and coherency in the information received via different channels.

In a technical sense, a virtual world setting typically consists of a *model server* from which participants can select the classes and instances (objects) of the virtual world(s) in which they want to participate. After the connection to a chosen virtual world is established:

Information about objects and participants is downloaded to a local workstation.

The selected model is fed into the model server for processing.

Information about changes in the position and viewpoint or movement of objects is distributed in real time to all participants in the shared session. The degree of reality in such a system can vary, depending on the software and hardware provided at a given location.

Participants, for example, can be represented by colored 3-D objects if the processing bandwidth of the hardware allows sufficient speed for rendering and if the setting permits the use of live video. Refinements may include mapping of eye movements, generation of facial movements, and so forth.

A diversity of different kinds of models of participants might exist, with some of them having more sophisticated virtual world representations than others.

However, the movement of entities (people and other objects) in the virtual world must be synchronized to ensure that everyone gets the same information.

There are different types of synchronizations that are essential, such as regular time-based media (in the case of video and sound) and aperiodic events. Therefore, synchronization mechanisms must be provided at the various locations to support basic functionality.

Vital to establishing a sense of presence are motor factors. In a virtual world setting, we try to achieve a wide range of sensor interaction and versatility in sensory movements.

Objects in the virtual world can be sensitive to all participants and all events.

Some actions, however, may depend on the timeliness of communication or other criteria.

As a design principle, processing tasks should be distributed as much as possible to reduce time lag. Movements of entities should be echoed immediately at each site, permitting the necessary feedback in the virtual world. Consistency problems also must be treated in a distributed system sense and, evidently, concurrency control must be provided.

16

Object Orientation, Hypermedia, and Semantic Modeling

16–1 INTRODUCTION

The main goal of the Integrated Office Information System (IOIS) project at the University of Arizona has been to develop an environment where diverse office information solutions containing data and knowledge can be integrated. By allowing access through a common interface, IOIS aims to improve office productivity.

A requirements analysis was done back in 1989 to establish properly IOIS implementation perspectives. It was based on a case study of the IOIS funding agency. The oultined knowledgebank requirements included:

- Procedures,
- Policies,
- Organizational structures, and
- Other knowledge pertinent to the office.

The requirements analysis found that this knowledge is characterized by a high rule-to-fact ratio. In other terms, most facts are highly interrelated and their interconnection has been mapped into the project.

From the outset, IOIS's intention has been to use a knowledgebank structure to support sophisticated queries and complex transactions beyond what is feasible with conventional database management systems. Among the goals has been effective navigation and integrity maintenance.

It was postulated, for instance, that the knowledgebank should be able to identify appropriate forms and procedures for a particular office action, such as a purchase order. Part of this effort has been aimed toward knowledge modeling with object-oriented properties, in a way permitting the capture of knowledge and information semantics.

The IOIS project looked into formalism for describing semantic databases. Other, similar research projects applied the object paradigm to multimedia design to develop enhanced search facilities through an object-oriented, knowledge-enriched architecture.

In the majority of these cases, solutions to the multimedia challenge address the capture, storage, retrieval, presentation, and manipulation of information in a hybrid environment which typically integrates data processing and knowledge engineering. The concepts guiding the implementation of multimedia solutions include:

- Callable entities
- Classes and subclasses
- Generalization hierarchies
- Attribute inheritance
- Metaknowledge capabilities

Among research findings has been the fact that multimedia approaches call for the implementation of a higher level database model enabling the designer, as well as the enduser, to incorporate a rich array of semantics into the database schema. Other research findings point to the fact that the current wave of digitization and compound electronic document implementation are not only complementary but also reinforce one another, making the development of more powerful solutions quite urgent, hence the interest in object-type implementation.

Multimedia is a domain where solutions have to be rich in semantics, reflecting descriptive and structural formalisms connected to data, text, graphics, image, and voice. Semantics should serve in applications modeling, leading to capturing and expressing the structure of the real-world environment to be mapped into the multimedia database.

16–2 OBJECT-ORIENTED MULTIMEDIA DATABASES

Multimedia communications are indivisible from the notion of distributed multimedia databases, while the latter depend on the former for their existence. One of the factors promoting multimedia databases is the development of software technologies emphasizing visualization, which has been advanced in response to management demands for improving mental productivity at enduser level.

Effective multimedia solutions have both prerequisites and aftermaths. The principal references in terms of prerequisites are shown in the six-layered structure of Figure 16.1. The characteristics of the top layer are user visibility and ad hoc queries, the latter supported through fuzzy engineering. This is needed to handle the increasing range of online man–machine communications which is involving a fair amount of vagueness and uncertainty.

The examples presented in Chapter 15 help us appreciate that the kernel of the multimedia database is best modeled as a collection of objects and interobject mappings, used to associate *multimedia objects* among themselves. This requires a significant amount of organizational work, which constitutes the second top-down layer in Figure 16.1 oriented towards system development. Such work should include:

- Normalization,
- Classification,
- Indentification, and
- Formatting.

Therefore, this second layer makes reference to organizational and procedural objects, representing entities that are executable (operations, meth-

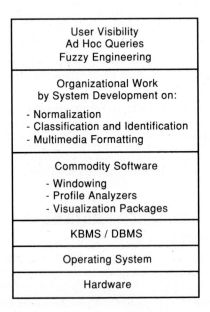

Figure 16.1   Answering requirements for multimedia solutions.

ods). Operations and methods are related to each other through the mapping of objects. At the present day, however, the latter are not treated in a uniform manner.

The reference to normalization and multimedia formatting is valid regarding communication protocols, semantic models, and programming languages as well. Within this perspective, kernel operations may be embedded into the primitives of a knowledge-based programming structure. High-level object-oriented data communications and database applications can be written in this language.

The host language must support data types such as objects, classes, signatures, and set operations. Variables can then be declared to be of these types with the kernel model consisting of objects in the distributed database.

As experience with multimedia-oriented solutions accumulates, the possibility should be kept open for addition of innovative features such as support of *object evolution*. This may concern changes to the fundamental semantics of objects, which can be essential in a database system in order to assure that its contents present a correct, accurate, and useful model of the application environment.

Another evolutionary reference is that the handling of multimedia documents requires polyvalent inference mechanisms associated with the different text/data types. A framework of plausible inference should allow us to interpret and combine the probabilities arising from various comparisons, with *uncertainty management* characterizing query and search. This will concern:

- Type of document
- Logical structure and contents
- Retrieval criteria

The retrieval process should be regarded as a form of *plausible inference*, the plausibility being quantified by some form of probability or possibility measure. On this concept is based ISO's Office Document Architecture (ISO/ODA).

A critical issue is that of assuring that multimedia operations can be added and dynamically modified. This is not necessarily supported by commodity software available today, yet for lack of better alternatives Figure 16.1 suggests such routines as windowing, rule-based expert systems for profile analysis, and packages of the word processing, graphics handling, and similar types.

Top to bottom, in Figure 16.1 the third layer emphasizes analysis and visualization, making reference to commodity software. Expert systems can play an instrumental role, particularly in the case of engineering databases and office management approaches which both impact and are influenced by multimedia solutions.

Looking at layer 4 of Figure 16.1, we should appreciate the contribution of the knowledgebank management system (KBMS) (as defined in Chapters 11 and 12) which determines the role each media can play in the database. This focuses the discussion on intelligence embedded into the fine tissue of the multimedia aggregate.

Within this fourth top-down layer, the KBMS constitutes the meta-level of the now classical DBMS. Let us repeat in a nutshell the concept of intentional and extensional functions as well as the roles of KBMS and DBMS discussed in Part Two:

> The KBMS looks after *intentional* activities, and functions on the basis rules in the knowledgebank.
>
> The DBMS handles the *extensional* information elements and needs KBMS assistance to address object-oriented multimedia IE.

As we have seen on many occasions, the contribution of a KBMS is fundamental because all DBMS presently available, including the most advanced relational types, have been designed to handle data—not multimedia. An exception to this statement is the object-oriented DBMS.

The effective handling of multimedia approaches needs a considerable amount of machine intelligence. In this connection, the role of a KBMS is better appreciated if we keep in mind that compound electronic documents are decomposable into more elementary units of information, more precisely objects described by:

- Characteristic attributes which they have
- Relationships they establish among themselves
- Mapping into queries and semantics which can be ad hoc and ephemeral

No DBMS commercially available at the present time is able to handle such a complex, temporal environment. This job is not doable without knowledge engineering, though part of it is approximated through the new breed of object-oriented DBMS.

At the KBMS/DBMS level, the kernel must provide integrity control. It must also make it possible to create meaningful relationships as well as a built-in mechanism for object classification. Such prerequisites should be understood by the system designer as well and they should be architectured into the system.

16–3 ARE THERE STANDARDS FOR DOCUMENT EXCHANGE?

The evolving concepts in connection to multimedia document standards are applicable both for communications purposes and for databasing. Norms that are in the making help describe a range of document artifacts which are permitted, as well as the relationships between *logical* and *layout* views of a document.

However, while different efforts are in process, solid document standards are not yet ready. Emerging norms like the Electronic Document Interchange (EDI) have many versions that are not necessarily compatible among themselves. What is more, means for assuring that the evolving standards will be enforced are still lacking, while a significant number of issues have not yet been settled in a normalization sense.

There are as well pseudo-standards in what regards multimedia sense. X.400, the ISO standard,[*] addresses itself primarily to data, not to multimedia documents. The same is true of IBM's DIA/DCA as well as of MAP by General Motors, TOP by Boeing, and, to a large measure, GOSIP by the U.S. Federal Government. Besides this, none of these approaches to normalization was made with object orientation in mind.

Electronic document interchange and EDIFACT[†] do address document structure but they are not true multimedia solutions either, nor has there been any serious effort to introduce object-based logic into them. And although EDI and its clones are seen by many as a closely related field to electronic funds transfer (EFT), so far there has not been a known object-oriented solution of EFT worthy of discussion.

This failure to develop a well-coordinated effort that can answer transmission, databasing, and query requirements for compound electronic documents is both surprising and distressing. This is particularly true as this domain is indeed one where:

- High technology can provide solutions rich in semantics, reflecting descriptive and structural formalisms connected to data, text, graphics, image, and voice.

These solutions should serve in applications modeling, leading to capturing and expressing the structure of the real-world environment to be mapped into multimedia databases.

---

[*]Designed for the applications layer of ISO's Open System interconnection (ISO/OSI). Not only X.400 is data oriented but the same is true as well of X.25, the packet switching protocol of CCITT. Neither is therefore fit for handling multimedia bit streams.

[†]EDIFACT stands for EDI Administration, Commerce, and Transport, developed under the auspices of the United Nations.

But contrary to what a rational systems approach would suggest, what exists today is a fair amount of incompatibility and inconsistency among the different efforts directed to protocol normalization, each being promoted as *the* standard. For instance, in regard to EDI,

> The X.12 protocol by the American National Standards Institute (ANSI) is used in North America, where nearly 10,000 companies employ it—an estimated 60 percent of the world's total in an implementation sense.

> By contrast, in Europe with more than 3000 estimated users, EDI-FACT seems to be nearer to becoming the norm—but companies also use X.12 for dealing with U.S. customers and suppliers, as well as different other EDI dialects.

All that does not make much sense in terms of universal document exchange, and this is felt not just in transmission but also in document processing, databasing, and retrieval.

At the same time, internal developments by different companies are still wanting, as most user organizations do not like to spend money on setting up an EDI department. They see that it is easier to handle transactions via a third party, whose core business is operating networks—and the third parties, like GEIS, have their own parochial EDI version.

In conclusion, due to the lack of generally accepted standards, whether we talk of networking, databasing, or taught a number of leading corporations that multivendor and multimedia communications would not be feasible without the use of the artificial intelligence constructs. An example is the handling of SWIFT messages, as practiced by leading financial institutions.[*]

16—4 OPTICAL INPUT AND ADVANCED SOLUTIONS

Long a bottleneck in data processing, and a very costly one for that matter, the punched card image of input (as well as of storage on magnetic disks) and the printed tabular data type of output are today strangling the company. They make *virtual office* solutions impossible and ensure that return on technology investments is limited.

Cognizant people in information technology suggest that, by all evidence, the fact that databases are still operated according to the image

---

[*]See also D.N. Chorafas and H. Steinmann, *Expert Systems in Banking*, Macmillan, London, 1991.

of punched cards permits the use of only 5 percent of available storage capacity—while the cost reflects 100 percent capacity. At the same time, the paper jungle continues to thrive because there is plenty of information stored on paper which cannot be put on magnetic disks. Yet,

- Probably nowhere are the old concepts of input, storage, and output more destructive than at the input/output ends.
- Legacy solutions are not just inefficient but also unacceptable in a world where through networked workstations the enduser now is at the frontline of information technology.

A dozen years or so ago, among leading-edge companies, data input and data access tools started to change, particularly in connection with enduser query and reporting. Examples are the point-and-click query, query by natural language interface, and applications integration among different desktop and office products to simplify input/output requirements.

Among the options presented to the user community have been terminal emulation, GUI screens, GUI frontends, and other enabling means.

However, while they have now entered daily practice and they are still necessary, these approaches are no longer enough.

New and much more efficient multimedia solutions are needed to redefine and revamp the whole process of computer input and output, which, in the majority of cases is still rather archaic. As such, it represents a situation full of errors, delays, and high cost. Fax-based optical information entry and processing is an example of an imaginative new departure.

Citibank Tokyo has developed an application that captures trade information using the optical processors built into standard facsimile machines. Trade data are captured through optical character recognition (OCR). Then, they are matched automatically with broker confirmations using a special comparison algorithm.

This solution, Citibank says, has been found to be a cost-effective way to implement trade processing.

The use of OCR for data entry and *auto-matching* significantly expedites trade execution.

The concept is interesting and holds good potential, while the required gear is not expensive. This innovative application uses PCs runnung DOS and Windows, Fax Grabber software, Intel's SatisFAXtion, Turbo C, Network Lite, and PC-Vax connectivity.

Multitasking is a key technology employed for this implementation. The source messages arrive continuously and the captured information must be processed by other applications as well. Therefore, the developers plan to incorporate into the imaging system a new software product: Windows for Workgroup. This enables *preemptive multitasking* permitting file sharing between the tasks of fax-capturing, OCR, and comparison matching.

Fairly close-coupled to the issue of the renewal of input chores is the use of optical solutions (photonics) for the storage of multimedia information elements. Since the late 1980s, leading-edge organizations have seen to it that *imaging* has become an increasingly important technology.

By enabling the conversion of physical documents into electronic form, imaging helps to reduce operating costs through greater efficiency. It permits the handling of compound electronic documents, makes retrieval much more comprehensive, and also

- Shrinks the company's storage needs in a significant way, and
- Enhances service quality by providing better accessibility to information.

Leading financial institutions, for example, have implemented imaging systems for a diverse group of banking activities, ranging from signature verification to trade processing. Management says that advanced imaging technologies are an opportunity to upgrade front desk and back office operations in a cost-effective manner that is also compatible with the longer term strategic direction in information technology investments.

16–5 A NEED FOR KNOWLEDGE-ENRICHED SOFTWARE

The problem is not only selection of appropriate software, hardware, and integration approaches, but also effective implementation. Although some of the necessary pieces for interconnecting networks and databases are in place, the knowledge-enriched software needed to solve problems associated with islands of automation does not yet exist and cannot exist without knowledge engineering.

Whether in the factory or in the office, an integrative approach to automation requires a tremendous amount of communications and databasing, as well as the creation and maintenance of large interactive systems focusing on:

- Clients,
- Suppliers,
- Equipment,
- Products,
- Prices, and
- Labor.

Every one of these entities can be handled in an object-oriented manner, facing the increasing demand for multimedia capabilities. With the sophistication of information technology steadily expanding, the number of cooperative functions becomes larger while:

- The functions themselves are distributed,
- New implementations are more demanding,
- The information structures are complex, and
- Processing must be adaptable to developing situations.

Thus more powerful mechanisms are necessary to design and implement the required systems, with multimedia and object-based approaches having a key role to play in this regard.

Figure 16.2 presents an example from a financial applications environment, based on the concept of *equity balance*. Eight classes of objects are identified, each of them requiring both information elements and rules in order to be handled in an able manner.

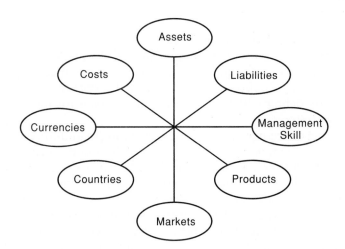

Figure 16.2   An object orientation in costing equity balance.

In past years, these information elements would have been mainly numeric, representing values—hence data. But in reality this was only a simplification, as in the real world each object class has the following items associated with it:

- Text in the form of rules and explanations
- Graphics presenting trends and tendencies
- Associated voice messages in some cases

This makes the financial application in reference a de facto multimedia environment, posing prerequisites to its integrative handling. No wonder, therefore, that American financial institutions are closely watching the results of a hyperdocument database project by the Defense Department's ARPA (Advanced Research Projects Agency). They foresee a hyperdocument impact in several implementation fields in banking, including marketing, where video images can be stored in the database, integrated with audio, text, graphics, and data, and managed in an object-oriented manner.

As this example suggests, document handling automation is a systems integration problem, where the most important aspect in putting the pieces together is finding the correct multimedia interconnect capability.

Interconnection is vital not only for the existing system functionality but also for that to be implemented in the future.

Today, an estimated 70 percent of important managerial and office work function is still not automated—and Japanese experts say it cannot be automated without knowledge engineering.

Closely connected to this reference is the issue of document modeling of which we spoke at the beginning of this section. It is a subject rooted in a pragmatic approach to document management, the use of data dictionaries, and the normalization of formats—as well as the broader examination of business modeling which should provide the basis for more intelligent information systems.

Speaking of prerequisites to the able handling of multimedia problems, in Chapter 15 reference has been made to the importance of *processing bandwidth*. We have seen how it can be enacted in a cost-effective way through the able use of high-performance computing and networked workstations.

There is also the need for *database bandwidth* that is able to handle the large volume of bit streams necessary for oncoming storage requirements—from vectorized raster images, to other graphics, text, data, and voice objects. In the not too distant future, terabytes will become the unit of measurement in database size. Eventually this, too, will be too narrow a bandwidth.

16—6 SERVICE PROVIDED BY HYPERMEDIA

Hypermedia is a flexible and effective approach to information management, permitting navigation in databases and posing bandwidth requirements. The basic principle is that entities are stored in a network of nodes connected by links. Such nodes can contain multimedia information meant to be viewed and manipulated *interactively*.

Hypertext solutions are a subset of hypermedia. They involve issues, systems, and applications mainly connected to text. Among the basic concepts are cognitive aspects of using and designing the primitives of hypertext systems, including:

- Means for supporting collaborative work,
- The management of complexity in large information networks, and
- Strategies for effective use of browsing.

Other issues are connected with copyrights and royalties. There are also social implications largely dependent on the specific use that is made of the system.

The facilities that hypertext and hypermedia provide come from the fact that the supported mechanism has intelligence embedded into it. This is as important with text as when we are combining information from various sources (text, data, graphics, audio, and video), in a nonsequential manner. Such information elements may lie in incompatible supports but must be presented coherently and in unison.

Typically, items on the display screen are associated with IE in a database, and they are linked to other related items. There is a direct analogy from printed literature, in which authors try to add nonsequentiality to their written works, this being done via "*see also*" footnotes, endnotes, bibliographic references, sidebars, and so on.

Hypermedia information typically consists of conventional text, data, and graphics, but is partitioned into discrete blocks or nodes. Generally,

- The first displayed document is in text form.
- Words and phrases are highlighted to indicate that more information is available related to them.

After obtaining information about a specific topic, the user may want to see connected topics. Automatic selection may, for instance, result in an access of information stored on videodisk. Subsequently, the user's reference is returned to the menu from which the selection was made and the search can continue.

In principle, a hypermedia system displays any type of information elements stored in accessible databases (e.g., graphic documents). Depending on requirements that develop interactively, a user can retrieve additional information pertaining to, say, a graphic display by simply choosing them with the mouse from a pull-down menu or from icons.[*]

Links between items of information are, by and large, transparent to the user, even for links that connect the enduser to remote databases. The only indication of the involvement of a remote database is a textual screen which displays the name of the database and, perhaps, special instructions.

In most common implementations of hypermedia, link sources are individual text items or icons.

Link destinations are nodes, and must be explored, as we will see in Section 16-6.

Some systems allow link sources or destinations to be blocks of text within a node.

Other systems do not allow links to be embedded within text, which is an inadequate approach for many applications.

Links provide an efficient and easy way to follow references between source and destination. They are usually forward directed, although it is possible to support going backwards along the link. Given such polyvalence in approach, it is always wise to examine in advance the capabilities of a proposed hypermedia solution.

In general, a hypermedia system provides a number of different link types in order to be flexible and agile in responding to evolving user requirements.

One type of link can be employed to connect the source with comments or annotations.

Another link may be used for cross-reference purposes.

Still another link can be used to place attribute/value pairs on links and query the network for them.

One of the useful features is to have procedural attachments to links so that traversing a link also performs some side functions, for instance, customizing the appearance of the destination node or running associated functionality making a hypermedia solution object-oriented.

---

[*]See also Chapter 14 on the GUI example.

Both actual practice and experiments have shown that people can retrieve information more accurately and more quickly with a hypermedia system than with conventional menu approaches, or, for that matter, with query languages such as SQL.

Query languages require more user training in language syntax than do hypermedia solutions, and they have limited application to nontextual material.

In contrast, footnotes, endnotes, and references can be modeled as automatic links in a hypermedia approach and graphics add considerable user-friendliness.

Through the latter solution, the user is able to follow the links by simply clicking the mouse. He or she does not have to flip pages, search for the endnote, or go to a library to find referenced documents. Neither does he or she need to learn the complex syntax of a programming language.

Figure 16.3 gives a bird's-eye view of the use of hypertext facilities by an author and casual user. Both address the same functions shown in the block diagram, but the means put at the disposition of an experienced author can be more sophisticated and he or she can be expected to contribute to database creation and maintenance.

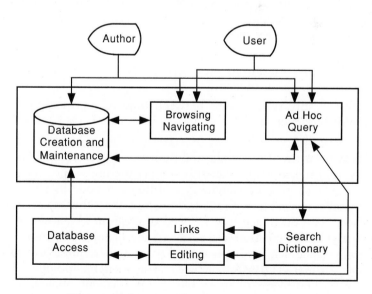

Figure 16.3   Using the facilities of hypertext.

16–7 CONCEPT OF NODES AND BROWSERS

Important in a hypermedia implementation sense is the concept of *node* size. In some hypermedia solutions, the node size is at the discretion of the author who can express an idea in as many words as seems appropriate. Typically, the author is using a single node to optimize the organization of information.

One of the constraints of this approach is that endusers do not think in terms of screenfulls, but of ideas and facts. This imposes a cognitive overhead on the author and/or user, who must try to partition their thoughts at screen-size level. Other factors that affect the optimal node length are:

- The nature of the task,
- Session duration, and
- Experience of the enduser.

When the node can exceed the size of the screen, some scrolling mechanism is necessary. This is not difficult to use since many users have scrolling experience from other, simpler database search systems and can employ it profitably with hypertext.

In the sense of any practical applications, the interconnected network of nodes in hypertext is a semantic network. The structure of a typical hyperdocument is similar to the semantic network scheme and can be used for representing knowledge. The semantic network is a collection of objects, expressed through nodes and links

Nodes represent objects and descriptors which provide additional information about objects.

Links identify relationships between objects, representing semantic interdependencies.

Apart from the use of links and nodes, a hypermedia solution must have ways and means of permanently storing the user's networks. We can implement nodes in a file system by storing each node in a file, making it individually accessible without locking out the other nodes from the other users. The drawback is that speed of creation and access is limited by the speed of file creation and access in the operating system.

Performance can be improved by using the facilities of a relational or an object-oriented DBMS. Database management technology is designed to address the problems of using files for permanent objects subject to concurrency control and query handling. These are commonly included in commercially available packages, although hierarchical, Codasyl, and relational DBMS do not address multimedia.

The drawback with a relational solution is that it does not necessarily provide a natural fit with the networking structure of hypertext. Therefore, commodity software follows a more efficient approach by incorporating a hypertext-specific editor.

In the latter case, links are introduced later to connect the newly created node with another node. By creating, editing, and deleting nodes and links, users can construct various database structures. In an object environment, hierarchical structures are ephemeral and can be dropped after the query has run its course.

What the latter reference technically means is that object-oriented solutions can be instrumental in automatic retrieval by navigation. This sort of approach is considered to be the primary means for accessing information in hyperdocuments. The user:

Moves through the structure by following links from node to node, and

Decides at each step which link(s) to traverse next, based on the information localized in, say, link icons as well as in the nodes displayed on the screen.

The whole process reflects browsing and *browsers* are among the most important navigation tools. As the application grows more complex, it becomes easy for a user to get disoriented. A browser helps to determine position in the hypermedia network by means of a visual presentation.

But although it is necessary, navigational access by itself is not sufficient. On applications characterized by large, unfamiliar, and heterogeneously structured networks, users tend to get lost while looking for some target information, hence the needed for knowledge-enriched guidance.

The more sophisticated hypermedia systems support a content search mechanism that permits the examination of hyperdocuments or other information elements for a match to a given query. The better part of this reference is the ability of a query mechanism to search for substructures or patterns in the network.

A different way of making this statement is that efficient query-based access mechanisms are needed to complement navigational access in large hypermedia databases, making feasible:

Free-text information retrieval, for which good methods have now been developed, and

Complex query operations performed in conventional database systems but enriched with AI capabilities.

One of the query-based approaches is structure search for hyperdocuments. The idea is to examine the hypermedia network for subnetworks that match a given *pattern*. A content search combined with a structure search can provide a first class filtering mechanism for the information that the user seeks.

All of this suggests that a major part of the effort in hypertext implementation should be directed at improving interaction between users and databases. Solutions should offer agile, friendly interfaces, enabling rapid and convenient access to large volumes of information.

Attention should be paid to the design and implementation of such interfaces. The optimal way of designing a user interface for hypertext is by:

Knowing how the enduser(s) seeks information in traditional database searches, and

Having an understanding of the basic cognitive processes that guide information searches.

Mechanisms for selection and feedback are critical to good design, and the use of common words and mnemonics should not be ignored. Grammatical variants of a word may need to be handled as equivalent, but synonyms and homonyms must be sorted out.[*] Compound terms need to be treated as a unit, and words of the same or similar meaning should be approached through data dictionaries.

These references constitute a simple form of natural language analysis, essential for effective information retrieval from multimedia databases. A similar statement can be made regarding the need for associative access and the incorporation of knowledge engineering supports.

16–8 A GROWING REQUIREMENT FOR SEMANTIC MODELING

We said that a hypermedia document is a collection of nodes interconnected by links. The nodes contain objects. The links assure direct connection between specific source and destination nodes, or are interactively instantiated at user request.

This functionality is very important with ad hoc queries, whose programmatic interfaces go beyond the structures that present-day database management and query systems handle. The required capabilities can be assisted through:

---

[*]See also the case study on Ciba-Geigy in Part One.

- *Semantic* data models, including entity-relationship, which can assure more flexible data structures, and
- *Object orientation* which helps provide facilities for storage, retrieval, and concurrency control.

Both are important in enabling the user interface to handle movements between concepts following runtime associations. We saw an example with informal browsing which permits the traversing of the database by following relationships from one object to another. This facilitates the task of the user in finding information, for instance, by browsing a class hierarchy or a version tree.

The first objective in the search for an effective solution tailored to user requirements is to close the semantic gap; the second is to support navigational aspects by traversing relationships. The third is to assure easier query access by selecting classes and their instantiation.

Closing the semantic gap is fundamental in browsing, as we often rely on exploratory searches when acquainting ourselves with a new artifact. However, not everything is to be found in semantics. Organizational perspectives may dominate and have to be expressed in a comprehensive form—that much the better if this form is rich in meaning.

Along that line of reference, each organizational entity may be mapped into an object form. The runtime instantiation of these objects can be handled as a logical expression for machine processing while the edges indicate relationships, such as annotations and references between nodes.

The complete hypermedia system must provide facilities for creating and editing nodes and links to form hypermedia documents, allowing any node to be connected to any other in a fairly complex network. A flexible interlinking of information elements can help provide exploratory browsing. This approach is useful as well for integrating unstructured or semi-structured information, and contributes towards the goal of reusable software.

But although achievements in hypermedia are significant, constraints and limitations exist. By and large, current connectivity offerings in hypertext and hypermedia:

1. Do not provide inference engines that automatically derive new information and enter it into the network.
2. Lack cross-database access capabilities, particularly so in a heterogeneous environment.
3. Are limited because the information and knowledge contained in a hypertext network is mainly entered by the user.

These limitations need to be eliminated from future offerings. By assuring both procedural and heuristics attachments as well as an AI-enriched inference mechanism, a hypermedia system may find much more rewarding implementation domains.

In conclusion, the advantages of hypermedia lie in the ability to organize information according to human cognition. Particularly important is the organization of memory as a semantic network in which concepts are linked together by associations or patterns. Such a solution permits the individual user to:

- Choose his or her own center of investigation and experience, and
- Determine how to move through the system as well as to determine the order of database mining operations to be done.

To widen their acceptance and their usefulness, multimedia solutions should be extensible and customizable. They should address internal functions of the database management system and cover performance as well as dynamic variations in requirements.

Knowledge engineering constructs should be employed to promote the concept of effective search in an intelligent distributed database. Browsing should answer ad hoc requirements supported through a multilingual environment under an open architecture.

It should also be feasible to customize and extend the kernel of the system, with users possibly adding application-specific database functions like image-join and voice-filtering. Knowledge-based constraints may as well need to be used to specify the integrity and checking procedures invoked with every system enhancement.

17

Multimedia and the Corporate Database

17-1 INTRODUCTION

A number of background factors have brought multimedia databases under scrutiny. Among them are user requirements that expand with the evolution in telecommunications—especially wideband optical communications (photonics)—but also expand because of applications reasons.

Another factor for the growing interest in multimedia databases is the increasing implementation of such storage devices as optical disks, supporting the new wave in office automation and document handling. A third lies in the fact that technology has an impact on graphics, text processing, facsimile transmission, and digitizers—providing the means for integration of bit streams.

As we have seen in Chapter 16, such integration has led toward compound electronic documents. It has also been instrumental in making us appreciate the fact that a multimedia implementation has characteristics that differ significantly from what we did for decades. Multimedia applications now feature:

1. Different types of objects
2. A rather large volume per object
3. Great variety in structure and representation
4. Sharing at the component (subobject) level

This definitely contrasts with, and even contradicts, the better known data-oriented, simple transaction handling and query environments that largely are characterized by:

- Relatively small object size,
- Rather standard structure and representation, and
- Sharing or nesting at whole-object level.

The evolving perspectives of multimedia implementation and their distinct requirements make it unfeasible, or at least unwise, to use approaches that we know from classical data processing and query handling. As the preceding two chapters have explained, object-based solutions are better fit for multimedia processing, but many more requirements must be met.

Semantic models and object-programming languages are necessary to integrate documents and their component parts for storage, retrieval, presentation, and exchange. The better conceived solutions are architecturally open-ended and extensible. They may be managed through relational principles at the base, but they require artificial intelligence constructs at the metalayer.

Reintegrating some of the basic notions we have seen in a user-oriented sense in the first chapters of Part Three, in this chapter we critically examine the notion of multimedia databases and what they mean to the organization employing them. In the following chapter, we extend this concept to cover the evolving aspects of text and image warehouses.

17–2 WHY SHOULD WE CARE ABOUT MULTIMEDIA DATABASES?

Multimedia application systems, such as electronic publishing, teleconferencing, visualization and visual simulation, have already become engrained in our professional practice. The same is true of multimedia storage on optical disks and multimedia transmission through optical fibers. There are, nevertheless, some issues connected to the design and implementation of multimedia databases and the applications using them.

What kind of model is suitable for storing multimedia information?
How can we best store and retrieve images and auditory information?
How much expense is reasonable for constructing a very large multimedia database?

To understand better the concept of multimedia databases, it is necessary to explain what the term *media* means in the database context. Like *data, media* is a singular noun. The Latin word *medium,*[*] has been widely

---

[*]There is also the Latin word *datum*. Both datum and medium have Greek origins. Respectively, δεδομενα and μεσα. In Latin, the plural forms of datum and medium are data and media. In information science, however, data and media are singular nouns.

used in the field of communications. However, this sense is not the same in database environments.

By definition, a multimedia database environment allows text, data, video, still image, dynamic image, and audio to become integral parts of database management—and this is a consequence of information retrieval. However, information retrieval and display take on new meaning when photorealistic images, charts, graphics, video, and audio can be added and played back directly from the database. This subject is still in its formative years, but with high definition television (HDTV) it will not take long to become complete.

Another subject now in its formative stage is how to use multimedia representation to communicate effectively the semantics and concepts that underline information elements and their aggregation. Contrary to hardware technology, where progress has been remarkable, conceptual and software developments are still lacking, and the same is true of new departures in database management.

> The ability to use audio and visual numeric values associated with other information in the database gives an entirely new meaning to databasing.

> The addition of multimedia semantics helps in terms of improved communications between databases and their users.

The reason for sophisticated solutions to multimedia databases is to satisfy the enduser and to achieve quality in information products and services. This is true from HDTV to enhanced semantics, but it can only be done through firm commitment to new and more effective departures in information technology.

In order to explain the type of such commitment, at least as far as present visibility permits to discuss, Part Three did not start with this chapter, but with GUI, graphic metafiles, frameworks, the use of objects, knowbots, virtual reality, and telepresence.

Some applications perspectives we have discussed are impressive. However, the employment of computerized multimedia systems remains a minor player in terms of percentages in the computer field. This is because what is presently available is more or less an improvement upon filing systems of image data.

For obvious reasons, different approaches have been taken to break through this bottleneck. They can be classified into roughly four categories that overlap somewhat.

1. *Hypermedia*, relating database contents from text to images, dynamically linking them together into a system, and permitting users to browse related parts through links

2. *Expert systems* providing knowledge about database contents, allowing for automatic searches for parts that users described in their query—the intentional approach

3. *Similarity retrieval,* making it possible for users to describe the features of desired images by samples or familiar objects (icons)

4. *Semantic* approaches capitalizing on the fact that drawings, such as diagrams and maps, indicate some meaning according to their syntax, each type of drawing being a kind of language

Even the same meaning may be represented by different ways in a variety of types of drawings. Alternatively, drawings help represent various types of information at the same time, with expert systems permitting users to focus on a few selected aspects of the drawings. In this way, various types of queries are possible depending on the aspects of the user's view.

Such exploitation is perfectly feasible, provided we have the right type of software. As we have seen, this is becoming available—but such a statement should not be interpreted to mean that existing hardware approaches the ingenuity technologists have shown with hardware developments.

Many functional VLSI (very large-scale integration) and ULSI (ultra large-scale integration) chips for signal processing, image handling, and text string pattern matching have been developed. These have enabled the high-speed processing of multimedia information with graphics and image-handling workstations, which use semiconductors now available at low prices.

Hardware breakthroughs are surely the more significant aspect in the developmental scale, although a software counterpart is becoming available. In regard to software technology, we can examine such media-processing functions as:

- Image handling,
- Voice recognition, and
- Voice synthesis.

All of these have made advances. However, much remains to be done to deal effectively with multimedia databases and multimedia representation, which remain current research topics.

From an implementation perspective, the emergence of image-compression standards for still and moving images and videoconferencing lowers costs in terms of communication and storage. In turn, this is driving the market for PC-based multimedia systems that in Europe alone are expected to grow to more than 6 million units by 1996, according to estimates by Dataquest, reflected in Figure 17.1.

This exponential market growth is not accidental. It reflects the need leading companies feel in terms of answering their growing implementation requirements. The more the industry is able to provide flexible, user-friendly, intelligence-enriched systems, the more the user community tends to capitalize from the sharp drop in costs.

17–3 ORGANIZATIONAL AND LOGISTICAL ASPECTS WITH MULTIMEDIA SOLUTIONS

In Section 17–2 it was mentioned that expert systems provide one of the better approaches to the exploitation of multimedia databases. The reader who has used artificial intelligence artifacts knows from experience that a characteristic of expert-based processes is tracking the transition in the knowledge space.

Artifacts can invoke procedures to trace from one symbol to the next, where each symbol and its meaning corresponds to a state of the knowledge space. As we have seen in Chapter 16, the whole concept of *hypermedia* rests on this notion.

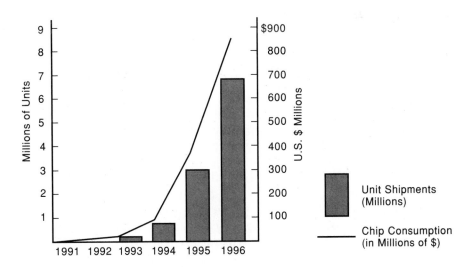

Figure 17.1   The European market for PC-based multimedia systems by 1996, according to Dataquest.

Three main component parts characterize the model that has been described, interacting and interrelating with one another, yet having their own specific characteristics.

1. *Multimedia databases* with text, data, graphics, and image (as well as index data), retrieved by structure matching and related data search
2. *Knowledgebanks*, containing the experts' knowledge about, say, plant observation and control, also used to retrieve multimedia in the database
3. *Agile user interfaces*, assisting endusers in telling retrieval conditions to the system by means of a graphic display and a pointing device

The system shows the result of the retrieval on the graphic display, as we examined in Chapter 14 when we discussed graphic user interfaces. The text in the Appendix documents the advantages of this approach versus the alternatives of character user interfaces.

Just as important are *organizational*, *legal*, and *logistical* issues. For example, in terms of the dynamics of multimedia storage and retrieval, an important topic is copyrights.

Video movies and publications are often used as sources of multimedia information.

Once they are into the system, they are edited and combined with other information.

Such operation results in the reconstruction of new information, but how are the rights of the information source, the indexer, and the editor related to each other? A new intellectual property concept for multimedia should be considered in a logistical sense, focusing on the information and knowledge age of this decade.

Because of the foregoing reasons, it is wise to distinguish between complex dynamic issues relating to multimedia databases, which are *still*, to a significant extent, and the opposite of it, the *dynamic* aspects. As far as still databases are concerned, we are dealing with simpler and more limited applications issues. Most of the existing implementation solutions may be satisfactory; however, these do not answer the much more demanding requirements posed by the dynamic database aspects.

Even for the more limited perspective of still data, new types of software are under development to help users easily append to existing or newly created database records. The latter may involve:

• Graphics and charts, and
• Photorealistic still images.

However, the movement toward dynamic data brings into focus a much richer array of handling needs with organizational, legal, and logistical aftermaths. Well-rounded solutions are necessary to address the manipulation of:

- Live video clips,
- Audio files with annotations, and
- Self-generated image sequences.

Runtime software is needed to help synchronize diverse elements to produce effective multimedia communications; for example, providing the pulse of the stock market in financial transactions through a radar chart;[*] producing dynamic graphics for board meetings; and ensuring concurrent information retrieval from CAD databases, electronic catalogs, and other systems.

Commodity software, which is emerging slowly, provides user organizations with tools to build, search, and present multimedia records from databases. Users can define the fields, merge local and remote files, and enter or import data from other databases.

Specific files can be identified through user-implied search criteria, employing friendly interfaces that are unique to all supported multimedia products. Endusers can browse their database by moving quickly between records, dynamically defining search criteria, and playing each corresponding record as demanded, case-by-case.

The dealer, for example, knows that he or she must take into account *24-hour trading* and *after-hours* networks. Increasingly, these will be multimedia services operating within a fully distributed perspective that can be handled in a dynamic, knowledge-intense basis.

As this process accelerates, it calls for very flexible and adaptable software that are only now emerging in the market. In contrast, as we saw in Section 17–2, at the device level, advanced VLSI technology has resulted in major capacity improvement and significant cost reduction.

These examples help to document that, not only are multimedia solutions increasingly in demand, but answering them is also a challenging, and often taxing, business. Classical data processing cannot respond to the integration of different media into one well-knit garment, to be manipulated in a comprehensive and efficient manner, despite futile attempts made in this direction.

In our architectural plans, we should also account for the fact that multimedia databases are open-ended and extendable. As a result, they require intentional constructs, as we have seen in Part Two.

---

[*]See D.N. Chorafas, *Simulation, Optimization, and Expert Systems*, Probus, Chicago, and McGraw-Hill, London, 1992.

17–4 CONCEPTUAL MODELS AND MULTIMEDIA SYSTEMS ARCHITECTURE

A multimedia systems architecture by necessity involves distributed, hetero-geneous databases, as well as the use of broadband channels and intelligent user interfaces. Successful professional work—from engineering design to securities and foreign exchange operations, as well as managerial-type applications—demand database systems that can incorporate text-and-graphics-oriented information, stored in diverse supports and accessed on a global scale.

Multimedia information is often expressed in nonformatted, complex structures. However, multimedia database systems are nearer to the notions we acquired in the past, whether they concern:

- Alphanumeric data,
- Figure and image databases, or
- Voice and sound.

However, dynamic multimedia solutions are not only a matter of wideband communications and high resolution in the presentation devices. They involve a new culture in information handling, including the need to include rapid change and uncertainty in retrieval.

Solutions must provide for the successful exploration of large volumes of information elements stored in distributed databases, keeping in mind that the capable handling of distributed multimedia databases constitutes one of the most significant implementations of artificial intelligence. In the architectural design of a multimedia database, the real world initially will be translated into a *conceptual model* (equivalent to the conceptual schema in ANSI/X3/SPARC), this being accomplished in two steps:

- *Cognition* realized by the acceptors, and
- *Modeling* proper, which is the perception of the real world.

The conceptual model represents how the database designer recog-nizes the structures (in this case, the text, graphics, and data structures) of the real world. As we know from other database implementations, the end result will be translated into another form—the *logical representation*.

To represent the real world as a conceptual model, we must describe our perception through a *symbol system* that goes well beyond the better known alphanumeric characters to include the following:

1. *Figures*, such as graphs, line drawings, plain and solid geometry, and icons

2. *Images*, involving paintings, carvings, photographs, films, and video frames

3. *Audio*, such as voice and other sounds

4. A *combination* of these references, helping to express a truly multimedia structure

The cognitive problem that has architectural aftermaths centers on how to recognize the real world, leading into model construction. A point often missed in relation to the evolution of databases is that the breadth of information that can be handled by computer has increased tremendously because of advances in digital representation of real world objects.

In the past, an object, such as a map or a voice recording, could not be stored in a computer database because of the inadequacy of input, storage hardware/software, and output. Today, it can be stored in a compound document, and it also can be interactively manipulated.

From a multimedia viewpoint, an object being designed can be described from several viewpoints. An electrical circuit, for instance, can be represented by its:

- Functional description,
- Circuit diagram, and
- General layout.

Often some descriptions are derived from others in the course of an interactive design activity. Hence, if the database is to be meaningful, the consistency between different descriptions must be maintained at the multimedia level.

The issue we are examining can become more complex by the fact that because engineering design is a trial and error process, it is necessary to store several alternatives of each description in the database. The system should maintain consistency among these alternatives.

1. Remembering which new alternative versions were derived from a particular original alternative.

2. Correlating such alternatives among themselves, both chronologically and in a multimedia sense

Figure 17.2 is a block diagram of a knowledge engineering-assisted graph analysis approach. The focal point is graph analysis control exercised on a range of functions from special context filters to smoothing, patterning, and graph interpretation.

A target position parameter helps to specify the exact location for an icon, so if an icon can fit at the target position, it will be placed there. Color specification is important when any region of the template may be colored. Size is vital because the template given for the description of an icon class may be scaled. This multifunctional viewpoint enhances the quality of the service, but it also increases system complexity.

17–5 PARAMETERS CONTROLLED BY CLASS DESCRIPTION

The solutions we provide must be instrumental in ensuring efficient multimedia capabilities. A graph- or icon-class description, for example, consists of a series of statements that specify the appearance of the graph or icon. Each statement performs some graphic operation, such as:

- Selecting a template picture,
- Coloring some region, or
- Inserting applicable text.

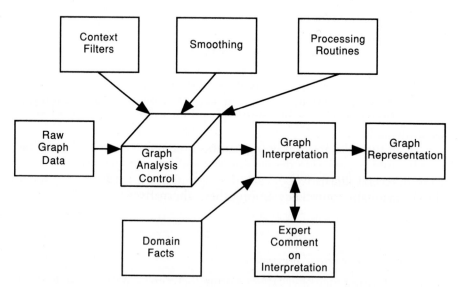

Figure 17.2   A knowledge engineering-assisted graph analysis system.

A graph constructed from a graph class may have its appearance defined at several levels of detail. This allows for zooming, by which a user sees a more detailed version of a graph by magnifying it, or, alternatively, looks at the macroscopic view.

Parameters that may be controlled by class description can be, for example, maximum size, choice of *picture* and *text*, target position, color, and so forth. Maximum size may be specified to prevent any graph or icon from becoming too large. A similar role is played by other constraints.

Choice of picture seems to be necessary because there may be several different references serving as templates, depending on the data in the tuple. Text may be added to the picture selectively, whether it is a simple string or data from one or more fields of the tuple.

Figure 17.3 shows a multimedia information-processing cycle. Authoring concerns the indexing and structuring of multimedia information. Multimedia authoring technology makes it possible to create, structure, and to input efficiently a large volume of information; however, this generates the problem of managing large multimedia databases.

A data model flexible enough for managing multimedia information elements in a unified way is crucial to database design, particularly when we must deal with distributed heterogeneous structures. In principle, the media have fundamental differences.

Motion pictures and auditory information have time dimensions. However, images and text strings do not.

The characteristics of each media should be reflected in a unified data model design. Therefore object-oriented data models and semantic data models are believed to be most promising in the implementation sense. However, in regard to multimedia information retrieval, factors used in

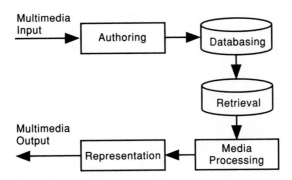

Figure 17.3   The handling of multimedia information.

compound document identification differ from those for simple text and data storage/retrieval.

Solutions can vary by implementation area. In engineering design, for example, a multimedia approach should support concurrent work where designers interactively communicate an image concept, including image retrieval, by using impression of documents as a clue. This assists designers to intuitively get images from the database. In a development by NEC (Nippon Electric Company):

> The internal model of the database represents the type of impression, as an axis in a semantic space.
>
> The images are represented as points in space and the queries as a subspace.

For ease of use, user interface design has been approached as a visual presentation of semantic space. The meaning of the axes is represented by concrete examples and the relation between the axes by the dispersion diagram of the images stored in the database.

Generally, when we talk of handling multimedia information, our primary goal is not merely to store the real-world object allowing the user to make changes to it. Our number one goal is to:

- Understand the function of the real-world object, and
- Use the computer system to execute that function effectively.

These two subjects become more important as global multimedia databases take shape, leading to identified requirements for their exploitation.

A complete model for describing multimedia information elements should include mechanisms for viewing them at different levels of detail. Through proper software, we should be able to decompose original descriptions, showing them graphically, as well as to represent complex behaviors, role-state transitions, dependencies and constraints between roles.

Such setting of facilities is fundamental in a growing number of domains for the support of ad hoc queries and for the visualization of answers to these queries. This is equally true whether we deal with simple cases or with complex ones to be decomposed into subqueries. Other characteristics also should be taken into account.

> Classically, queries have been crisp, addressing an equally crisp database and giving a crisp response.

A crisp query asks for a YES/NO answer; it is typically cast in a black or white form, accepting no tonalities of gray, such as those implied by fuzzy queries.

Increasingly, however, queries are not crisp. They are fuzzy and so is the specification of the databases they address.

Classical, record-based data processing chores cannot handle queries involving vagueness and uncertainty. Fuzzy engineering approaches are much better suited for this task, thus increasing the utility of a computer,[*] and helping to determine how effectively a user can employ the system to carry out required multimedia jobs.

17—6 RELATIONAL EXTENSIONS AND BINARY LARGE OBJECTS

In Chapter 16 we discussed the advantages of object-oriented solutions present in a multimedia environment. However, it has also been claimed that improved relational models can play a role. This section presents the case of relational extensions.

The basic suggestion behind the relational model is that conceptually all data is represented by simple tabular data relations, and that users access data through a nonprocedural declarative query language.

Instead of writing an algorithm to obtain desired records one at a time, the analyst or programmer specifies a predicate identifying the desired records or their combination.

A query optimizer in the DBMS translates the predicate specification into an algorithm to perform the necessary database access to the records.

As Part Two outlined, through a relational approach, data structures can be created that are easily understood and independent of each other. This helps in eliminating complex linkages and reducing volatility. Relational structures help in controlling data redundancy, and they are rather flexible for database modifications.

A query language helps to model data in a relational structure, with operators applying to the tables as a whole. *Relational Algebra* is an example of a relational query language. It consists of a set of operators that are composed to form expressions, and it can be applied to existing relations to create new relations.

Such expressions constitute the query that guides a man–information communications procedure by means of basic relational operators. One

---

[*]See also D.N. Chorafas, *The New Information Technology. A Practitioner's Guide*, Van Nostrand Reinhold, New York, 1992.

criticism of the relational approach, however, is that the model does not lend itself to efficient processing because there is no provision for the user to move quickly through access paths in his or her data.

Improved structures address this problem with database models combining a two-dimensional relational table with such solutions as main memory directory system. The result is more flexibility for database views and faster online terminal sessions.

Records can be hashed into information elements and may be partially or completely inverted in cross-referenced tables, depending on how the items will be searched.

When a record is placed in a hash table, its position becomes its record number.

These record numbers act as switches within the cross-reference tables.

A bit vector can be maintained for all inverted items and used to keep track of records with common characteristics.

A threaded binary search tree can be maintained by the user on any inverted item. Such a method facilitates single-record retrieval, sorted retrievals, and proximity searching, provided the tree is system maintained.

Other improvements are the so-called *relational extensions* and *entity-relationship* databases (e.g., *Portgress* and *Adabas Entire*). They allow connections and relationships to be expressed in the data, but behaviors still are not stored in the database.

Object values are converted into relational storage formats, but this approach retains the inefficiency of join processing. However, because it constitutes an improvement that became known as *Binary Large Objects* (BLOBS), it is now being added to almost all the popular relational DBMS to help them store unstructured, large objects, as required by multimedia handling.

BLOBS were introduced to accommodate such multimedia record types as digital video and sound sequences that can have huge record sizes. This approach not only can help to provide multimedia information to users, but it can store some of the unwieldy more classical data structures also.

Therefore, with distributed database technology, the advent of BLOBS makes it feasible to handle multimedia and other large data types; for example, to provide a number of distinctive services based on the data from real-time feeds. An application featuring graphs of stock prices could include, for example, two horizontal lines:

- The bottom one representing a buying price, and
- The top representing a selling price.

Should the stock price graph hit one of the lines, it could sound an alarm or trigger a transaction program automatically.

To make this approach feasible, software is necessary to support a tie-in to the backoffice system. Also, decision support routines are needed that permit current information to be compared with historical information, allowing the implications of fluctuating prices on portfolios to be explored.

Other real-time programs should enable a significant number of port-folios to be modeled with investments broken down into, say, geographic and indistrial sectors, with values represented in dynamic graphs. BLOBS also can be used to hold a series of historical data on stock behavior.

A bank may want to hold 20 years' of history of prices for a number of stocks.

Prices typically change many times a day, but for a given application, it may not be sensible to have each price change as a database record.

By holding a stock's price history as a BLOB, the record can be added to the daily reference, stored, and manipulated as any other database record. This approach is also being used to store certificate information where the letters are scanned and stored against an event.

The handling of reference information in BLOBS permits scanning and storing files as free text. This gives analysts and fund managers access to a wider range of support information online.

17–7 AUDIO AND VIDEO INFORMATION ELEMENTS

We have seen evidence sufficient to support the notion that text, data, graphics, and the emergence of digital audio and video technologies pose a challenge to the database community. Solutions for effectively handling audio/video are needed, not only in a classical database sense, but also in ways to enable management of very large capacity storage systems.

Photonics plays, and will continue playing, a key role in the technology leap of the 1990s; some examples are advances in high bandwidth transmission and very significant improvements in storage. In turn, this leads to greater availability of audio and video systems, a process enhanced by special purpose computing.

In principle, audio/video storage must benefit from online database functionality, allowing shared use and efficient access. Solutions must account for the fact that audio/video often goes through an editing (postproduction) process, during which particular segments are selected and combined.

Typically, edited segments consist of links to the original information elements. Hypermedia application increasingly will feature interlinked objects. Moreover, an object may be referenced in many places, with dependencies managed by a database system so that referenced information elements are neither deleted accidently nor unnecessarily duplicated.

The database management approach under discussion leads to the need for design and production tools capable of handling media* in such a way that it can be easily combined and reused. However, as designers acquire and augment multimedia object collections, they:

- Face the need to organize and query clip media, but
- They encounter basic problems in database management caused by the limitation of current tools.

This is particularly true as the solutions horizon for storing and retrieving multimedia information elements is enlarged. Typically, current approaches have been projected per application area; hence, they provide domain-specific functionalities and features.

One of the best examples of handling multimedia information comes from office automation; most particularly from processing compound electronic documents through:

- High definition raster images,
- Graphics software, and
- Audio annotations.

Work along this line has focused on modeling and complex object structures, as well as on content-based retrieval. Study of the results different projects have reached helps to identify certain features generally valid for multimedia databases.

Although content-based retrieval is possible for text and data components, this approach is much more difficult with images and audio. In the latter case, content-based retrieval typically is limited to conditions of the information elements' existence and type.

As a result of such limitations, some multimedia document systems do not put much emphasis on content-based retrieval, but rather they focus on:

- Tools for *authoring*, that is, creation of multimedia documents; and

---

*Noun singular, like data.

- Tools for *interlinking* media components through such solutions as hypermedia.

Whichever approach they choose, multimedia database management systems must be able to handle the growing range of requirements posed by image processing. This starts with image recognition, where typically image structures and features are extracted from images, while the original images are kept in a different image store.

A query-by-pictorial-example interface tries to answer a query using the extracted information.

This approach capitalizes on the fact that knowledge-enriched software is capable of storing and retrieving a large number of multimedia values.

Such software must have the necessary facilities for controlling concurrent access and providing real-time transfer to applications. The production and processing of audio and visual values includes format conversion, filtering, compression, and rendering—often requiring such hardware as:

- Analog-to-digital (AD) and digital-to-analog (DA) converters,
- Digital signal processors, and
- Graphics-pipelining capabilities.

Scheduling of multimedia usage should be under application program control. Concurrent access to audio and visual objects brings up the need for resource preallocation, in connection with a given applications environment.

Applications may specify data placement. At the same time, the representation of multimedia objects may be based on quality factors. There are also alternatives for encoding and compressing digital video and audio.

In principle, applications should specify data representation indirectly, in terms of such quality factors as audio fidelity and video resolution. Formats should be handled in a flexible manner.

There are some emerging data formats allowing the combination of digital audio and video. The same is true of transfer such mechanisms as asynchronous, stream-based interfaces to applications.

The temporal nature of such multimedia information, as audio and video values often requires specialized devices capable of real-time handling of data streams, as well as protocols facilitating online transfer of digital audio and video. Also needed are fast rendering rates for graphics hardware making feasible real-time animation.

Much of the work that has been done in this domain tends to favor the object-oriented approach, but objects are only part of the requirements. Because storage needs for multimedia information are large, compression techniques are required to minimize storage space on the physical level. Data sharing through aggregation is important at the logical level, and this is also true of multimedia query and browsing tools.

18

Text and Image Warehouses for Document Management

18–1 INTRODUCTION

Despite the huge growth of computer use in the last 35 years, data input is still an inefficient and expensive task. This is even more true in terms of text input. Therefore, there is an acute and growing need for systems that make the capture and storage of large volumes of documents simple. Moreover, this need brings into the discussion the twin issues of:

1. Document image storage, and
2. Document image processing.

Both areas command an increasing interest in the user community. They are also integral parts of the new wave of databases, providing low-cost, high-capacity solutions to online archiving requirements— from data processing to office chores, engineering, manufacturing, marketing, and finance.

Document image processing cannot be left out of any serious database architecture. Also known as *imaging*, document image storage involves the integration of existing technologies to meet the growing online access needs of applications rich in text and picture-handling requirements.

Given that all major organizations must solve document image problems, it comes as no surprise that the leading systems suppliers are active in this market, which is expected to double in size over the next 2 years.

Users who have experimented with imaging tend to extend its applications to all parts of an organization.

The spreading characteristic of imaging brings into focus the urgent need for reliable answers to key questions affecting the future of document handling. Basic queries go beyond the costs and benefits of using image technology to focus on the technical subjects of integration among the different media increasingly stored in databases.

How will imaging work in unison with existing database structures?

Which applications developments will be most important in widening the use of imaging?

Where should the line be drawn between text and document handling on one hand, and data processing on the other?

How can we develop homogeneous query procedures to facilitate the task of the enduser when he or she interacts with multimedia?

All major manufacturing organizations and financial institutions I have talked to during the last 2 years expect the handling of compound electronic documents to be one of their focal points in the 1990s. We should, therefore, ensure that the solutions we provide are cost effective, user friendly, and virtually homogeneous.

18–2 CONTENT LABELS AND INFORMATION SYSTEM VISIBILITY

As far as the enduser is concerned, the information system's visibility starts with a query. Then, it continues with cross-database searches, and it ends with the response the user gets to the query, especially via visualization.

Therefore, whether we talk of data, text, or graphics, one of the subjects attracting a great deal of attention within the database community today is the subject of ad hoc queries. In the new competitive environments, such as interactive computational finance or concurrent engineering, the database is for the enduser. He or she must be able to query without the constraints inherent in obsolete data models or inefficient languages.

This is as true of compound electronic documents as it is of data alone, but the former pose more challenges than the latter. Figure 18.1 shows a document-handling procedure implemented by a leading financial organization with optical media (imaging) for electronic documents as the centerpoint.

Content labels have been used to route a query automatically to the multimedia databases where the query can be processed. This approach is

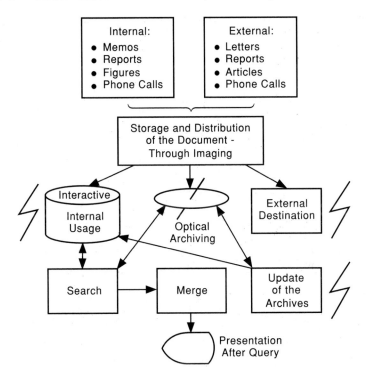

Figure 18.1   Creation and usage of a compound electronic document.

AI supported, and it is engineered through a knowledgebank management system (KBMS), of which we spoke in Part Two.

A *content label* is a description of text and data pertinent to a specific user's database.

Database queries are expressed using *predicates* and content labels.

Content labels are also used to *route queries* and updates, as necessary.

A simple theorem prover typically is employed to route queries to appropriate multimedia databases that exist within a distributed environment. If a *query predicate* implies a database content label predicate, then the KBMS knows that the query can be processed at this particular information resource. Database updates are sent to all databases whose content label the updates satisfy.

This reference helps underline the fact that access to multimedia databases increasingly means much more in terms of service than it did in the past. An integral part of the query is personalized filtering, made necessary because of:

- The large volume of text and data in storage, and
- Multimedia streams pumped in by information providers.

The content label of a personalized database is a user's *filtering* list. Because this filter precisely describes what is to be retained in the user's microfile (his or her personal database), or to be presented on his or her screen, it helps to determine the link between queries and visualization.

To operate effectively along this line, we should visualize a comprehensive view of a networked system involving workstations, multimedia database servers, gateways and, say, a digital market feed. The latter is processed through a *market data filter* that extracts the information necessary for each professional workstation according to labels. As shown in Figure 18.2, the market data filter is pruning for market feed and database contents, a systems approach applicable to many implementation domains.

For housekeeping purposes, in this particular implementation, the content labels of file server computers were kept in the data dictionary and used by the workstations' database management system. The latter sends queries to the local servers, and if these queries could not be processed locally, they were forwarded to the central text and data warehouse.

During the evaluation of the original prototype, a thorough investigation of requirements suggested that systems designed to support multimedia within new and growing applications domains should:

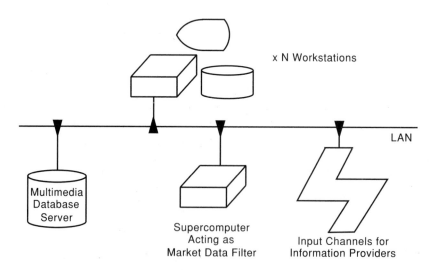

Figure 18.2   Comprehensive view of a networked system in practical applications.

1. Make it possible to manage the evolution of text, image, and data in the system in various ways;
2. Provide both local solutions and a repository for persistent information, drawn from a variety of implementation environments;
3. Support cooperation and sharing between different multimedia resources; and
4. Cope with the growing demands of users for multimedia information operating in a distributed sense.

Therefore the chosen design approach has been one capable of supporting these features. It provided an interface between the needs of complex and varied application domains, as well as the diverse, distributed media on which information elements reside.

The demanding nature of these requirements gave rise to the principle that an extensible, adaptable, and flexible design is the best approach. Enriched through artificial intelligence, the adopted federated database solution[*] ensured that independent local databases would not be visible from outside the server. However:

Once a query entered the server, a second level of query routing has been used to dispatch the query to appropriate local databases.

Served through a data dictionary, this procedure permitted local database contents to be moved between servers as a unit, when necessary.

This and similar architectural approaches will be needed increasingly not only because of the heterogeneity of the databases today available in major organizations, but also given the transition that occurs in storage technology:

- From magnetics to photonics, and
- From data-centered to text- and graphic-centered solutions.

In this environment, semantics can be used ably for manipulating the complex data objects that are required by the different operational procedures and other reasons inherent in the application domains. As we have seen in Chapter 16, semantics also can be used to support sharing, and at the same time to provide the mechanism for data management and multimedia database access.

---

[*]See also D.N. Chorafas and H. Steinmann, *Solutions for Networked Databases*, Academic Press, New York and San Diego, 1993.

18–3 CONQUERING THE TEXT FRONTIER OF THE 1990s

No workable answers can be provided for the problems of compound electronic document handling without bringing into the discussion the text frontier with which every company will be confronted in the 1990s. This is particularly true of organizations that find themselves awash in documents.

In the research I did from 1991 to 1993, many financial and industrial organizations, from Tokyo to New York and London, commented that recently their data-processing equipment and aged procedures were making matters worse, not better. They were churning out briefs, memos, patent filings, and reports in record numbers. Copies of all those documents were dutifully filed away, but this did not help.

> How can an investment advisor or an accountant locate relevant information buried in documents created years before?
>
> Who can grasp the content of so much spoken and written information well enough to cross-index all of it successfully?

Textual material: letters, memos, electronic mail, telexes, faxes, other messages, and field reports pour into a company's office system each day from many sources. This flood of information is not altogether useless, because it includes elements that may provide management with a competitive edge, but only if the elements can be located quickly and correlated to a pattern.

However, the ways and means provided by classical data-processing cannot answer the database mining needs. The tools DP typically uses are too primitive for sophisticated multimedia applications. Although in a data-processing sense:

> Mainframes may be good in handling data that fits naturally into lists of structured records.
>
> Mainframes and their aged operating systems and DBMS are *quite ineffective* in handling text, image, and voice objects.

Capable handling of compound electronic documents is a totally different matter than were old data-processing chores—but it is an integral and fast-growing part of a dynamic organization's daily operations.

Many of the problems managers and professionals must solve, ranging from cost control and project administration to CAD, marketing, finance, and legal duties—in short, all significant applications—are largely text-oriented, not of the DP type. That is why some 75 percent of important management jobs in the United States, Western Europe, and Japan have not even been touched by computers.

- Contrary to data that fits into some preestablished file and field formats, and can be indexed for retrieval,
- Text documents generally are long, unindexed strings of words, whose sentences and paragraphs *convey ideas not numbers.*

However, solutions do exist in the form of a variety of practical examples help document, but we must prepare for implementing them through high technology—not naive DP. We must also stress that all efficient solutions to text handling involve knowledge engineering.

One of the better examples regards the use of the Connection Machine[*] at Dow Jones public databases. As customers access these text databases, the supported expert systems are able to handle ad hoc noncrisp queries through a memory-based reasoning (MBR) approach.

A similar solution can be applied to the responsibilities of any manager who searches documents in a noncrisp manner. It can be implemented effectively through fuzzy engineering, as we have seen in Chapter 3.

Dow Jones now feeds text and databases and serves the demands of its customers through *Dow Vision.* This is a thoroughly restructured newswire that delivers a daily stream of some 10 megabytes of business information. Dow Jones says it could not be handled without AI and supercomputers.

In order to appreciate the advantages offered by new technology, it is proper to bring into discussion the competitive strong points of this solution.

Assisted by AI constructs, customers can receive reams of information without having to decide previously how to organize or search for it.

In contrast, in traditional computing of the data-processing type, data must fit into a database's predefined slots.

Another example of the use of knowledge engineering for text retrieval comes from IBM and involves an application known as the Capital Asset Expert System (CASES). It exploits a textual database involving factory rules and regulations that have accumulated over 65 years; that is, since the mid-1920s, when the Endicott manufacturing facility was first built.

Written for factory asset management purposes, CASES is a good example of the use of AI in administrative duties. Its goals can be expressed in the following terms:

---

[*]A supercomputer by Thinking Machines, Cambridge, MA, delivering 10,000 MIPS peak power for about $3 million.

1. Simplify operating procedures in ordering, acquisition, transfer to/from, storage, utilization, disposal;

2. Give an all-encompassing advice on asset management;

3. Provide comprehensive answers over the whole interdepartmental area of procedural applications;

4. Cut through different types of procedures and directives (cut red tape);

5. Integrate signature authorizations for transaction validation; and

6. Avoid wasting time and reduce current level of frustration.

Solutions provided by CASES include online consultation dialog, interactive provision of information pertinent to the user, and merging procedures and forms from many sources. In addition, CASES creates a factory knowledgebank for written operations procedures and directives.

The years of utilization of this expert system have documented the assurance which it provides in terms of one cohesive course of action, while customizing its response to individual queries. It has guaranteed a unique ability to handle company directives, and its system availability is 24-hours per day, 7 days per week.

18–4 OBJECT APPROACHES TO DOCUMENT HANDLING

As we have seen on many occasions through practical examples, object-oriented designs provide many advantages in a complex implementation environment, starting with a common denominator across the system. One of the most significant contributions is that the database servers need not be homogeneous; however they must to have full knowledge of all the possible types of files, formats, and messages.

It is a sound principle of systems design that information elements are self-describing in terms of their implementation as objects. There is also a need for flexibility in introducing into the system new types of IE, changing or eliminating old types, and generally managing the global features.

In a document environment with its associated database search, object-oriented systems provide necessary flexibility for making changes. New objects can be defined and existing ones modified. In traditional programming situations, there is a dichotomy between user agents:

- The procedures or files that are activated by them; and
- The messages or files that are manipulated by such procedures.

In contrast, object-based systems ensure that user roles, procedures, and messages can be implemented in a dynamic sense. Roles can act on messages, but messages (and files) can also act on roles. This is a significant advantage when we execute a document search.

Figure 18.3 presents a configurator for object-based, ad hoc queries that imply document search. Depending on the needs of the enduser, including queries that involve vagueness and uncertainty, such a document management system provides procedures and heuristics to build and edit text, data, graphics, and images. It is also useful for handling missing values and transforming search variables.

Companies with experience in this field commented during the 1991/1992 research that for building and editing document files, software should assure among other functions:

- Defining information elements;
- Correcting or editing information elements;
- Entering multimedia values; and
- Deleting values, listings, and so forth.

Basic file manipulations must also be provided for sorting and merging documents by cases or by variables, copying or renaming multimedia information, and creating files and subfiles.

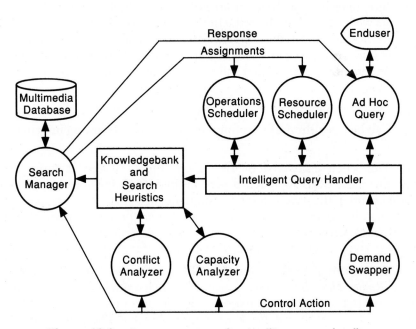

Figure 18.3   Component parts of an intelligent query handler.

In such an applications environment, heterogeneity should be looked at as a fact of life. Differences may exist in the data description languages (DDL) being employed, the data manipulation languages (DML), the data models of interest to the global manager, transaction handling at the distributed operating system level, as well as protocols for communications.

Internetworking has an impact on DBMS implementation and vice versa. Communicating databases do influence the design and operation of computer networks; however, the inclusion of primitives for communicating databases is vital because online access enhances the multimedia workstation level with services not otherwise available to the enduser.

The provision of widespread access capabilities also underlines the need to control both centralized and local files, as well as the access to them. This brings into the discussion the requirement of enhancing reliability in a system wide sense, because a physical or logical failure has an impact on the interactivity of the enduser—even if such failure can be confined to one subnetwork.

Access capabilities must be AI-enriched because document-oriented queries may be not only crisp but also fuzzy (as we have seen with examples in Chapter 3).

1. *They Are* Crisp *When They Are Amenable to Sharp Definitions With Answers Clearly Pointing to an Unambiguous Direction*—A thing is black, or it is white. In real life, such situations exist very rarely, if ever at all. For nearly 40 years we have dealt with abstractions, not necessarily understanding that they are nothing more than approximations of real-world situations.

In this sense, a crisp query is a special case. It is crisp only when it asks for something specific, an information element that either:

- Exists in memory as such, for example, a contractual document; or
- Can be algorithmically computed on the basis of existing information.

This is practically what SQL's "Select...From...Where"is doing; however, this naive SQL approach is very limited. SQL specifies in a black or white manner the type of information needed from the storage space, conveniently bypassing the real problems that are present in man–machine communications.

2. *A Query is* Fuzzy *in the Case When it Involves Vagueness and Uncertainty, Rather Than Two Crisp Alternatives*—Such a query may have embedded in it a hypothesis; it may express a doubt; or it may respond to another query without exclusive black or white choices. There may be fuzzy responses to crisp queries, as well as fuzzy answers to fuzzy queries.

Enriched with fuzzy query capabilities, distributed online access to document-oriented databases brings benefits through centralized query functions well beyond what was thought to be possible in the past.

A *thesaurus* permits the contents of a referenced section to be accessed effectively and applied to the job on hand.

A *web of links* would allow for direct connection between workstations among themselves and toward the global multimedia database.

Our goal in using object-oriented solutions within such an environment, should be that of ensuring a dependable, robust system operation despite fuzzy queries and data, and despite component node failures. Such solutions should evolve in a modular fashion and with appropriate consideration to a whole range of security issues:

1. Uncertainty as to the exactness of the required search;
2. The eventuality of an improper use of facilities and the objects they contain;
3. Disclosure or modification of information contained in sensitive objects; and
4. Loss of resources of either a temporary or permanent basis, making objects unavailable.

Any study concerning multimedia databases must account for requirements and constraints, policy guidelines, and implementation perspectives, not only access routes and logs. The identification of system components must receive proper attention. This covers machine-sensable identification; defining and identifying users and workstations, as well as all documents handled by the system.

Evaluation must be made of ways and means for monitoring; recognition of violations; user accessibility to system information; possible vulnerability of database(s); integrity constraints; and of audit tools and audit trails.

Privacy locks can be symbolic names or names of database rules and procedures. Protection algorithms should define who can extract information for which purpose, with identification and authentication being done networkwide.

Up to a point, object-oriented privacy requirements applicable to multimedia databases sound similar to those valid for data systems. However, the fact is that distributed multimedia documents present, many difficulties in the implementation of security measures—we are still learning how to implement such measures.

18—5 MEMORY-BASED REASONING AND DOCUMENT SEARCH

Let us start with the premise that *uncertainty* is a better mechanism for database search than is certainty. No doubt this is an evolutionary thought, but there is now enough evidence to document its validity.

Developed at Brandeis University, *memory-based reasoning* (MBR) is a good approach to search strategy. This statement is generally valid, provided supercomputer power is available for its implementation. We tradecomputer cycles for greater accuracy and flexibility.

In principle, five methods constitute the toolkit for memory search, ranging from classical approaches to AI-controlled idea databases. Each can be employed as it best fits. Written in increasing order of sophistication, these are:

1. Boolean queries
2. Select-From-Where
3. Relevance feedback
4. Speed document search
5. Memory-based reasoning

MBR is the ideal way of searching object-oriented databases that contain multimedia information elements representing values, situations, and outcomes or actions. Although values are expressed in data form, situations may involve polyvalence; may include text; and may have moving images, dynamic graphics, and voice.

The global user view within such setting will still be a logical schema specified in terms of:

• Database description,
• Structuring formalism, and
• Operations creating a database model.

Superficially, this looks not unlike classical databases, but in reality the latter have significantly limited capabilities for expressing meaning or for presenting multimedia documents. The same is true in regard to relating a database to its corresponding application landscape.

The *semantics* of a multimedia database must be readily apparent from the *schema*. This requires a *metalevel* model that enables database designers and users to proceed with description and structuring formalisms that can serve as a natural application mapping mechanism.

Semantically enriched memory-based reasoning has wide implementation domains, and it basically involves two phases.

1. *Hypothesis Formation*—In this, situations that are similar to the instantiated one, which we want to understand, are selected by the system from a large database.

It is important that the database be large, so that a number of instances will be found that are generally similar to the instantiated situation.

2. *Filtering*—The hypotheses suggested by the returned instances are examined one-at-a-time and evaluated using Bayesian or possibilistic theory.

Although semantic and object-oriented concepts dominate, supercomputers make a major contribution to memory-based reasoning through their ability to search in a parallel mode for similar instances—making them tractable. In addition, they ably support different models of hypothesis testing.

As we have seen, in terms of cost effectiveness, supercomputers are vastly superior to mainframes by a ratio of 80:1. When a metric changes by an order of magnitude, management must change the way in which it makes decisions. Here we have a change of nearly 2 orders of magnitude in cost benefit. What we used to do with the now slower-and-slower classical computers is not only obsolete—it can also be counterproductive.

Ossified concepts and low MIPS are an impedence to future progress. New departures are necessary, MBR and teraops computers being two of them.

A different way to state this is that the slow speed of current mainframes makes memory-based reasoning impractical, and the same is true of other rigorous search models based on semantic reasoning.

The now available serial machines cannot do the job required to match fast-moving document search heuristics. In contrast, massively parallel computer architectures are capable of deep searches, which they can perform quite effectively in an object-oriented sense.

18–6 BENEFITS TO BE DERIVED FROM LOGIC MODELING

MBR is logic modeling, and it deals with the rules that control the search process. Such rules are largely heuristic, reflecting the fact that many business system functions are stochastic in their behavior. Search actions cause retrieval events that will be more effective if the following prerequisites are observed.

1. *Speed*—Documents must be retrieved at a much faster rate than can be done by the classical search methods for data processing.

2. *Accuracy*—In large databases, calculations and manipulations should be performed accurately, and this can be done by means of euristics.

3. *Density*—Multimedia information can be stored in photonics (optical disks) more cost-effectively than in magnetic form.

4. *Utility*—It must be possible to present document contents in different formats for different user purposes.

These are among the advantages to be obtained from the evolving multimedia database technology over more classical processes. The need for such solutions has prompted a number of firms to focus on the efficient, reliable manipulation of large volumes in information storage.

It is increasingly recognized that understanding and describing the structure of an episodic memory and its semantics can lead to major implementation advantages. This is not the case with traditional methods because they were developed to allow the data to be manipulated with a repeating, record-oriented structure. Therefore, relatively little attention was given in the past to:

1. Providing richer data description languages;

2. Designing systems with more flexible data structures; and

3. Assuring more effective search mechanisms.

As a result, today's dominant database management paradigms are not well suited for handling text and data warehouses rich in graphics and images. They are oriented toward the storage and retrieval of volumes of data with a known, repetitive structure, handled through a more or less deterministic approach.

Although the databases of the last 20 years can still be used for keeping existing records, the newly developing requirements make such approaches obsolete and unwise for usage with new applications; hence, the interest in object orientation, semantic models, and multimedia and memory-based reasoning approaches. We also must to face another challenge: global multimedia database management, which, as we saw in Part Two, can be done through KBMS.

An example of needed functionality is given by the Knowledge APPlication-oriented Advanced Database and Knowledge Base Management System (KAPPA). We have already spoken of KAPPA in Part Two as a development by ICOT, the Japanese New Generation Computer Project.

The knowledgebank layer of KAPPA has been designed on a framework of deductive and object-oriented approaches to serve in demanding applications environments. A list of software functions supports the layers in Figure 18.4, in recognition of the fact that document handling must make the functionality of existing DBMS subserviant to the KBMS.

This approach should be combined with the concept of disciplined relationships leading to a schema for the evolution of database schemata in terms of multimedia interactions. Patterns must be identified and mapped onto the database schema, and there is a need for monitoring queries to understand the requirements of the enduser.

Pattern development should avoid an excessive computational burden and provide a practical identification method. This is important both for administrative reasons and for learning purposes because multimedia implementation is still a new discipline.

18–7 OFFICE DOCUMENT ARCHITECTURE AND TEXT PROCESSING

A manuscript and the formatted document produced from it bear a mathematical relationship. This can be seen as an algorithmic description of the formatting process. On this premise rests the office document architecture (ODA) of the International Standards Organization (ISO). ODA specifies two separate hierarchies for any combination of document type and layout style:

- Logical hierarchy of the document's content
- Physical or layout hierarchy of the formatted document

Given these two hierarchies, we aim to specify the transformation of objects in their logical representation to the corresponding object in a physical representation. An interactive environment requires that this transformation to be reversible, permitting the user to find, for a given layout object, the logical objects it represents.

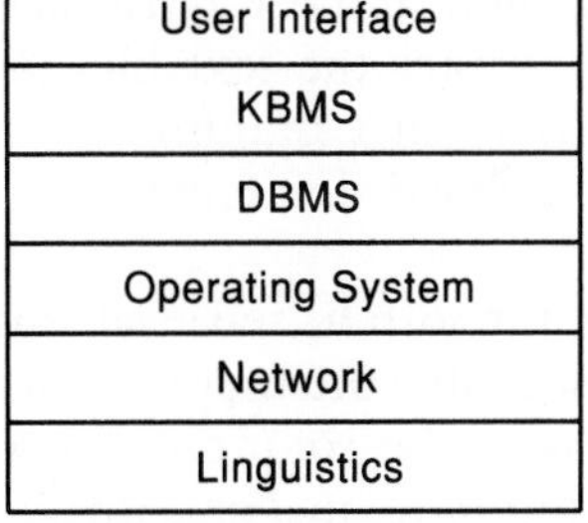

User Interface
KBMS
DBMS
Operating System
Network
Linguistics

Figure 18.4   A layered open architecture for document-handling purposes.

Typically, the formatting process starts with the logical structure of the document obtained by parsing. This produces a document in some syntax, where structure is kept but lexical detail may be eliminated. The best way to look at parsing is as a process similar to compiling. In more specific terms, parsing:

- Augments the existing structure by objects extracted from it via some homomorphism;
- Then, it puts into order the as yet unordered parts of the document.

Sorting of unordered sets of document components may be performed before, after, or intermixed with these homomorphic mappings. This permits us to specify different layout styles and supports an implementation-oriented specification method.

With emphasis increasingly placed on practical implementations of an office document architecture, the developing document retrieval theory specifies the properties for query language in office environments.

1. Incomplete specification of assertions: About <Report,Text>
2. Flexible specification assertions: Range of queries; Look-alike approach
3. Means of relating assertions about different views of documents

The provision of such functionality calls for a manipulation language associated with multimedia models. In all cases, query specification must ensure an agile interface for the specification of query predicates and associated uncertainty.

As we have seen in Part One, uncertainty is a very important part of retrieval. By all indications, it will become a cornerstone in office studies of the future, and it also will be a basic ingredient in managerial and professional productivity.

A document management and text retrieval system should be available to help organize and administer the text files we create or acquire. The chosen solution must ensure that multimedia information contained in magnetic and optical disk-based documents is always quickly and easily accessible.

Tools and methods for search, retrieval, manipulation, sorting, and organizing functions must enable the user to treat his or her text and image files as a *free-form* database. The solution should be flexible enough to manage just about any kind of textual and image information that cannot be handled conveniently by conventional database programs; for example it should be able to:

1. *Find multimedia information fast,* searching any number of objects or files at a time for specific information content in full-text context;
2. *Connect documents by content,* gathering related extracts of information automatically into one object or file from any number of them;
3. *Permit viewing files instantly,* scanning contents of any number of files at a time, browsing through records with full scrolling control; and
4. *Compress and decompress,* restoring compressed files back to their exact original form at a fast rate.

Other vital functions are adding, deleting, copying, and renaming multimedia information, of any number of files, of any type, within any directory.

The provision of these services must always keep in focus the fact that text and data have different characteristics. The structure of text and image is not necessarily known in advance, and it evolves over time.

It typically contains heterogeneous data types.

Information may be generated and managed directly by the enduser.

Therefore, many programs designed to run personal text files have adopted a completely unstructured approach. They are treating all information elements as free text that is searched and displayed in response to ad hoc queries.

Hypermedia systems, which we discussed in Chapter 16, provide a simple structuring mechanism, ensuring links between information elements. They allow the user to create a topological space of adjacent elements. Structure, however, arises out of the grouping of similar items and relationships defined among those groups, not the simple linking of individual items together.

Current solutions have their limitations. In relation to the issues raised in this section, most hypertext systems assume that the information of interest resides exclusively in the IE rather than in the structure. As a result, they do not provide the user with the means to:

• View and manipulate the structure itself, or
• Create relationships among groups of information elements.

This can be detrimental to the user's search. The solutions we need in the 1990s must be capable of handling compound electronic documents, self-monitoring information, permitting interactive graphic reports, sharing electronic agendas, and assuring hypermedia information access—all based on object-oriented technology.

Object identifiers can be used to build up hypertext-type links among multimedia objects. Such an approach permits users to navigate freely amid text, graphics, images, voice, and other forms of information. The best results can be achieved through knowledge-enriched solutions and object orientation. This has been the main thesis of this book.

Appendix: A Comparison of GUI and CUI

The Graphic User Interface (GUI) for workstation software contrasts to the Character User Interface (CUI)[*] in terms of performance and user-friendliness. Sponsored by Microsoft and Zenith Data Systems, a study was done by Temple, Baker, and Sloan (TBS) in 1990 comparing GUI and CUI. This study found that:

> GUI users work faster and better, completing their tasks more accurately than CUI users.
>
> Therefore, GUI users have a higher productivity than CUI users.

On average, when compared to CUI users, experienced GUI users completed 50 tasks versus 37 tasks over the same time period; a 50 percent greater throughput.

In another experiment, GUI users correctly completed a higher proportion of the exercises they attempted: 91 percent versus 74 percent for CUI users. They also expressed lower frustration and perceived less fatigue after working with personal computers.

> The tasks being accomplished were clerical, professional, and managerial.
>
> It was also found that as the knowledge intensiveness of work grows, the value of GUI to the user increases.

Other research results point to the fact that GUI users are more able than CUI users to teach themselves and explore opportunities and to learn

---

[*]Not to be confused with CUA, or common user access, which refers to the use of a common interface for all enduser-oriented applications.

more in terms of applications. In addition, graphic user interfaces help in generating higher output per man-hour, as well as in reducing frustration and fatigue. In turn, this means that GUI has a greater return on information technology investment than CUI. GUI users also suggest that there is a need for standardization. Areas in which users indicated that there are urgent normalization requirements include:

- The control keys and graphics symbols in the keyboard
- Character size, graphic symbols, and graphic images in screen layout
- Help commands as well as computer language elements, particularly for simulation

There are also other domains where conflicting standards exist and therefore there is need for standardization. These include the character sets and coding recognition in keyboards; font, color, and character type aspect of screen layout, and so on.

In spite of these shortcomings, GUI has advantages. Since with GUI endusers master more capabilities and require less training and support, organizations can realize greater benefits. Established by a number of user organizations, experimental results help in documenting the notion that the easier a piece of software is to learn, the more likely the enduser will explore the more advanced features of a given application.

To measure the likelihood that a user would attempt to implement such features, some companies surveyed their personal computer users about their expectations before, during, and after the tests. Queries posed focused on the enduser's confidence in teaching himself or herself more of available advanced features. Studies found that GUI novices felt greater confidence in their abilities than CUI novices, both before the tests began and afterwards.

When asked how long it would take in terms of practice to feel really comfortable using these applications environments to accomplish their ongoing work,

GUI participants said it would take up to a few weeks.
CUI users felt that 1 to 6 months would be necessary.

Quite significantly, in terms of enduser response, experienced GUI users reported little need for documentation or aids by software vendors. By contrast, CUI users expressed the opinion that their performance could greatly improve if such aids were available.

In terms of personal response, GUI users liked the consistent feel of graphic software. CUI participants were confused by the multiple combinations of function keys and other characteristics of character-based approaches. Multimedia and GUI were found to facilitate learning and subsequent usage, both within an application and among applications.

Many companies fail to consider the major advantages of GUI when, because of inertia and resistance to change, they stick to obsolete tools and naïve protocols. Management should not be lenient in regard to this failure. Quoting an Athenian senator in Shakespeare's "Timon of Athens," "Nothing emboldens sin so much as mercy."

Acknowledgments

The following is a list of organizations and their senior executives, specialists in computers and communications, and faculty members who contributed to the research projects on which this book is based. The list is subdivided by country and the organizations are arranged alphabetically within these subdivisions.

United States

American Airlines

Jeffrey A. HARTIGAN, Managing Director, Advanced Technology and Enduser Technology
Mary ALEXION, Managing Director, Corporate Data Management
4200 Amon Carter Blvd., CP2 Mail Drop 2517, Ft. Worth, TX 76155

Susan L. DUNLAP, SABRE Computer Services
Todd FITZGERALD, Manager, Database Administration
Warren ELLIOTT, Manager, Data Models
Brenda MORYAN, Manager, Data Planning
Sam ANTURI, Technical Planning
Phil HARTLEY, Advanced Technology, Object-Oriented Applications
P.O. Box 619616, Dallas/Fort Worth Airport, TX 75261-9616

Anderson Counsulting

Bruce B. JOHNSON, Director of Research
Michael DE BELLIS, Center for Strategic Technology
100 S. Waker Drive, Chicago, IL 60606

Stanton J. TAYLOR
69 West Washington Street, Chicago, Illinois 60602

Charles W. McDONOUGH
400 Renaissance Center, Detroit, Michigan 48243

Associative Design Technology

John C. EDWARDS, President
Two Westborough Business Park, Westborough, MA 01581-3199

Bankers Trust

Dr. Carmine VONA, Executive Vice President
One Bankers Trust Plaza, New York, NY 10015

Beatrice/Hunt-Wesson

John L. ESTES, Director, Information Systems and Services
Elaine M. GIDCOMBE, Manager, Systems Development
1645 West Valencia Drive, Fullerton, CA 92633-3899

BBN Communications Corporation

Jeff MAYERSOHN, Senior Vice President
Dr. Gilbert FALK, Director, Telecommunications Consulting

A. LYMAN CHAPIN, Chief Network Architect
150 Cambridge Park Drive, Cambridge, MA 02140

BBN Systems and Technologies Corporation

Steve JEFFREYS, Staff Scientist, Laboratories Division
10 Moulton Street, Cambridge, MA 02238

Chemical Bank

Frank A. KORAHAIS, Vice President, Information & Technology Management Division
96 Wall Street, New York, NY 10005

John E. CANTELLA, Vice President, Systems Development Department
55 Water Street, New York, NY 10041

Chicago Board of Trade

Glen W. BELDEN, Vice President, Information Systems
James D. WHITE, Vice President, Computer Systems and Operations
Richard N. LEE, Manager, Administrative Information Systems
Frank CHERECK, Manager, Network Computing
Veronica MURPHY, Database Administrator
Mark JESSKI, Supervisor, Administrative Systems
LaSalle at Jackson, Chicago, IL 60604

Citibank

Colin CROOK, Chairman, Corporate Technology Committee
399 Park Avenue, New York, NY 10043

Daniel SCHUTZER, Vice President
Sholon ROSEN, Vice President
Dr. Alexander J. PASIK, Assistant Vice President
909 Third Avenue, New York, NY 10022

John DAVIES, Vice President
Robert HSU, Vice President
1 Huntington Quadrangle, 4th Floor, Melville, NY 11747

Harvard Software (HSC)

Thomas GUTCHIGIAN, Vice President, Software

Jim DUDMAN, Product Manager
1661 Lincoln Blvd., Suite 101, Santa Monica, CA 90404

Hewlett-Packard

Dr. Ming-Chien SHAN, Manager, Cooperative Information Management, Hewlett-Packard Laboratories
Prof. Witold LITTWIN, University of Paris (currently at Hewlett-Packard)
Abbas RAFII, Manager, Database Technology
Philippe DE SMEDT, Database Technology
Weimin DU, Database Technology
Dr. Rafi AHMED, Database Technology
1501 Page Mill Road, 3U-4, Palo Alto, CA 94304-1126

Douglas DEDO, Product Line Manager, Commercial Systems Division
Hewlett-Packard Company, 19111 Pruneridge Avenue, Cupertino, CA 95014

Hughes Aircraft

Bhadra K. PATEL, Senior Scientist, Systems Technology Laboratory
Mae MA. Project Leader, Database Integration
Command and Control Systems Division, Bldg. 618, MS P325, P.O. Box 3310, Fullerton, CA 92634-3310

Hughes Research Laboratories

Son DAO, Senior Staff, Knowledge Based Systems, Artificial Intelligence Center
M/S RL 96, 3011 Malibu Canyon Road, Malibu, CA 90265

Inference Conference

Dr. Alexander JACOBSON, President
Dr. Philip KLAHR, Vice President, Professional Services
550 N. Continental Blvd., El Segundo, CA 90245

Kendall Square Research (KSR)

Alex DONNINI, Director of Marketing
Dr. David S. REINER, Director of Commercial Software Development
Rober H. DORIN, Manager of

Technical Support Commercial
Products Group
170 Tracer Lane, Waltham, MA
02154-1379

LAC-USC Medical Center

Dr. Bharat N. NATHWANI, Professor
of Pathology, President Intelligraph
1200 N. State Street, Los Angeles,
CA 90033

Lotus Development Corporation

Peter HARRIS, Systems Architect
55 Cambridge Parkway, Cambridge,
MA 02142

Steven L. SNEDDON, Chief
Technologist
One Rogers Street, Cambridge, MA 02142

Microelectronics and Computer Development
Corporation (MCC)

Dr. P.E. CANNATA, Manager, Carnot
Project
3500 West Balcones Center Drive, Austin,
TX 78759-6509

National Association of Securities Dealers
(NASD)

Rober N. RIESS, Senior Vice President
Technology & Development
1735 K Street, N.W., Washington, D.C.
20006

Santa Clara University

Dr. Mohammad A. KETABCHI,
Director of Engineering Design
Center
Santa Clara, CA 95053

Security Pacific Automation Company

Dale P. TERRELL, Executive Vice
President
Security Pacific Plaza, 333 S. Hope Street,
Los Angeles, CA 90071

Terryhill Associates

Meir BARTUR, Partner
Marc D. GUREN, Partner
1900 Sepulveda Boulevard, Los Angeles, CA
90025-5620

Thinking Machines Corporation

Dr. Craig W. STANFILL, Senior Scientist

245 First Street, Cambridge, MA
02142-1214

TRW Systems Engineering

Dr. Anthony T. MATERNA, Manager,
Data Integration Systems
Software & Systems Laboratory, DH6/2753,
P.O. Box 6213, Carson, CA 90746

UBS Securities, New York

Dr. KRAENZLIN, Manager of
Information Technology
299 Park Avenue, New York, NY
10171-0026

University of Southern California, School of
Business Administration

Dr. Jack R. BORSTING, Dean
Prof. Dr. Alan ROWE, Professor of
Management
Dr. Dennis McLEOD, Professor of
Computer Science
Los Angeles, CA 90089-0871

University of Virginia

Prof. John ROSENBLUM, Dean
Prof. Brandt R. ALLEN, Director, The
Executive Program
Prof. William W. SIHLER, Executive
Director, Center for International
Studies
Prof. Robert J. SACK, Chairman,
Information and Technology
Committee
Frank MORGAN, Manager, Executive
Education
Darden Graduate School of Business
Administration, P.O. Box 6550,
Charlottesville, VA 22906-6650

Dr. Anita K. JONES, Professor and
Department Head, Computer Science
Dr. John L. PFALTZ, Professor and
Director, Institute for Parallel
Computation
Thornton Hall, Charlottesville, VA 22903

Philip M. NOWLEN, Dean, Division of
Continuing Education
P.O. Box 3697, Charlottesville, VA 22903

Karl G. HAHR, Director, Information,
Technology & Facilities Department
Emmitt S. SUMMERS, Jr., Chief,

Services and Systems Support Division,
Cash Management Department
Pilarisetty MADHUSUDAN, Manager,
Systems Programming
*The World Bank, 1818 H Street, N.W.,
Washington, D.C. 20433*

Xerox Corporation

Mark C. MALETZ, Manager, KBS
Competency Center
*780 Salt Road (Building 845-20C),
Webster, NY 14580*

Japan

*Bank of Japan, Institute of Monetary and
Economic Studies*

Yoshiharu ORITANI, Chief Manager
Masahi NAKAJIMA, Assistant Manager
Nobuko KUWATA, Researcher
*2-1-1 Hongoku-Cho, Nihonbashi,
Chuo-ku, Tokyo 103*

*Center for Financial Industry Information
Systems*

Shigehisa HATTORI, Executive
Director and Member of the Board
Masao TAKAYANAGI, Director,
Electronic Banking Research
Fumitaka HAYASAKA, Deputy
Director, General Administration
and Planning
*16th Floor, Arc Mori Building, 12-32, 1-
Chome, Akasaka, Minato-ku,
Tokyo 107*

Dai-Ichi Kangyo Bank

Shunsuke NAKASUJI, Assistant General
Manager and Director, Information
Technology Division
Kiyomo AKAHANE, Database
Administrator
Misako YOSHIDA, Systems and
Operations Planning
*1-5 Uchisaiwai-cho, 1-Chome, Chiyoda-ku,
Tokyo 100*

DEC Japan

Dr. T. KOBAYASHI, Director of
Research and Development
Yoji OGINO, System Engineer,
Integration Services
Yasuko MORI, Database Specialist

Kikuzo ABE, District Sales Manager
Takao NODA, Financial Sales Division
*134 Goudo-cho, Hodagaya-ku,
Yokohama 240*

EOS Hardware

Takeharu KOBAYASHI, President
Sumio ISHIZAKI, Professor at Sanno
College and Consultant to the
President
*1-12 Sumiyoshicyo, Shinjuku-ku,
Tokyo 162*

Fuji Bank

Yasuo FUNAMI, Deputy General
Manager; Chief, Systems Planning
Division
Otemachi, Chiyoda-ku, Tokyo

Fujitsu and Fujitsu Research Institute

Masuteru SEKIGUCHI, Member of the
Board, Fujitsu Research Institute
Tatsuji IGARASHI, Manager, Research
and Planning Division, Fujitsu
Kazuaki WATANABE, Manager,
Technical Support center, Fujitsu
Takashi KIMOTO, Manager, Systems
Laboratory
Kiyoshi ASAKAW, Chief Researcher,
Neural Networks
*1015 Kamikodanaka, Nakahara-ku,
Kawasaki 211*

Hitachi

Dr. Fumihiko MORI, Manager, System
Development Laboratory
Haruyoski YAMANOUCHI, Manager,
Banking Systems
Kazuo MASAI, Senior Engineer,
Database Department
*5030 Totsuka-cho, Totsuka-ku,
Yokohama-shi 244*

Institute of Space and Aeronautical Science

Prof. Dr. Kozo FUJII
*Yoshinodai 3-1-1, Sagamihara,
Kanagawa 229*

*Japan Electronic Directory Research Institute
(EDR)*

Dr. Toshio YOKOI, General Manager
*Mita-Kokusai-Building Annex, 4-28 Mita,
1-Chome, Minato-ku, Tokyo 108*

Japan Research Institute, Subsidiary of the Sumitomo Bank

Koji SANO, Manager, Software Development Division
Akihito SAKAI, Vice-Chief, Software Development
3-1-31 Minamiaoyma, Minato-ku, Tokyo 107

Laboratory for International Fuzzy Engineering

Prof. Dr. Toshiro TERANO, Executive Director
Dr. Tomohiro TAKAGI, Deputy Executive Director
Itsuko FUJIMORI, General Manager, Research Administration
Siber Hegner Building, 3rd Floor, 89-1 Yamashita-cho, Naka-ku, Yokohama-Shi 231

Mitsui Taiyo Kobe Research Institute and Mitsui Taiyo Kobe Bank

Teruhisa TAKASHIMA, General Manager, System Consulting
Yoshiaki IWAMARU, Deputy GM, Financial Systems
16-6 Shinjuku, 2-Chome, Shinjuku-ku, Tokyo 160

Masato FURUKAWA, Senior Vice President, Systems Development Division, Mitsui Taiyo Kobe Bank
4-1-4 Kami-Osaki, Shinagawa-ku, Tokyo 141

NEC and NEC Management Systems Research Institute

Kotaro NAMBA, Senior Researcher, NEC MSRI
Isao KAMOI, Engineering Manager, Database Development
Takeshi YOSHIMURA, Manager, Basic Technologies Research Lab
Yutaka KIMURA, Researcher on Object-Oriented Database
5-29-11 Shiba Minato-ku, Tokyo 108

Nippon Telegraph and Telephone

Dr. Fukuya ISHINO, Executive Manager NTT, Director of the

Communications and Information Processing Labs
1-2356 Take Yokusuka-Shi, Kanagawa 238-03

Masao KIMURA, Division Manager, Building Design and Construction
No. 21 Mori Building, 4-33 Roppongi-Chome, Minato-ku, Tokyo 106

Sanwa Bank

Shoji SAKAMOTO, Deputy General Manager
Toshio HORIKAWA, Assistant General Manager–Databases
Akira FUJIWANA, Database Expert
1-1 Otemachi, 1-Chome, Chiyoda-ku, Tokyo 100

Sumitomo Bank

Akimoto TANAKA, Director, Operations Administration Department
Shigeo MORIWAKI, Assistant General Manager, Domestic Banking Planning
3-2 Marunouchi 1-Chome, Chiyoda-ku, Tokyo

Tokyo International University

Prof. Dr. Yoshiro KURATANI
FI Bldg., 6F, 1-26-5 Takadanonaba, Shinjuku-ku, Tokyo 169

Tomin Bank

Kuwiki MASAI, General Manager, Systems Development Division (Tomin Bank)
Hideo KOISHIAWA, General Manager, TCS Systems Development Company (Subsidiary of Tomin Bank)
3-11 Roppongi, 2-Chome, Minato-Ku, Tokyo 0106

Toshiba

Tadahiro OHASHI, Manager, Computer Applications Department
Kazuo KAWAMURA, Manager, Financial Sector Systems
Willie SHA, Stock Trading System Analyst
Miss SATO, Bond Trading System Analyst
1, Toshiba-Cho, Fuchu-Shi, Tokyo 183

Toyo Information Systems (TIS), Subsidiary of the Sanwa Bank

Yukio URATA, General Manager, Business Systems Division
Katsutoshi YAMASHITA, Deputy GM, Business Systems Division
Hiroshi SHUNOHARA, Assistant GM, Systems Consulting Division
Kumiko TOTSUKA, Manager, Systems Integration
4-6-1 Ginza Chuo-ku, Tokyo 104

UBS Tokyo Area Office
Peter BRUTSCHE, Executive Vice President and Chief Manager
Helmut LASKA, Director of Regional Logistics
Graham MELLOR, New Director of Regional Logistics
Dr. Peter BERWERT, Manager, Regional Information Systems
Masaki UTSUNOMIYA, Manager of IT, UBS Investment Banking
Dan CERRI, IT UBS Trust Bank
Tom KOZLOSK, IT UBS Trust Bank
Fukoku Seimei Building 5F, 2-2-2 Uchisaiwaicho, Chiyoda-ku, Tokyo 100

Yamaichi Securities
Morihiro MATSUMOTO, Deputy General Manager, Strategic Planning and Product Development
Toshihiro HATTA, Manager, Financial Strategy
Masaaki HASHIMOTO, Deputy Manager, Systems Planning
Norio KOMAKO, Assistant Manager, Systems Planning
Fukuoka Bldg., 4F, 8-7 Yaesu 2-Chome, Chuo-ku, Tokyo

United Kingdom

Abbey National
Mac MILLINGTON, Manager, Group Systems
Nick GOODMAN, Project Leader, Finance & Banking System
Management Services Division, Chalkwell Drive, Shenley Wood, Milton Keynes MK5 6LA

Anderson Consulting

Hugh MORRIS, Partner
Dr. Gilles LAFUE, Director, European Research Division
2 Arundel Street, London WC2R 3LT

Associative Design Technology
Mathew TOMAS
23 Forthbridge Road, London SW11 5NX

Bank of Scotland U.K. Banking (East)
Colin S. McGILL, Divisional General Manager
P.O. Box No. 12, Uberior House, 61 Grassmarket, Edinburgh EH1 2JF

Barclays Bank
Peter GOLDEN, Information Technology Director, Markets Division
Brandon DAVIES, Head of Financial Engineering Global Treasury Services
Graeme M. SKELLY, Manager, Financial Engineering, Global Treasury Services
Murray House, 1 Royal Mint Court, London EC3N 4HH

George BIGBY, Chief Data Architect, Group Information Systems, Technology Organization
Radbroke Hall, Knutsford, Cheshire WA16 9EU

Barclays de Zoete Wedd
Neil G.A. EVERINGHAM, Director
Ebbgate House, 2 Swan Lane, London EC4R 3TS

Chemical Banking
Graham BLAND
180 The Strand, London WC2R 1EX

Coopers Lybrand Deloitte
Ian L. BRIGGS, Manager, Knowledge Engineering Applications
Samit KHOSLA, Manager, Object-Oriented Systems
Plumtree Court, London EC4A 4HT

County Natwest
Sam GIBB, Director of Technology
Cyril KILBRIDGE, Business Systems Analyst

Chris BAKER, Business Systems
135 Bishopsgate, London EC2M 3UR

County Natwest Investment Management

David MAGUIRE, Manager,
Information Technology
*43/44 Crutched Friars, London
EC3N 2NX*

County Natwest Securities

Don F. SIMPSON, Manager,
Information Technology
135 Bishopsgate, London EC2M 3UR

London Stock Exchange

John D. SCANNELL, Head of Network
Operations/SEAQ
Diane IMTHRUN, Network
Operations/SEAQ
*London Stock Exchange, London
EC2N 1HP*

National Westminster Bank

Andy F. MILLER, Senior Manager, IT
Planning, IT Strategy & Policy
Department
10/11 Old Broad Street, London EC2 1BB

Noesis Ltd.

G.J. MASKELL, Director
*10 Cobden Road, Brighton, East Sussex
BN2 2TL*

UBS Phillips and Drew

Hansruedi WOLFENSBERGER, Vice
Chairman
Dr. Peter JACKSON, Area Director of
Information Technology
Urs BRYNER, Former Area Director of
Information Technology
100 Liverpool Street, London

Sweden

Irdem HB

Gian MEDRI
19, Flintlasvagen, S-19154 Sollentuna

Nordbanken

John LUNDGREN, Project Manager,
Business Systems
24, Smalandsgatan, S-10571 Stockholm

Skandinaviska Enskilda Banken

Mats ANDERSON, Manager of Systems
Architecture and Technology
2, Sergels Torg, S-10640 Stockholm

Svenska Handelsbanken

Lars O. GROENSTEDT, Senior Vice
President
Peter ININBERGS, Systems Analyst
11, Arsenalgatan, S-10670 Stockholm

Swedish Bankers Association

Bo GUNNARSSON, Technical Director
and Coordinator of Bank Automation
Box 7603, S-10394 Stockholm

Other Countries

AVT/Eurosept

José MOREJON, Director of AVT
13, rue Gilbieri, 69002 Lyon, France

Bank of Norway

Lars Erik RUSTAD, Data Security Chief
*Bankplassen 2, Postboks 1179 Sentrum,
0107 Oslo 1, Norway*

Banque Scandinave en Suisse

François JEANNET, Director
*Cours de Rive 11, P.O. Box 901, 1211
Geneva 3, Switzerland*

Ciba-Geigy, AgroDivision

Pamela Ann BATHE, Director of
Logistics
Stefan JANOVJAK, Information
Manager
Meike BUEGLER, Information
Architect
Schwarzwald Allee, 4002 Basel, Switzerland

Bim Systems

Olivier DECLERFRAYT, General
Manager
Didier HECK, Technical Director
30, rue de Lisbonne, 75008 Paris

Fellesdata AS

Forde IHLEN, Chief Consultant
*Nedre Skoyenvei 26, P.O. Box 248, Skoyen,
0212 Oslo 2, Norway*

Union Bank of Switzerland

Ulrich RIMENSBERGER, Director of
Telecommunications
Kurt WOLF, Director of IT Technology
in Investment Banking/Area Europe
Hans WALTHER, UBILAB (Union
Bank of Switzerland Research

Laboratories)
45 Bahnhofstrasse, Zurich, Switzerland

University of Ottawa

Dr. John Scott COWAN, Vice Rector,
Resources and Planning
*550 Cumberland, Ottawa, Ontario, Canada
K1N 6N5*

Index